HITLER'S RAID
TO SAVE MUSSOLINI

■

HITLER'S RAID
TO SAVE MUSSOLINI

■

THE MOST INFAMOUS COMMANDO
OPERATION OF WORLD WAR II

Greg Annussek

Da Capo Press
A Member of the Perseus Books Group

Set in 11.5-point Berkeley by the Perseus Books Group

Library of Congress Cataloging-in-Publication Data

Annussek, Greg A.
   Hitler's raid to save Mussolini : the most infamous commando operation of World War II / Greg Annussek.—1st Da Capo Press ed.
     p. cm.
   Includes bibliographical references and index.
   ISBN-10: 0-306-81396-3 (alk. paper)
   ISBN-13: 978-0-306-81396-2 (alk. paper)
   1. World War, 1939–1945—Commando operations—Italy. 2. Mussolini, Benito, 1883–1945—Captivity, 1943. 3. Germany. Luftwaffe. Fallschirmjägerdivision, 2—History. I. Title.
D794.5.A56 2005
940.54'1245—dc22

                                      2005012566

Published by Da Capo Press
A Member of the Perseus Books Group
http://www.dacapopress.com

Da Capo Press books are available at special discounts for bulk purchases in the U.S. by corporations, institutions, and other organizations. For more information, please contact the Special Markets Department at the Perseus Books Group, 11 Cambridge Center, Cambridge, MA 02142, or call (800) 255-1514 or (617) 252-5298, or e-mail special.markets@perseusbooks.com.

1 2 3 4 5 6 7 8 9—08 07 06 05

CONTENTS

■

Acknowledgments vii

Prologue   Mussolini Falls from Power 1

Chapter 1   Into the Wolf's Lair 9

Chapter 2   Treason in the Air 21

Chapter 3   An Early Friendship 37

Chapter 4   A Dangerous Game 59

Chapter 5   Tonight No Sleep for Anybody 81

Chapter 6   The Odyssey of Benito Mussolini 99

Chapter 7   Hitler Takes Control 109

Chapter 8   The Raid on Santo Stefano 123

Chapter 9   The Mystery of Maddalena Island 137

Chapter 10   The Badoglio Shuffle 155

Chapter 11   The Highest Prison in the World 169

Chapter 12   The Double Cross 183

Chapter 13   A Simple Plan 199

Chapter 14   Freeing Mussolini 213

Epilogue   The Aftermath 237

The Story of Operation Oak 261
Notes 265
Bibliography 307
Index 315

ACKNOWLEDGMENTS

———————— ■ ————————

MANY THANKS ARE DUE TO MY AGENT EDWARD KNAPPMAN, WHO helped to refine the concept of the book at the outset. I am also indebted to Robert Pigeon, my editor at Da Capo, for his advice on narrative structure as well as his overall enthusiasm for the project.

Anastasia Schüle, who translated the German and Italian source material into English, went the extra mile by working tirelessly to meet tight deadlines.

I am also grateful to friends and family who offered their feedback on early drafts of manuscripts and book proposals. This group includes my parents, Robert and Rosarita Annussek, as well as Angel Annussek, Rosa Michnya, Lana Zannoni, Jeffrey Stanley, and David Bourla.

Mr. Cameron Archer, Director of the Tocal Agricultural Centre (Paterson, NSW, Australia), Mr. Dan Hunt, and Mr. Peter Bardwell were gracious enough to allow me to use several of their photos in this book.

In the final stages of book production, copyeditor Jennifer Blakebrough-Raeburn made a number of helpful suggestons.

SWITZERLAND

A L P S

Brenner Pass

AUSTRIA

Dongo Lake
Mezzegra Como Lake
Garda Tarvisio
Salo Feltre
Milan Verona Venice

YUGOSLAVIA

Po River

A

Genoa

P

Spezia

E

Forli

Bologna

Arno River
Florence

N

N

Tiber River

Elba

Corsica

Lake
Bracciano

L'Aquila Assergi
Pescara

I

Rome

N

Frascati

Anzio

Cassino

N

Adriatic
Sea

La Maddalena Is.
La Maddalena

Gaeta

E

Sardinia

Ponza
Ventotene
Santo Stefano

Naples

Salerno

S

Taranto Brindisi

Italy, 1943

N

= mountains

Straits of Messina

0 km   100   200
0 miles   50   100

RLP

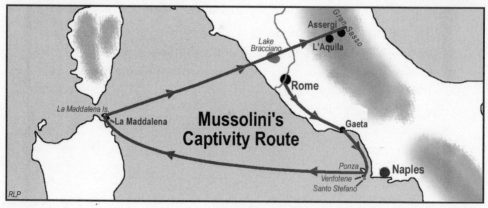

Assergi

Gran Sasso

Lake
Bracciano

L'Aquila

Rome

La Maddalena Is.
La Maddalena

Gaeta

Mussolini's
Captivity Route

Ponza

Naples

Ventotene
Santo Stefano

RLP

PROLOGUE

■

MUSSOLINI FALLS
FROM POWER

Mussolini's Headquarters in Rome, Italy—July 25, 1943

CLOSE TO 9:00 A.M. ON A QUIET SUNDAY MORNING, BENITO MUSSOLINI stepped out of the brilliant sunshine and into the austere beauty of the Renaissance-era Palazzo Venezia in the heart of Rome.[1] He went up to his second-floor office, a cavernous hall known as the *Sala del Mappamondo,* and sank into a chair behind his massive desk. If the Italian dictator looked even more pale and haggard than usual on this day, it was not without good reason. The events of the previous evening had left Il Duce with little time for sleep. During a stormy all-night session of the Grand Council of Fascism, the lofty name given to a glorified gang of Mussolini's political henchmen, a small band of rebellious subordinates had staged a dramatic and unprecedented revolt.

One after another, several of the Duce's top lieutenants criticized the weary fifty-nine-year-old despot and his disastrous conduct of the war. "You have imposed a dictatorship on Italy," declared Dino Grandi, the ringleader of the bunch. "You have destroyed the spirit of our Armed Forces. . . . For years when selecting someone from among several candidates for an important post, you have invariably

1

selected the worst."[2] With such a frank airing of grievances, it was no wonder that some of the conspirators had stuffed hand grenades into their briefcases as a precaution against arrest.[3]

They need not have worried. Long depressed in spirit and suffering from severe stomach pains, Mussolini listened impassively to the growing chorus of dissent without making a move to silence his detractors. The exhausting ten-hour meeting broke up at 2:40 A.M. on Sunday, but not before a majority of council members had voted in favor of the so-called Grandi Agenda.[4] This ominous resolution proposed to abolish the Duce's personal one-man rule and transfer his most important powers, such as control of the armed forces, to King Victor Emmanuel III of Italy, who had remained on the throne largely as a figurehead during the life of the Fascist regime. To the dictator's chagrin, one of the men who voted against him that night was none other than Count Galeazzo Ciano, Mussolini's playboy son-in-law and onetime foreign minister.

The Duce had concluded the meeting with a bitter announcement: "You have provoked a crisis of the Régime."[5] And yet, to all appearances, he did not seem overly concerned by this flagrant insurrection on the part of his Fascist brethren. Undaunted, he had shown up promptly for work a few hours later to resume his stewardship of the broken-down Italian Empire. "As I had regularly done for the last twenty-one years," he wrote afterward, "I settled down to my working day—the last!"[6] As Mussolini well knew, the Grand Council was merely an advisory board, a bit of democratic window dressing that in his mind did not count for much.

Moreover, he also doubted the mettle of his Fascist flunkies, some of whom had already expressed a desire to retract the votes they had cast just a few hours earlier. "Too late," the Duce had said over the telephone that morning in response to one such entreaty.[7] Not long before the Grand Council meeting, he had neatly summed up his view of the yes-men with which he had often chosen to surround himself.[8] "Believe me . . . these Grand Council members," the dictator had remarked to his chief of police, "are of low, very low intelligence, wobbly in their convictions, and without much courage. These people live in someone else's shadow: if the source of light should disappear, they too would be cast back into the darkness from whence they came."[9]

Though his star had dimmed in recent months, Mussolini could assure himself that he was still the brightest object in the murky constellation of Italian politics. The shadow men may have turned their knives on the modern-day Caesar, but the Duce felt only pricks: irritating perhaps, but not fatal. Nevertheless, he planned to visit the king later in the day to discuss the vote and its implications.

At 1:00 P.M., Mussolini received a visit at the Palazzo Venezia from the Japanese ambassador, Shinrokuro Hidaka. The Duce spent an hour giving Hidaka an account of his recent war conference with Hitler, which had taken place just six days earlier. The immediate crisis, then and now, was the Allied invasion of Sicily. This large mountainous island, which had once provided the setting for legendary battles among the ancient Greeks, was the scene of desperate fighting between the Axis and the Western alliance.

The Anglo-Americans had made their landings on the island on July 10 (among them was a gung-ho American general named George Patton) and were quickly overwhelming most of its German and Italian defenders, the latter offering only a token resistance. An invasion of the Italian mainland could not be far off, and Mussolini knew that he would be helpless to stop it. It was this dilemma, and its inevitable effect on his political viability, that had been eating away at him in recent months and aggravating his longstanding— and somewhat mysterious—health problems.

During his conference with Hitler, he had hoped that the Germans would agree to send reinforcements and supplies to shore up the defense of Sicily—and to bolster the Duce's own domestic political standing—but substantial aid was not immediately forthcoming. The Nazis' resources were already stretched to the limit, and Hitler was having grave doubts about the Italian will to fight. In the intervening days, Mussolini decided to take a harder line with his

German ally, and he wanted fellow Axis partner Japan to back his position.

"Please tell Tokyo urgently," Mussolini told Hidaka, "of my decision to send a note to Berlin on Wednesday that will say that if Germany does not furnish all the war material Italy has requested, we will be forced to declare that we can no longer fulfill our duties within the alliance. I ask that the Japanese ambassador in Berlin support my request very forcefully. Unfortunately, this is the situation, and Berlin must understand. In order to fight, one must have weapons."[10] Three years after plunging Italy into World War II at Hitler's urging, the Duce was scrambling to stave off the inevitable.

After his meeting with the Japanese diplomat, Mussolini departed the Palazzo Venezia and drove through the working-class district of San Lorenzo, which had been badly damaged during a recent Allied bombing raid. The Italians, it must be said, had never wanted Mussolini's war—despite the ubiquitous presence of such unequivocal slogans as "Mussolini is always right"—and when the conflict finally arrived on their doorstep they privately cursed his decision to throw in his lot with the detested Nazis, whose racial policies they had always abhorred.[11]

As Mussolini stepped out of his car, he was greeted with several obligatory salutes from the weary men and women who were still sifting through the rubble.[12] Or as he remembered it: "I was at once surrounded by a crowd of the victims, who cheered me."[13] He returned the favor by instructing General Enzo Galbiati, who had accompanied him, to empty his wallet and distribute money to the people.[14] (Mussolini did not generally carry cash.)[15]

He seems to have taken some pride in his reception that afternoon among the ruins of Roman neighborhoods, which would not be surprising.[16] The solitary dictator had always derived more gratification from his rapport with the masses, real or imaginary, than from the intimacy of personal relationships.

It was a particularly steamy summer in Rome that year, and by mid-afternoon on Sunday the city was beginning to wilt under the

Mediterranean sun.[17] "An oppressive and sultry heat burdened the souls of men," remembered Mussolini, a onetime journalist who in his younger days had fancied himself a novelist, "and pressed down from a motionless sky on the city of Rome."[18] At 3:00 P.M. he pulled up to the Villa Torlonia, his comfortable estate in nearby Frascati, where, bearing a bowl of soup and Cassandra-like prophecies, his wife, Rachele, awaited him.*[19]

"I had my usual breakfast," he recalled, "and spent an hour chatting with Rachele in the little music room. My wife was more than depressed, and her fears that something was going to happen were very great."[20] The suspicious Rachele begged her husband to cancel his meeting with the king, whom she distrusted, but the Duce shrugged off her warnings.[21] He had nothing to fear from Victor Emmanuel, he told her.[22] The king was a friend.[23]

Mussolini had no inkling that his friend the king, in league with a cabal of Italian generals, was the prime mover of a separate conspiracy designed to topple the dictator from power and sweep away his twenty-year-old Fascist regime. To the king's mind, the Grand Council vote was simply a convenient pretext for springing his own trap, which was far more extreme than anything envisaged by most of the Duce's minions in the *Gran Consiglio,* who wished to provide the country with new leadership without committing political suicide by destroying Fascism altogether.[24] Mussolini's last-minute request to call on the royal residence had upset the timing of the coup d'état, which was scheduled to occur the following day. But the king and his men decided to accommodate the Duce, who unknowingly hastened his own exit from the stage.

At about 5:00 P.M., Mussolini's Alfa Romeo passed through the iron gates of the Villa Savoia, Victor Emmanuel's residence on the outskirts of the capital.[25] The Duce, who was dressed in a dark-blue

---

*Cassandra is a figure from Greek mythology known for making accurate predictions that no one believed.

suit and black felt hat, saw members of the carabinieri, the Italian military police, standing here and there on the grounds.*[26] Others were hiding behind the king's shrubbery, unseen by the dictator.[27] But the presence of armed guards was not out of the ordinary and failed to pique his curiosity. Mussolini thus walked into the heart of the spider's web without the slightest trace of foreboding.[28]

As he approached the villa, he saw Victor Emmanuel waiting for him on the steps. The diminutive king—he was about five feet tall—was wearing a gaudy marshal's uniform.[29] After a brief exchange about the hot weather, the Duce followed Victor Emmanuel into a drawing room where the two men could be alone.[30] Mussolini began to describe the Grand Council meeting, minimizing the importance of the vote as well as its legal ramifications, when the king cut him short.[31]

"My dear Duce, it can't go on any longer," the king said. "Italy is in pieces. Army morale has reached the bottom and the soldiers don't want to fight any longer. The Alpine regiments have a song saying that they are through fighting Mussolini's war."[32] In what must have been a surreal and uncomfortable moment for the Duce, the king recited the chorus ("Down with Mussolini, murderer of the Alpini") as the dictator listened in silence.[33]

"Surely you have no illusions," he continued, "as to how Italians feel about you at this moment. You are the most hated man in Italy; you have not a single friend left, except for me. You need not worry about your personal security. I shall see to that. I have decided that the man of the hour is Marshal Badoglio."[34]

The name cut Mussolini to the quick. Pietro Badoglio was a former chief of *Comando Supremo* (the Italian High Command) who had been sacked by the Duce in 1940 after Italy had suffered its biggest military humiliation of the war. The two men were considered enemies. Yet the king was now telling Mussolini that he had

---

*The carabinieri, a military organization, and *polizia,* the civil police, were the two primary law-enforcement agencies in Italy.

selected the old soldier to be the head of a new Italian government. "He will form a cabinet of career officials," Victor Emmanuel added, "in order to rule the country and go on with the war. Six months from now we shall see."[35]

The Duce seemed crushed by the blow, according to the king. "Then my ruin is complete," the dictator muttered, lowering himself into a chair.[36] "I'm sorry," said the king, who had developed a genuine admiration for Mussolini over the years, "but the solution couldn't have been otherwise, I'm sorry."[37] When the Duce had recovered his composure, he voiced some mild protest, then added: "I am perfectly aware that the people hate me. I admitted as much last night before the Grand Council. No one can govern for so long and impose so many sacrifices without incurring more or less bitter resentment."[38]

The meeting had lasted a mere twenty minutes.[39] At 5:20 P.M., Victor Emmanuel, whose monarchy had collaborated closely with the Fascist regime for two decades, escorted Mussolini to the door.[40] The two men shook hands. "His face was livid," the Duce later observed wryly, "and he seemed even shorter than usual, as if he had shrunk."[41]

But the biggest surprise was yet to come. As he walked to his car, the unsuspecting Mussolini was placed under arrest by a captain of the carabinieri and bundled into a waiting ambulance, which sped off at high speed with its bewildered cargo. The strutting dictator of Fascist Italy was now a prisoner of his own people.*

Once Mussolini had been spirited away to a secret location, the king and his fellow conspirators proceeded to round up some of the leading Fascists in Rome, dismantling what remained of the Duce's political regime in the process. Despite what he told Mussolini in the Villa Savoia, the king had no intention of allowing Italy to

---

*No one knows for certain what was actually said during the meeting between Mussolini and King Victor Emmanuel of Italy. The above account is pieced together from the contrasting versions later provided by the participants; both accounts are considered suspect to some degree by historians.

bloody itself any further in the war. When the time was ripe, Victor Emmanuel was prepared to break away from the Axis and seek the mercy of the Allies. The ex-Duce might prove to be a valuable peace offering to the would-be invaders of Italian shores.

Though Mussolini and his followers were neutralized without much fuss in the days immediately following the coup, the possibility of German interference posed a far greater danger to the king's new government. The regime change was bound to be viewed with malevolence by Hitler, who was known to call the Duce his friend and who also harbored a deep distrust of the monarchy and its attitude toward the war (and not without good reason).

An Italian surrender, should such an event occur, could prove catastrophic for the Nazis, who were counting on their Mediterranean partner to help defend the southern front against the Allies. If the Italians suddenly threw open their gates to the enemy, the Germans feared that British and American forces might make a dash up the peninsula and launch an assault on the Third Reich itself, which was already engaged in a desperate struggle against the gargantuan Russian army in the East.

To avoid German reprisals, the king was planning to conceal his peace offensive from Hitler while reaffirming Italy's commitment to the Axis. Such dissimulations were conceived as a temporary measure designed to keep the Nazis at bay long enough for the Italians to enter into covert negotiations for a promise of military support from the Allies. But therein lay the rub. Until such time as it secured a deal with the enemy, the new Italian regime would have to rely on its wits if it was to forestall a possible attack by the Germans.

In the early evening of July 25, as Mussolini's captors began the task of blotting out Fascism and consolidating their control over the country, they did so in an atmosphere of grim suspense. How would the Nazis react, they wondered nervously, to the sudden disappearance of the Duce—stalwart supporter of Germany and Hitler's personal friend?

1

INTO THE WOLF'S LAIR

Mussolini must be rescued, and speedily, otherwise they will deliver him up to the Allies.[1]
—Hitler, speaking in the Wolf's Lair on July 26, 1943

THE LARGE FIGURE OF CAPTAIN OTTO SKORZENY WAS A CONSPICUOUS presence in the surprisingly comfortable lobby of the Tea House, a spacious room furnished with several armchairs and a few tables. The Tea House was part of the *Wolfsschanze,* or Wolf's Lair, Hitler's military headquarters in the forests of East Prussia.* The stocky, six-foot-four Skorzeny was accompanied by five other German officers whom he had never met before—three lieutenant colonels and two majors from various branches of the military.[2] Like Skorzeny, they were all leaders of special units. They all out-ranked him.

The six men had converged on the Wolf's Lair from various parts of war-torn Europe. Having been urgently summoned without explanation, they now milled around the lobby. Skorzeny stared down at the looped-wool carpet covering the floor.[3] The thirty-five-year-old felt slightly uneasy in the rarified atmosphere of his surroundings. The Wolf's Lair, as he well knew, was the inner sanctum of the German High Command. From this isolated and heavily

---

*"Wolf" had been one of Hitler's nicknames during his younger days.

9

guarded complex, Hitler and his war chiefs struggled to manage the conflagration they had unleashed on the world almost four years earlier, but now it was gradually imploding on Germany itself.

The pleasant décor of the Tea House did little to ease Skorzeny's ill-defined anxiety. When one of the other officers mispronounced his name, Skorzeny, who was known for his cool head, reacted with the impulsiveness to which he was occasionally prone.

"It's not so very difficult," he snapped. "All you have to do is break it up: Skor-zay-ny—it's quite simple!"[4] It was, in fact, an odd name for a captain in the Waffen SS, the so-called politically elite branch of Germany's fighting forces. The response of the offending officer has not been recorded, but it is easy to imagine his quick apology and perhaps a faint smile betraying Skorzeny's remark as a transparent show of nerves.

It was Monday evening, July 26—one day after Mussolini's sudden disappearance from the Italian scene. Skorzeny and his fellow officers had no knowledge of the Italian coup d'état. Official announcements in Germany indicated that the Duce had resigned from office for reasons of poor health.[5] Italy's new government had publicly pledged to continue the war at Germany's side.

Skorzeny had nearly missed the mysterious summons altogether; indeed, for much of the day, he had been happily incommunicado. In the afternoon, Skorzeny had donned civilian clothes and visited the lounge of the Hotel Eden in Berlin, about 350 miles west of the Wolf's Lair.[6] He sipped ersatz coffee (an "indefinable brew") with a friend who taught at the University of Vienna (a professor who apparently had been untouched by the Nazi purges of the university system).[7] When he finally decided to check in with his office at the Friedenthal Battalion, the commando outfit he had created just several months earlier, he learned over the phone that his staff had been desperately trying to reach him for hours.

"You are summoned to the Führer's headquarters, Chief," his secretary told him excitedly.[8] Her sense of urgency was understandable: Skorzeny had never before been called to the Wolf's Lair. Like most

Germans, in or out of the military, he was not even privy to its secret location. He knew only that it was located somewhere in East Prussia.

Skorzeny needed to go to Berlin's Tempelhof airport right away, she told him, where a special plane had been sent to fetch him. To save time, he decided to go directly to the airport, but he told Lieutenant Karl Radl, his thirty-one-year-old aide de camp, to pack a bag for him and meet him there. "You have no idea what all this is about?" he asked his secretary.[9] But she had no clue.

A little after 5:00 P.M., Skorzeny was hastening eastward across Germany as the sole passenger of a Junkers 52. Large and box-like, the three-engine cargo plane resembled a winged corrugated-tin shed. Now a workhorse of the Nazi war machine, it ferried troops and equipment to and from the far-flung German dominions. It had received its baptism of fire during the Spanish Civil War, when Ju 52s in the service of General Francisco Franco's Nationalists dropped thousands of tons of bombs on Republican forces and Spanish civilians.[10]

Skorzeny's Ju 52 was a modified VIP plane equipped with a small bar. The young officer downed two glasses of cognac while contemplating what awaited him at Hitler's headquarters: Had he been summoned to the Wolf's Lair to report on the progress of his fledgling commando unit? It seemed unlikely to him that any of his ongoing operations warranted such a high-level invitation. While Skorzeny was changing into his uniform at the airport, he and Radl had discussed the strange goings-on in Italy; but neither man saw a definite connection between this piece of news and Skorzeny's flight into the great unknown.[11]

Soon after take-off, Skorzeny discovered that Radl had slipped a map of Germany into his briefcase. He decided to make use of it. Before long, he was sitting next to the pilot and eagerly tracing the flight path of the sluggish Ju 52 as it approached its destination. In a few hours, the plane had traveled about 320 miles and was nearing Masuria, a low-lying region of East Prussia known for its forests and large lakes.[12]

The area possessed significance for Skorzeny. Decades earlier, during World War I, the German army had scored a spectacular victory over the Russians at the nearby village of Tannenberg. Like many Germans of his generation, Skorzeny could recite the history of World War I with the same zeal that his American counterparts reserved for baseball trivia. Germany's bitter defeat in that conflict and the harsh peace terms imposed by the Versailles Treaty had not only dominated the German psyche for much of the interwar period but also paved the way for Hitler's rise to power.

■ ■ ■

As dusk descended, the Ju 52 finally touched down at Rastenburg airfield, just southwest of Hitler's HQ. Skorzeny stepped off the plane and approached a shiny black Mercedes parked in front of the airport's hut-like office, where a sergeant was awaiting his arrival. The car would take Skorzeny on the last leg of his journey to the Wolf's Lair, which was located about five miles east of Rastenburg (modern-day Kêtrzyn in northeastern Poland). Built in anticipation of Operation Barbarossa, the Nazis' massive invasion of Russia in 1941, this dreary compound was Hitler's home (with numerous interruptions) between June 1941 and the fall of 1944.

Nestled in a swampy forest of fir and pine trees, the sprawling headquarters did not look impressive from a distance.[13] Visitors had to pass through several security zones and checkpoints before reaching the nerve center known as Sperrkreis I (Restricted Zone I), where Hitler's personal bunker was located as well as lodgings for some of his closest aides. Access to Sperrkreis I, as opposed to other sections of the headquarters, was limited to a select few.

Shortly after leaving the airfield, Skorzeny's car approached the first concrete barrier. The officer in charge asked to see his I.D. and the special pass issued to him at the airport. Skorzeny signed the register, the barrier swung open, and the car proceeded. The road narrowed and crossed railroad tracks. When the Mercedes arrived at the second checkpoint, Skorzeny presented his papers to another guard. After making a telephone call, the officer asked Skorzeny who had sent for him. Skorzeny said he did not know.

He had been summoned by the German General Staff, the guard informed Skorzeny, whose curiosity was growing. "What the deuce did they want of *me* at headquarters?" he wondered silently.[14] After traveling a final few yards, the Mercedes passed through a portal and entered the grounds of Sperrkreis I. For Skorzeny, the place was the holiest of holies.

At first glance, he thought Sperrkreis I resembled an "old park," although one surrounded by a high barbed-wire fence.[15] Small buildings and huts were scattered about the grounds in no discernable pattern, connected only by winding, tree-lined paths. He noticed the green carpet of grass blanketing the rooftops and what appeared to be small trees taking root there. (This was the handiwork of a Stuttgart landscaping company, which had installed artificial trees and moss on the tops of the buildings.)[16]

Camouflage nets strung high in the trees provided a canopy that blocked the sunlight and deepened the primordial gloom.* The rooftop lawns and camouflage screens were designed to make the compound invisible to enemy bombers flying overhead. Dozens of antiaircraft (AA) guns and a series of surface bunkers, their walls several yards thick, also served to protect Hitler and his staff from air attack.

It was almost dark when the Mercedes pulled up in front of the Tea House, a single-story building composed of two wings linked by a covered passageway. Skorzeny was escorted into the lobby of the right wing, where events were about to take an unexpected turn.

■ ■ ■

Lieutenant Otto Guensche, an officer from the Wolf's Lair, entered the room to make a startling announcement to Skorzeny and the

---

* "Anyone coming from the sunny expanses of the surrounding countryside to this encampment in the gloomy East Prussian forest found the atmosphere oppressive," recalled Hitler's interpreter, Paul Schmidt. The place "reminded one of the fairy tale of the wicked witch." Schmidt, 239.

other men: "Gentlemen," he said, "I am about to take you into the Führer's presence."[17] The six officers could scarcely believe they had actually been summoned to meet with Adolf Hitler himself!

At first, Skorzeny thought his ears had deceived him. "Then an unreasonable fear almost swept my legs from under me," he recalled, making no attempt to disguise his awe. "In a few moments, for the first time in my life, I was to stand in the presence of Adolf Hitler, Führer of Greater Germany and Supreme Commander of the German Armed Forces! Talk about your surprises."[18]

Skorzeny had seen Hitler twice before—but from afar. The first time, in Berlin, had been 1936 at the Olympic Games, where Jesse Owens made a mockery of the Fuehrer's racial theories by winning four gold medals. Two years later, perched on a scaffolding with some workmen, Skorzeny had witnessed Hitler's triumphant entry into Vienna after the *Anschluss,* Germany's annexation of Austria. Like many Austrians, Skorzeny had delighted in Hitler's bloodless coup.

Lieutenant Guensche, Hitler's SS adjutant, led the six men out of the Tea House and into a nearby wooden building; here, Skorzeny found himself in another lobby that resembled the first. Guensche opened a door and the six men filed into a large room of twenty feet by thirty feet. It was infused by an aura of power. In his heightened state of awareness, Skorzeny took note of every detail: the "monumental" fireplace, the large wooden table covered with maps, a row of pencils lined up neatly on a desk.[19] He also noticed a painting by Albrecht Dürer, *Bouquet of Violets,* in a shiny silver frame. Almost certainly part of a cache of looted artwork used to decorate the Wolf's Lair, this delicate still-life from the hand of Germany's most famous Renaissance artist (he was one of Hitler's personal favorites) must have seemed incongruous in the bowels of GHQ.

"I was just musing," Skorzeny remembered, "so this is where the great decisions of our epoch are worked out, when a door facing us opened."[20] The bodies of the six men stiffened as Hitler entered the room. He was wearing a gray officer's jacket, a white shirt, and a black tie. Two medals earned during World War I—the Iron Cross and the Wound Badge—were visible on the left side of Hitler's simple uniform, which lacked the insignia of rank. After taking a few steps, the dictator raised his arm in the characteristic salute so familiar to the men from photos and newsreel footage.

Starting at the far right of the line, Guensche presented the officers, each of whom gave a brief summary of his career. As the lowest-ranking soldier in the group, Skorzeny stood at the opposite end, patiently waiting his turn. Though the reason for the interview remained obscure, the commando leader was eager to make a favorable impression. To this end, Skorzeny, who was not without ambition, began to master his emotions.

A few moments later, Skorzeny stood face-to-face with Adolf Hitler. His notorious blue-gray eyes, alive with diabolical energy, seemed to pin the commando chief to the wall.[21] After a brief bow, Skorzeny listed some basic facts about himself: his birthplace (Vienna), education (he had an engineering degree), and military career, including his present duty as commander of the Friedenthal Battalion. As Hitler looked upward at the giant, he could not help but notice the large dueling scar that ran down the left side of Skorzeny's face.

Hitler stepped back and gazed down the line.

Which of them, he wanted to know, was familiar with Italy?

None replied but Skorzeny.

"I was there twice before the war," he said. "I rode by motorcycle as far as Naples."[22]

Hitler said nothing. Instead he immediately posed a second question to the six men.

"What," Hitler asked, "do you think of Italy?"[23]

A pause. It was a strange question to ask about Germany's comrade-in-arms. The sheer vagueness of it probably made the officers wary. Responding in turn, most of them simply regurgitated phrases from Hitler's formidable propaganda machine: Italy was Germany's partner in the Axis, an ideological ally, and so forth.

Skorzeny, it appears, decided to gamble. The drift of Hitler's questions and the mysterious happenings in Italy prompted him to take a tack different from that of his fellows. What did he have to lose?

"I am an Austrian, Führer," Skorzeny replied.[24] Hitler continued to stare at the hulking captain, but the latter said nothing more.

This pithy response was probably a touch of drama on Skorzeny's part. His shorthand expression was meant to reflect the traditional enmity that existed between Austria and Italy, which had sharpened since World War I. As a loser in the conflict, Austria had been obliged to hand over a large chunk of territory to the Italians in 1919. The so-called South Tyrol (or Alto Adige, as the Italians referred to it) was home to some 200,000 German-speaking ex-Austrians.[25]

"Indeed," Skorzeny explained in retrospect, "I had always judged this answer sufficient to expose my point of view, for any good Austrian must suffer deeply at the loss of the South Tyrol, the most beautiful region we ever possessed."[26] As he was aware, Hitler was himself an Austrian in origin—not to mention an irrepressible gambler in politics and war.

Without another word, Hitler told the officers that they were dismissed. "As for you, Captain Skorzeny, you will stay. I have to talk to you."[27]

■ ■ ■

The two men were now alone. Skorzeny's impromptu strategy had apparently paid off; yet because the dictator had divulged nothing during the group interview, the captain was unaware of what was required of him. As they faced each other, Skorzeny, who was taller than Hitler by several inches, noticed that the Fuehrer had a slight stoop.

"I have a mission of the highest importance for you," Hitler began. "Yesterday Mussolini, my friend and our loyal partner in the struggle, was betrayed by his king and arrested by his own compatriots. Now I cannot and will not abandon the greatest of Italians in his hour of peril."[28] Mussolini was nothing less than a modern-day Caesar, he told Skorzeny, but the leaders who had taken his place could not be trusted. With the Duce out of the way, the new Italian government (the Badoglio regime) could soon be expected to switch sides in the war.

Hitler grew more animated as he spoke, his hands slicing through the air with short, compact gestures.[29] "But I shall not go back on my word: Mussolini must be rescued, and speedily, otherwise they will deliver him up to the Allies. I therefore entrust you with this mission; its successful outcome will be of incalculable bearing upon the development of future military operations. If, as I ask you, you bend every effort and face every risk to attain your goal, then you will succeed!"[30] For the duration of the mission, Hitler said, Skorzeny would be placed under the orders of General Kurt Student of the Luftwaffe, the German air force, who was scheduled to fly to Rome as soon as possible with a contingent of crack paratroopers.

Hitler had in mind an undercover operation—one that must be kept secret not only from the Italians but also from most of Skorzeny's fellow Germans. "There is one more essential point," Hitler explained. "You must consider this the most absolute of secrets. Outside of yourself, only five persons are to be in our confidence." Even Marshal Albert Kesselring, the top German commander in Italy, and Hitler's diplomats at the embassy in Rome were to be kept in the dark. Hitler gave Skorzeny a warning: "[These men] have a completely false conception of the situation and they would only act counter to our interests."[31] As shall be seen later, Hitler was quickly losing faith in the German officers and diplomats based in the Eternal City, who, he believed, had become too cozy with the Italians.

Not surprisingly, Skorzeny was receptive to the Hitler mystique. "The more the Führer spoke," he later admitted, "the stronger I felt his hold upon me. His words seemed so persuasive that, at the moment, I did not even question the success of our enterprise."[32] Hitler's voice had filled with emotion, Skorzeny noticed, when he spoke of his friendship with Mussolini.

The two men shook hands. Skorzeny walked to the door, then turned to salute the German warlord before making his exit. Hitler's gaze had never left him.

■ ■ ■

Skorzeny returned to the lobby of the Tea House bewildered by the experience. He could still feel Hitler's glance upon him, "a glance of unbearable intensity, the glance of a hypnotist."[33] Skorzeny lit a cigarette and greedily inhaled the first few puffs. Before long, Guensche appeared again and told him that Student was waiting to see him.[34]

Skorzeny entered a small office and presented himself to General Student, the well-respected commander of Germany's airborne forces. (German airborne troops belonged to the air force, unlike their counterparts in Britain and the United States, who belonged to the army.) Hitler had charged Student with overseeing the mission to find and rescue Mussolini, which had been dubbed Operation Oak. Skorzeny thought the general had a friendly face, even though it was marred by a deep scar that ran along his forehead (where he had been hit by a sniper's bullet in 1940).[35]

Skorzeny had barely begun to speak when another visitor appeared at the door. It was Heinrich Himmler. A onetime chicken farmer, Himmler was now the dreaded chief of the SS (and therefore Skorzeny's boss), not to mention one of the most powerful men in the Third Reich. After being introduced to Skorzeny, whom he had never met before, Himmler told the two men to be seated. He appeared to be anxious.

Himmler, his eyes darting behind his trademark pince-nez, proceeded to analyze the political situation in Italy and the events behind Mussolini's fall from power. The new Italian government, headed by Marshal Pietro Badoglio at the king's request, had vowed to continue fighting alongside the Nazis. Himmler suspected that Badoglio would betray the Axis at the first opportunity by making a separate peace with the Allies.

The SS chief began to list a series of Italian misdeeds, showering Skorzeny with names and dates. Though some of those in the Italian camp remained loyal to Germany, Himmler contended, many others were out-and-out traitors. With increasing agitation, he then discussed dozens of Italian notables by name—military men, politicians, and members of the Italian aristocracy—and gave them widely varying grades of reliability. The list was endless. When Skorzeny began to take notes, Himmler flew into a fury.

"Have you lost your mind?" Himmler cried, throwing a glance at Student in disbelief.[36] "These things must all remain top secret. Remember them, for God's sake!"[37] Skorzeny ceased his scribbling.

"Italy's defection is certain," Himmler continued. "The only question is: when will it occur? It may well do so tomorrow."[38] The Italians, Himmler informed them, had already sent envoys to Portugal (a neutral country with foreign diplomats in residence) to start peace talks with the West.* After exhausting the subject with another flurry of names, Himmler began to discuss other matters with Student. Skorzeny checked the time. Seeing that it was almost 11:00 P.M., he decided to telephone his office in Berlin and let his staff know what was happening.

As he stood in the hallway waiting for his call to go through, Skorzeny lit another cigarette. Himmler appeared almost at once.

"This is unbelievable!" Himmler shouted at him. "Don't you have enough willpower to stop smoking? Always these stinking cigarettes! I can see that you're not the right man for this job!"[39] Before Skorzeny could respond, the SS chief had stridden off.

"A promising beginning," Skorzeny thought to himself, putting out the cigarette with his heel.[40] He wondered whether he had already been fired.

---

*This statement was untrue, at least during the month of July.

2

TREASON IN THE AIR

The English will take advantage of this, the Russians will cheer, the English will land [on the Italian mainland]; one might say that in Italy treason was always in the air.[1]
—Hitler, referring to the Italian coup, July 26, 1943

SKORZENY MAY NOT HAVE KNOWN IT, BUT THE WOLF'S LAIR HAD BEEN in turmoil during the twenty-four hours preceding his arrival on July 26. The bald truth was that Mussolini's abrupt fall from power one day earlier had caught Hitler and his military chiefs off guard.

The Germans were not oblivious to the potential for political intrigue in Italy; indeed, Hitler had become increasingly suspicious of the Italian royal house in recent months as the Axis army in North Africa crumbled and an Allied invasion of Italy loomed large. The German dictator had railed for years about the dangers posed by the king and the court circle—he had a lifelong contempt for the bourgeois and upper classes in general—whom he portrayed collectively as an aristocratic fifth column.*[2] The Nazis also worried about

---

*In August 1939, on the eve of World War II, Hitler emphasized to his generals that the very existence of Mussolini was "decisive" and warned that if he were removed from the political equation "Italy's loyalty to the [Axis] alliance will no longer be certain. The basic attitude of the Italian Court is against the Duce." Even before this date, Hitler and the king of Italy had grown to loathe each other. *Nazi Conspiracy and Aggression*, vol. 3, 582.

Mussolini's failing health, which seemed to threaten the stability of the Fascist regime in Italy.

"One has to be on the watch like a spider in its web," Hitler had remarked dramatically just two months earlier. "Thank God I've always had a pretty good nose for everything so that I can generally smell things out before they happen."[3]

But despite increased vigilance, the timing of the Duce's sudden overthrow by the king came as a bitter surprise to the Germans. When it came to Italy, Hitler depended for information on his men-on-the-spot in Rome, who consisted primarily of diplomats at the German embassy and agents working for the Third Reich's police and intelligence services. They had been caught napping.[4] The German ambassador to Rome, Hans Georg von Mackensen (the son of a famous field marshal), had badly misjudged the state of affairs in the capital. Not only did the ambassador and his subordinates fail to anticipate the royal machinations behind the coup; they were also grossly ignorant of lesser schemes being hatched by Mussolini's cronies in the Grand Council of Fascism.

It is ironic that on July 25, the day the Duce was arrested at the king's villa, Mackensen had informed his superiors in Germany that Mussolini had the political situation in Rome under control. The Nazis received his optimistic analysis at about the same time they learned of the Italian coup. "Von Mackensen's report reached its destination just as Benito Mussolini became a prisoner of his King and Emperor," recalled Eugen Dollmann, an SS man who was with Mackensen when the latter sent off his report. "The German Foreign Minister [Ribbentrop] was wild with fury when he heard the news."[5]

Hitler was juggling other developing crises on the war front around the time of the Duce's fall, the latest in a series of military disasters and demoralizing reverses for the European Axis powers. Though most of Europe remained firmly in Hitler's grip by July, when Il Duce was arrested, the Allies were beginning to press hard around the edges.

Stalin's armies were hotly contesting Germany's newly conquered Lebensraum, or living space, in the East. Things had begun to unravel there for the Germans early in the year. The Battle of Stalingrad, one of the most brutal episodes of the war, had finally ended in February 1943. It was Germany's most devastating defeat to date. When the dust cleared, several hundred thousand Axis soldiers, casualties of Hitler's muddle-headed no-retreat policy, had been killed or captured by the Russians. Stalingrad was a major psychological turning point in the war, not to mention a grave loss to the Reich of much-needed manpower.

An even larger catastrophe (if that were possible) soon followed on the southern front. In May that year, the Anglo-Americans were victorious in the arid deserts of North Africa, scene of earlier exploits by Marshal Erwin Rommel, the Desert Fox. The Allied success in Africa deprived the Axis of 250,000 Italian and German soldiers, who had surrendered with Mussolini's reluctant blessing, and prepared the way for a July 10 invasion of Sicily.[6] "After their covering positions in Africa had been removed," recalled General Siegfried Westphal, a high-ranking officer in the Italian theater, "the southern flank of the 'Fortress Germany' was exposed, and an assault could be made on the 'soft under-belly' of Europe, as Churchill called it."[7] Axis misfortune in the Mediterranean also stiffened the resolve of Italians in high places who were contemplating the ouster of the Duce.

In the West, where the war was being fought on the seas and in the skies, the Axis was faring little better. The Battle of the Atlantic, a deadly cat-and-mouse game that pitted German submarines against Allied cargo ships and their defenders, had turned sharply in the Allies' favor by spring. Hitler's only choice was the temporary withdrawal of his once-dreaded U-boats from the North Atlantic, an action that allowed thousands of merchant vessels to cross from the United States to Britain that summer.[8] From the Axis point of view, the situation was unacceptable and presented more than just a setback. "We had," Admiral Karl Doenitz, chief of the German navy, concluded in retrospect, "lost the Battle of the Atlantic."[9]

For the urban populace of Germany, 1943 was the year the Allies brought the war home to the Third Reich with a vengeance by stepping up their bombing campaigns against major German cities.

Taking off from their bases in Britain, which began to resemble an enormous aircraft carrier, Allied bombers flew endless sorties into Germany during the first half of the year (and beyond).*[10] The Casablanca Conference, an Allied summit attended by Winston Churchill and Franklin Roosevelt in January, had officially sanctioned the use of carpet-bombing to destroy strategic targets and undermine the morale of the German people.[11] Confident of ultimate victory, the Allied leaders at Casablanca also formally pronounced the endgame: They would accept nothing less than "unconditional surrender" from Germany, Italy, and Japan.[12]

■ ■ ■

Though Hitler was far from finished—the Russians would not win the race for Berlin until April 1945—the stress of the war had begun to take its toll on the fifty-four-year-old German dictator by the time of Mussolini's fall. Early in 1943, for instance, Hitler noticed trembling in his left arm and leg.[13] His attempts to control these chronic tremors, which grew worse despite treatment, gave rise to new mannerisms: He would cross his right hand over his left and push his foot against any stationary object that happened to be nearby.[14] At about the same time, Hitler developed a slight limp and had to drag his left foot behind him as he walked.[15]

Though he did not smoke or drink alcohol, the abstemious dictator was a hypochondriac who found it difficult to function during these increasingly dark days without frequent doses of various drugs, vitamins, glucose injections, hormones, and more exotic concoctions.[16] His personal physician, a certified quack known as Professor (Theodor) Morell, maintained a vast pharmacopoeia in the Wolf's Lair for this purpose and became indispensable to Hitler and other members of his staff.[17] The ministrations of the inept pro-

---

*About 200,000 tons of bombs were dropped on Germany during 1943 alone. That was five times as much tonnage as was dropped the year before.

fessor, who sometimes used his gullible master as a guinea pig for the testing of new drugs, may very well have contributed to Hitler's deterioration.[*][18] (Between 1941 and 1945, Morell gave Hitler a staggering number of medications and supposedly therapeutic preparations: seventy-seven in all.)[19]

Infrequent visitors to the Wolf's Lair were often shocked by Hitler's decline. On July 7, 1943, just a few weeks before Mussolini's fall, Wernher von Braun, who was the architect of Germany's rocket program, arrived at the compound for a meeting. "Hitler's physical appearance was frightening," recalled Braun, who instinctively linked Hitler's failing health to the recent downturn in the war. "I had last seen him in 1939. He looked tired but still radiated an almost magic strength. His eyes had something diabolical in them, but his face was pale, and he looked like a beaten man."[20]

Or, as Rommel put it succinctly to his wife at the end of July 1943: "Sometimes you feel that he's no longer quite normal."[21]

■ ■ ■

Hitler and the Germans learned of the Italian coup a few hours after it took place on July 25, though deceptive measures taken by the Badoglio government continued to obscure the details for weeks to come. The first indications of trouble south of the Alps had surfaced during the afternoon Fuehrer Conference at the Wolf's Lair.

As it happened, part of this conference, which began in the late morning, coincided with the meeting between Mussolini and the Japanese ambassador, Shinrokuro Hidaka, at the Palazzo Venezia in Rome. The same afternoon that the Duce was complaining to Hidaka about Italy's lack of military resources, Hitler was sitting in a conference room of the Wolf's Lair enduring yet another round of

---

*The decline in health that Hitler experienced during the last few years of his life has never been fully explained. It has been suggested that an onset of Parkinson's disease could account for some of Hitler's symptoms, though no one can rule out the effects of sheer psychological stress.

depressing status reports. One of these revealed a serious shortage of reserves on the eastern front, where Germany and Russia had been locked in a titanic struggle for more than two years.

On July 5, the German army had launched a massive new offensive in the Kursk region—it was referred to as the Citadel plan—involving 500,000 men and thousands of tanks. The attack had made little progress, so little, in fact, that the Russians were emboldened to launch an offensive of their own in mid-July.[22]

"Operation Citadel was more than a battle lost," recalled General Walter Warlimont, "it handed the Russians the initiative and we never recovered it again right up to the end of the war."[23] On the day of his arrest, Mussolini gave an explanation to Hidaka: "It is urgently necessary that Germany and Russia stop making war on one another. It's not that Germany does not want to help us, but she is so bogged down on the eastern front as to be unable to send us any help."[24]

Hitler's mind was also grappling that afternoon with his old nemesis, the English (those "arrogant islanders"), whom he had failed to subdue in 1940.[25] The previous evening (Saturday), while Mussolini was facing a rebellion in the Fascist Grand Council, the Allies had staged a major bombing raid against Hamburg, Germany's second-largest city.[26] It was the violent herald of a devastating, multistage air attack dubbed Operation Gomorrah. The explicit aim of the operation, as specified by Bomber Command, was to destroy the city.[27]

This goal was nearly accomplished. Two days later, on July 27, another air raid on Hamburg ignited an enormous sea of fire that prompted the Hamburg Fire Department to coin the term *Feuersturm,* or firestorm.[28] The inferno reached temperatures of 1,400 degrees Fahrenheit, killing tens of thousands and destroying eight square miles of the city—an area about half the size of Manhattan.[29] Some of the German victims were roasted alive within the confines of bomb shelters; others were trapped in the melting asphalt of city streets before succumbing.[30]

But on July 25, the true horrors of Hamburg lay in the future. At about 1:30 P.M., Hitler was arguing with an officer from the air force about how Germany, with its ever-shrinking resources, should respond to the Saturday-night bombing and similar outrages. Having withdrawn their submarines from the North Atlantic, the Nazis were contemplating a scheme that involved laying mines in English coastal waters (via airplane) in an attempt to disrupt Allied supply lines. But with Hamburg weighing on his mind, Hitler was in the mood for more violent means of retaliation. The conversation was taken down verbatim by Wolf's Lair stenographers.*

"I have already told you, when we discussed this a few days ago, that terror can only be broken by terror," Hitler said to Colonel Eckard Christian. "One has to counter-attack, everything else is nonsense. In my opinion all this mining is worthless, it gives no lift to our people and it doesn't affect those people over there either. . . . In my opinion we should use our planes for attacking them directly, especially since they are putting so many planes into the air."[31]

As on many other occasions during the war, Hitler's first instinct was to strike with overwhelming force. But in 1943, the deadly whims of the German warlord were constrained by shortages of men and machines. Christian gently pressed the point—the Luftwaffe simply did not have enough bombers available to carry out large-scale raids against England. At least the mine-laying operation, he argued, would have an "indirect" effect on the enemy.[32]

"Terror can only be broken by terror," Hitler repeated firmly. "We can only stop this business if we get at the people over there. Otherwise our own people will gradually go crazy. . . . It is going to work only if we attack their cities systematically. But all the time I am told things like 'We couldn't find that place' or 'We don't have enough planes'; but then it turns out we do have enough to do something else . . . the usual excuse I get to hear is, 'We can't find it.' You can't find London! A God-damned shame!"[33]

But Germany simply did not have enough planes available, Christian said.

---

*According to Albert Speer, Hitler began to employ stenographers at headquarters in the fall of 1942 and so provide "evidence for posterity that he had always issued the right orders." Speer, 305.

"That's not true," Hitler countered. "The important thing is to make them feel something. It seems to me that if there are 50 bombers over the center of Munich it is quite enough; not a single person can sleep that night. At any rate, it is better for you to put 50 of our planes over a city like that than to drop mines. That's a lot of tripe!"[34]

The Luftwaffe officer continued to argue his point, but Hitler had heard enough.

"Instead of monkeying around," Hitler replied, "let's attack, get ready here, and pick out a target—it doesn't matter what target. We can't go on this way. Eventually the German people will go nuts. . . . Terror can only be broken by terror, and in no other way."[35]

When Hitler learned that the Allies had lost only twelve bombers during the Hamburg raid, he asked Christian to determine exactly the points at which they had been shot down.* Christian's response revealed that bombers were not the only commodity in short supply in the Germany of 1943:

"Yes," Christian said, "but that takes longer now because we don't allocate any gas for that. They just send people out with bicycles."[36]

"That has to be done," said Hitler, who suddenly sounded like a scolding headmaster, "or else you won't be able to make a report. You'll have to send them out with bicycles."[37]

■ ■ ■

Such were the exigencies competing for German attention on the day Mussolini walked into a trap at the king's villa in Rome.

It was later during this same conference that Hitler received the first hint of the power struggle underway in the Eternal City. It came in the form of a report from Walter Hewel, Ribbentrop's man at Hitler's headquarters, who had been in touch with Ambassador

---

*The minimal losses suffered by the Allies (who had put 791 bombers in the air) were largely due to the debut of Window, a new development in the ongoing radar wars: Thousands upon thousands of thin aluminum strips had been dumped over Hamburg in an effort to jam German radar.

Mackensen in Rome.[38] Hewel confirmed that the Duce had convened the Fascist Grand Council the previous evening, Saturday,
July 24. As Hitler was aware, the council was little more than a
rubber-stamp committee in the service of Mussolini, who had not
even bothered to convene it since 1939.

"He heard from different sources that the meeting was extraor-
dinarily stormy," said Hewel, referring to Mackensen. "Since the
participants are sworn to secrecy, he hasn't heard anything authentic yet; only rumors."[39] The Germans did not know it at that point,
but the Grand Council had essentially voted to abolish the Duce's
dictatorship. Because the Council had no legal powers and lacked
the brute force necessary to enforce its resolution, the vote was
largely a symbolic gesture. Only a coup supported by the Italian
military was likely to succeed, but the army had decided to back the
king of Italy's more radical change of regime.

In the absence of additional information, the gravity of the situation in Italy was not readily apparent. Hitler seemed more puzzled
than alarmed. "What's the use of councils like that?" he asked.
"What do they do except jabber?"[40]

■ ■ ■

By early evening, however, news of the Italian coup had exploded
upon the Wolf's Lair like a thunderbolt. Though the finer points remained sketchy, even the bare fact of the power grab was enough to
send shock waves through the compound. Around 9:45 P.M., Marshal Wilhelm Keitel, Hitler's sycophantic chief of *Oberkommando
der Wehrmacht* (OKW)—the German High Command—was hurry-
ing to a conference room where the Fuehrer and a few others had
assembled to discuss the matter.

"The Duce has resigned," Hitler announced. The words were directed at Keitel, who had just entered the room, but it seemed as if
Hitler were still trying to convince himself of the news. "It is not
confirmed yet. Badoglio has taken over the government. The Duce
has resigned."[41]

That evening, shortly after King Victor Emmanuel had arrested the Italian dictator, Badoglio contacted the Germans and issued a cover story: Mussolini had stepped down of his own accord and Badoglio had been charged by the king to head a provisional Italian government.[42] Badoglio emphasized that the regime change was purely a domestic matter and did not affect its alliance with Germany.[43] He assured his Axis ally that Italy would continue to fight against their common enemies.[44] Disgusted, Hitler did not even bother to reply.[45]

"The decisive thing is," asked General Alfred Jodl, chief of operations for OKW, "are the Italians going to continue fighting, or not?"[46] ("Decisive" was something of a pet word among the Nazis.)

"They say they will fight," Hitler answered, "but it is certainly treachery. We must realize that this is open treachery. I'm just waiting for information about what the Duce says . . . I want the Duce to come to Germany right away."[47] No one in the German camp was having success in tracking down Mussolini.

"If there is any doubt," Jodl said, "there is only one thing to do."[48]

It was only hours since the Duce's downfall, but Hitler was contemplating a forced takeover of Rome and the swift reinstatement of Mussolini: "I have been thinking about ordering the 3rd Panzergrenadier Division to occupy Rome and to capture the whole government," Hitler said, referring to a motorized division stationed about thirty-five miles north of Rome near Lake Bolsena.[49]

Military discussions between Hitler and his advisors followed. He was especially concerned about the large number of German troops fighting in Sicily. By July 25, the Allies had squeezed these soldiers into the northeastern corner of the island.[50] Hitler feared that if the Italians switched sides in the war, German units trapped in Sicily would be surrounded by an enemy coalition of Italian and British-American forces.

"The fellows down here have to be saved under all circumstances," Hitler said in reference to the troops in Sicily. "They are of no use down here. They have to get back. . . . Their equipment doesn't matter a damn. Let them blow it up or destroy it; but the men have to get back. There are 70,000 men there now. . . . We can handle the Italians with side arms."*[51] Recent history had convinced Hitler that he could safely underestimate serious resistance on the part of the Italian army.

"We really ought to wait for exact reports about what is going on," said Jodl.[52]

"Certainly," said Hitler, "but still we have to plan ahead. Undoubtedly, in their treachery, they will proclaim that they will remain loyal to us; but that is treachery. Of course they won't remain loyal."[53]

For Hitler, the implications of the Duce's mysterious vanishing act were clear from the beginning. Having disposed of Mussolini—practically the only leading Italian who still maintained fidelity to the Axis—the Badoglio government would move quickly to negotiate a separate peace with the Allies. Or perhaps, as Hitler feared, Badoglio had made a deal with the enemy *before* the coup. As things stood on July 25, the Allies could easily swoop into mainland Italy (which was practically bare of German troops) with Badoglio's consent and take over the country.

"Has anyone spoken to this fellow Badoglio?" Keitel asked.[54]

"Although that so-and-so declared immediately that the war would be continued," Hitler said, "that won't make any difference. They have to say that, but it remains treason. But we'll play the same game while preparing everything to take over the whole crew with one stroke, to capture all of that riffraff. . . . The climax will come at the moment when we have mustered enough strength to go in there and disarm the whole gang."[55]

The meeting was interrupted by Hitler's telephone call to Hermann Goering, the corpulent chief of the Luftwaffe. Goering had been planning to pay a visit to the Duce to celebrate his sixtieth birthday on July 29, just a few days hence. Hitler's war chiefs listened as

---

*German forces on Sicily included the SS-Panzerdivision "Hermann Goering," the Fifteenth Panzergrenadier Division, and elements of the Twenty-ninth Motorized Infantry Division and the First Parachute Division.

the dictator personally delivered the bad news to his disbelieving longtime lieutenant. Though they could hear only Hitler's part of the call, the drift of the conversation was clear enough.

"Hello, Goering?" Hitler asked. "I don't know—did you get the news? Well, there's no direct confirmation yet, but there can't be any doubt that the Duce has resigned and that Badoglio has taken his place. In Rome it is not a question of possibilities, but of facts. That's the truth, Goering, there's no doubt about it. . . . At any rate, under these circumstances I think it would be a good idea for you to come here right away. What? I don't know. I'll tell you about that then. But adjust yourself to the fact that it's true."[56]

Hitler hung up the phone. "I only hope they didn't arrest the Duce," he said. "But if they did, it is even more important that we go in there."[57]

Even when outside the conference room, Hitler seems to have spent much of the evening huffing and puffing about the Italians. "Hitler swore," recalled Traudl Junge, one of Hitler's female secretaries. "He was furious about the [secret] secession of Italy and Mussolini's mishap, and that evening he didn't hide his bad temper even from us women. He was monosyllabic and absent-minded. 'So Mussolini is weaker than I thought,' he said. 'I was giving him my personal support, and now he's fallen. But we could never rely on the Italians. . . . They've cost us more in loss of prestige and real setbacks than any success they brought us was worth.'"[58]

The Duce's disappearance was all the more disturbing to Hitler because he had seen his fellow dictator and "friend" just one week before his fall. The two men had met at Feltre in northern Italy for a military conference, their thirteenth in nearly ten years.*[59] The meeting was precipitated by the chaos following the Allied invasion of

---

*The first Allied bombing of Rome occurred on this same day. Rome was a major transportation hub (road and rail), which made it a tempting target for the enemy. Most of the supplies reaching the Germans in Sicily and southern Italy ran through Rome.

Sicily.* Almost immediately after the Anglo-Americans had landed on the beaches, the two Axis powers began to clash.

For the Italians, the key issue was military aid—or rather the lack of it. Their outnumbered, demoralized, and ill-equipped forces were no match for the massive Allied assault, especially in the air. On July 12, just two days after fighting had broken out on the island, the Italians urgently requested that Hitler send them 2,000 fighter planes to help stem the tide. Hitler balked at this and other large requests for military support, which in turn outraged many in the Italian camp who had hoped that the Nazis would rally to Italy's side.

For them, Hitler's standoffishness was proof that the Fuehrer was intending to "leave Italy in the lurch"—to sacrifice his Mediterranean partner to the Allies so that he could wear down the enemy, conserve German forces, and delay an assault on the Third Reich itself.[60] Dino Alfieri, the Italian ambassador in Berlin, spoke for many on the Italian side of the Axis when he expressed the view that Hitler looked on Italy and the Axis satellite countries merely as "bastions of the German fortress."[61] Germany could "never commit herself fully against the Anglo-Americans in Italy because she wants to reserve her main effort for the Russian campaign and does not yet possess sufficient forces to wage total war on both fronts simultaneously."[62]

Hitler, meanwhile, was deeply disturbed by reports he had received—and these reports were accurate—indicating that the Italians were offering only a token resistance to the Anglo-American attack (and in many cases were surrendering or simply melting away). "The Fuehrer's worries are heavier than ever," lamented the fanatical Martin Bormann, Hitler's aide, in a letter written to his wife during July. "The Italians are bolting, exactly as they did in Russia, or they simply let themselves be taken prisoner. In actual

---

*Rudolf Semmler, who worked in the Propaganda Ministry, recorded Goebbels's first reaction to the news. "On our journey back to Berlin in the train," wrote Semmler in his diary on July 10, "we heard at Erfurt, at three in the morning, that the enemy had landed in Sicily. Goebbels looked black and once again cursed our alliance with the 'macaroni eaters.'" Semmler, 90.

fact Sicily is now being held only by our handful of Germans."[63] That meant that Hitler's 60,000 or so soldiers were left to fend off an Allied invasion force of half a million men.[64]

On the evening of July 12, just two days after the Sicily invasion, Hitler sent Mussolini an angry message through General Enno von Rintelen, the military attaché at the German embassy in Rome. Rintelen, who served as a military liaison between the Nazis and the Italians, told the Duce that Hitler had no intention of sending more German soldiers to Italy if the Italians were not willing to defend their own country. This sparked a flurry of exchanges between the Axis partners.

On July 18, Mussolini wrote Hitler a lengthy telegram.* The Allied successes in Sicily, he argued, had nothing to do with a lack of fighting spirit on the part of the Italians. But Italy was reaching the end of her tether and required help. "Germany is stronger economically and militarily than Italy," the Duce wrote. "My country . . . has step by step exhausted itself, burning up its resources in Africa, Russia, and the Balkans."[65]

Mussolini also included an ominous warning: "The sacrifice of my country cannot have as its principal purpose that of delaying a direct attack on Germany."[66] The same day, the Duce received an urgent invitation from Hitler to attend an Axis summit scheduled for the following morning, July 19. After grumbling over the short notice, Mussolini agreed.

The stakes at Feltre had been high for both men. With the defense of Sicily in doubt, Hitler worried with some justification that even the Duce, as staunch an ally as he was, might consider backing out of the war altogether. Using a combination of bluff and bluster, Hitler meant to whip up the martial spirit of his drooping Axis ally without promising too much in the way of direct German aid, now in short supply.[67] On the Italian side, Mussolini faced an equally daunting challenge. He was under intense domestic pressure to obtain

---

*It is unclear whether this missive was actually sent.

speedy military support for the defense of Italy or, failing that, to end his country's participation in the war—if possible, by seeking Hitler's permission to pursue a separate peace with the enemy.

However, as had happened so often in the past, the Duce did not quite muster the courage to speak frankly with Hitler when the two men were standing face-to-face in northern Italy. Whether out of fear or shame, Mussolini could not bring himself to admit that Italy had finally reached the end of the line.

It was the Duce's inexplicable silence at Feltre that had prompted the king of Italy to remove him from power one week later on July 25.

3

AN EARLY FRIENDSHIP

*The man is hysterical. When he told me that no one had
lived through and shared my anguish more intensely than he
had there were tears in his eyes. All that is an exaggeration.*[1]
— **Mussolini, referring to Hitler's behavior
during a 1941 Axis summit**

HITLER'S DETERMINATION TO RESCUE MUSSOLINI FROM THE CLUTCHES
of his fellow Italians was a dramatic reminder of how much had
changed since the early 1920s when the two men first made tentative contact.[2] At that time, Hitler was a little-known right-wing
agitator, but Mussolini was the leader of Fascist Italy and an increasingly visible figure on the world stage.* The young and ambitious
Hitler looked up to Il Duce in those days, and it is not difficult to see
why. The Fascist revolution in Italy was a source of inspiration and a
potential model for what Hitler fervently dreamed of accomplishing
in Germany.

"In this period—I openly admit—I conceived the profoundest
admiration for the great man south of the Alps," Hitler wrote in *Mein
Kampf,* referring to the year 1923, "who, full of ardent love for his

---

*It is sometimes forgotten that, before he gravitated toward Hitler, Mussolini was
the darling of many of the world's conservative politicians and opinion makers.
He counted Winston Churchill among his admirers.

people, made no pacts with the enemies of Italy, but strove for their annihilation by all ways and means. What will rank Mussolini among the great men of this earth is his determination not to share Italy with the Marxists, but to destroy internationalism and save the fatherland from it."[3] (That the Duce had succeeded in getting the Italian trains to run on time was mere icing on the cake.)[4]

However, the attraction was not necessarily mutual. True, Mussolini occasionally (and quietly) doled out cash to Hitler's fledgling Nazi Party during its bid for power and offered it other forms of assistance.[5] But the cautious Italian dictator, while claiming to be flattered by Hitler's admiration, generally kept the angry Austrian at arm's length.[6]

In 1926, for instance, when Hitler contacted the Italian embassy in Berlin asking for a signed photograph of his idol Mussolini, his request was promptly turned down.[7] "Please thank the above-named gentleman for his sentiments," read a message from Rome to the Italian diplomats in the German capital, "and tell him in whatever form you think best that the Duce does not think fit to accede to his request."[8] Hitler had to make do with a bronze bust of Mussolini, proudly displayed in his office at the Brown House, the Munich headquarters of the Nazis.[9]

The dynamic between the two men began to change when Hitler came to power in the early 1930s. Germany was disarmed and politically isolated at the time, and Hitler, who became chancellor early in 1933, was determined to strengthen the country's military might and divide (and thereby weaken) the major European powers.[10] Though the Duce had mixed feelings about the new Fuehrer—a resuscitated Germany could certainly pose dangers for Italy—he also believed he could use Hitler for his own ends: namely, that by exploiting the West's fear of Nazism he could extract territorial concessions for Italy in the Balkans, the Mediterranean, or North Africa.

Naturally, Mussolini feared that Hitler would attempt to unite Germany and Austria, thereby erasing in one blow the security buffer (Austria) between Italy and the Third Reich.[11] But the Duce was confident that he could control his adoring protégé and overrule attempts to create the so-called *Anschluss* (forbidden by the Treaty of Versailles).[12] As Mussolini remarked at this time (1933), "[Hitler is] simply a muddle-headed fellow; his brain is stuffed with philosophical and political tags that are utterly incoherent."[13]

Having spent the previous decade dodging Hitler, the Duce finally agreed to meet with the German dictator in Venice in June 1934. Even at this early date, Hitler did much of the talking, expounding on the two themes closest to his heart: aggressive war and race.[14] Hitler even went so far as to cast bizarre aspersions on what he viewed as the less-than-pure race of the Italians!

"I was afraid I'd have difficulties with the German language," admitted the Duce, who spoke several languages, including German. "But I had none whatever. He gave me no chance to speak."[15] Mussolini was not much impressed by the effusive Nazi, whom he compared to a broken record that repeated itself endlessly.[16] "He [Hitler] is a violent man with no self-control," he concluded, "and nothing positive came out of our talks."[17]

It was a prophetic comment. Though no stranger to violence, the Duce was shocked when, just a few days after the conference, Hitler murdered several hundred Nazi comrades and political enemies during a bloody purge later dubbed the Night of the Long Knives. "Look at his," Mussolini said in disgust to his wife, Rachele, pointing to newspaper accounts of Hitler's brutal handiwork. "That person makes me think of Attila the Hun. Those men he killed were his closest supporters, who raised him to power."[18]

He was even more flabbergasted in July by a Nazi attempt to seize power in Vienna (Hitler did not like to waste time). Hitler quickly backed down when the Duce made threatening gestures by placing four Italian divisions on the Brenner Pass (on the frontier between Italy and Austria). But relations between the two men had hit an all-time low. Shortly after the Austrian fiasco, Mussolini referred to Hitler as a "horrible sexual degenerate" and a "dangerous fool."[19] Nazism was nothing less than "savage barbarism" in his eyes.[20] "Murder and killing, loot and pillage and blackmail are all it can produce."[21]

■ ■ ■

Over the next several years, England and France encouraged the Duce's hostility toward Germany and sought to cultivate an alliance with Italy to counter the potential threat posed by the Nazis. But Hitler also began an elaborate courtship of Mussolini, who dreamed of reviving the power and glory of the ancient Roman Empire, by slowly drawing him into Germany's orbit and playing on the dictator's vanity and greed. Being an opportunist by nature, the Duce was content to play both sides against each other and so obtain the maximum advantage for himself and his nation.

Hitler's aggressive swagger continued to give Mussolini cause for concern.[22] In March 1935, Hitler mocked the Treaty of Versailles by announcing his intention to create an army of half a million men. One month later, Italy joined England and France in condemning Hitler's actions and voicing its support for Austrian independence. This momentary alliance was referred to as the Stresa front, and it was aimed squarely at Germany. By joining ranks with the democratic states, the Duce had provided himself with a measure of security on Italy's northern border. And keeping Hitler in check was particularly important for Mussolini because the Italian dictator was contemplating a land grab of his own—in Africa.[23]

In October 1935, the Duce launched his brutal and unprovoked invasion of Ethiopia (then known as Abyssinia). "I had to wage the Abyssinian campaign," Mussolini remarked privately (and grandiosely) during the war. "Italy needs new colonies, the Italian people require more land, Italy has become too small for us."[24] England and France had already gobbled up large parts of the world, he was wont to argue, so why should Italy not do the same? With the Duce's approval, General Pietro Badoglio, who was running the military operation, used poison gas against the Ethiopians to speed the progress of the invasion.

Europe was divided over Mussolini's blatant act of aggression. Hitler was delighted, but the Western Powers found themselves in a more awkward position. Although they were loath to allow Mussolini's invasion of Ethiopia to go unpunished, they were also hesitant to alienate the Italian dictator, whom they viewed as a possible counterweight to Hitler. England and France therefore decided to issue sanctions against Italy (through the League of Nations), but made certain that they had no teeth. Though this compromise solution failed to prevent the rape of Ethiopia, it did succeed in antagonizing the Duce and driving him closer to Hitler.

■ ■ ■

Their partnership began to coalesce in 1936. Early in the year, Hitler snubbed his nose at the West by sending German troops into the Rhineland, which had been demilitarized. Though England and France could have easily stopped Hitler in his tracks (and Hitler was aware of this), they declined to force the issue.

In May, the Italians took the Ethiopian capital of Addis Ababa and effectively completed their conquest of that country, after which the League of Nations admitted defeat and cancelled its sanctions. The war against the Ethiopians made Mussolini more popular than ever among the Italians, who were now informed that they were the proud owners of a new Italian Empire.[25] On the heels of this victory came another, more private (and longer-lasting) conquest: Claretta Petacci.

Claretta was then twenty-four years old (half the Duce's age).[26] Their affair began shortly after the Ethiopian war, although they had known each other for several years.[27] Her fascination with Mussolini had started much earlier: As a young girl, she had slept with his photograph under her pillow.[28] Though the Duce kept many mistresses during the Fascist era, it was his steady relationship with this attractive, husky-voiced, green-eyed brunette that captured the imagination of the Romans and caused tongues to wag.

Another notable event that took place in 1936 (in June) was the elevation of Count Galeazzo Ciano to the position of Italian foreign

minister. The thirty-three-year-old Ciano, who had spent the previous few years working in the Press Office, was married to Mussolini's favorite daughter, Edda.[29] Though Ciano was not without
intelligence—or cunning, for that matter—he was also young and
frivolous, a handsome playboy who worshipped the Duce and
shared his father-in-law's ambitious aspirations for Italy.[30]

"He was by nature extremely vivacious, whimsical, imaginative,
ironical and sentimental," wrote Dino Alfieri, a Fascist diplomat. "He
always had a ready retort and his wit was facile and spontaneous. In
Ciano contrasting qualities blended and often clashed."[31] Like Mussolini, Ciano believed that the Western powers were weak and on the
decline.[32] Though he favored an alliance with the Nazis on practical
grounds, he was never hypnotized by them in the way the Duce was.[33]

In October 1936, Ciano and Hitler met for talks. Hitler was lav-
ish in his praise for Mussolini, calling him "the leading statesman
in the world, to whom none may even remotely compare himself."[34]
Hitler also bragged about the great things that could be accomplished if the Germans and Italians joined forces. Carving up the
world in his mind, Hitler explained that the Nazis could dominate
Eastern Europe and the Duce could expand his empire in the Mediterranean and North Africa.[35] Ciano did not need much convincing.
He returned to Italy naïvely thinking that he and Mussolini could
easily manipulate the Fuehrer to their own advantage.[36]

A few days later, on November 1, speaking in Milan's Piazza del
Duomo, the Duce referred to the growing relationship between Italy
and Germany and employed the metaphor of an axis: "This vertical
line between Rome and Berlin is not a partition, but rather an axis
around which all the European States animated by the will to collaboration and peace can also collaborate."*[37]

In 1936, Mussolini also began to boast irresponsibly of Italy's
"eight million bayonets" (a phrase he often repeated thereafter), a

---

*Mussolini did not coin the term. A Hungarian politician had used the word
"axis" in this same context two years before Mussolini adopted it as his own.

wildly misleading reference to the number of Italian troops that could be mustered in the event of war.[38] In reality, the Duce could raise only about 1.5 million soldiers, and the country was generally unprepared for a major European conflict.[39] Italy's tanks were too light by the standards of the day, its warplanes and artillery were woefully out of date, and many of its soldiers were armed with antiquated, 1890s-style rifles more suitable for the American Wild West than for a modern-day battlefield.[40]

■ ■ ■

In September 1937, wearing a brand new blue-gray uniform that he had ordered for the occasion, Mussolini visited Germany at Hitler's invitation.[41] The Nazis spared no expense in attempting to woo the Duce with shows of pomp and pageantry and demonstrations of Germany's increasing military might.

On the Maifeld in Berlin, near the Olympic stadium, the two dictators made speeches to a cheering audience of nearly a million people (some of whom had been coached on the intricacies of proper cheering).[42] Hitler praised Mussolini as "one of the lonely men in history who are not put to trial by historic events but determine the history of their country themselves."[43] The Duce responded with a fateful promise: "When one finds a friend, march along with him to the end."[44]

Though Mussolini continued to flirt with England and France in the years to come, his visit to Germany had made a profound impression on him.[45] Psychologically he had chosen sides. "From now onwards Mussolini clung to the myth of probable German invincibility," observed the historian Denis Mack Smith, "and this reception in 1937 was a fateful and fatal event in his life."[46] Or as the SS man Eugen Dollmann put it: "Megalomania is infectious."[47]

In March 1938, Germany annexed Austria; but even though Mussolini had repeatedly sworn to protect Austria from Nazi intrusion, he looked the other way. Hitler could barely contain himself when he learned that the Duce had offered no objections.

"Then, please tell Mussolini," Hitler said over the telephone to his envoy in Rome, "I will never forget him for this! Never, never, never, no matter what happens! . . . As soon as the Austrian affair has been settled I shall be ready to go with him through thick and thin—through anything! . . . You may tell him that I do thank him from the bottom of my heart. Never, never shall I forget it. I shall never forget him for this, no matter what happens. If he should ever need any help or be in any danger, he can be convinced that I shall stick to him whatever may happen, even if the whole world gangs up on him."[48]

The Duce accepted Hitler's fervent gratitude. The murmurs of the Italian people, on the other hand, were less accommodating. "For the first time since the murder of Matteotti," wrote Mussolini biographer Christopher Hibbert, referring to a great scandal that had occurred early in the Duce's reign, "a general and deep sense of disenchantment swept over them; and although the Axis survived the *Anschluss,* the Duce's hitherto unquestionable popularity did not. Apart from the sudden and seemingly abject change of policy to please an unwanted ally, no intelligent observer could fail to realize the dangers for Italy in allowing a strong and militant Germany to extend its frontiers to the Alps."[49] (These dangers became clear during the summer of 1943 when Hitler began sending the German army into Italy via Austria and the Brenner Pass.)

Hitler was keen on obtaining a formal military alliance with Italy before making his next brash (and illegal) move—an invasion of Czechoslovakia—but Mussolini was not yet ready to sign on the dotted line. He did, however, take other steps during 1938 to strengthen ties between the two countries. For one thing, he forced his fellow Italians to adopt the Nazi goose step, which the Duce renamed the *passo Romano* (Roman step) and demonstrated in public.* (The borrowing occasionally went both ways. The Nazi raised-

---

*Throughout his political career, Mussolini made a point of showing off his physical vigor, and could often be seen shirtless in press photos. By way of contrast, Hitler avoided almost all forms of exercise (aside from short walks) after 1938 in the mistaken belief that he suffered from a bad heart.

arm salute, for example, was modeled on the Roman salute adopted by the Fascists.)[50]

More important, during the summer and fall of 1938, Mussolini introduced a series of anti-Semitic racial laws that affected the 40,000 to 70,000 Jews living in Italy.[51] He had already laid the groundwork for this legislation by instructing the Italian press to denigrate Jews in the media.[52] According to the new restrictions, Jews were to be expelled from Italian schools (whether they be teachers or pupils), purged from the military, forbidden to marry gentiles, and excluded from owning land or certain types of businesses.[53]

By all accounts, the Duce's racial laws (though not energetically enforced) were not well received by the open-minded Italian people.[54] Mussolini's own beliefs about race—to the extent that he had a well-defined point of view at all—are harder to decipher. Over the years, for instance, the dictator had worked with Italian Jews, many of whom were Fascists and looked fondly on the Duce, and had indulged in affairs with Jewish women.[55]

During the early 1930s, in fact, he had shown contempt for Hitler's racial theories, which he had dismissed as the ravings of a crank. "Here in Italy we have practically no Jewish question," Mussolini remarked at the time. "We too have our Jews. There are many in the Fascist Party, and they are good Fascists and good Italians."[56] Hitler's views on race were "nonsense."[57] The very notion of anti-Semitism was "stupid and barbarous."[58]

"Thirty centuries of history," the Duce proclaimed during a public speech in September of 1934, "enable us to look with majestic pity at certain doctrines taught on the other side of the Alps by the descendants of people who were wholly illiterate in the days when Rome boasted a Caesar, a Virgil, and an Augustus."[59]

Regardless of Mussolini's true feelings on the subject, in practice he approached the so-called Jewish question with the same sort of opportunistic spirit that he applied to other aspects of political life. That is to say, he was never inclined to make an issue of race except in circumstances where it was politically expedient to do so—for example, in trying to justify his conquest of African peoples (such as the Ethiopians) or in cementing the bond between Italy and her new would-be ally, Germany.

By the late 1930s, when Hitler had become a dominant factor in world politics, he began to treat the Duce as his junior partner. Even at this early date, Mussolini was beginning to chafe at his subordinate role in the Axis; he complained bitterly that Hitler failed to ask his opinion and informed him of Germany's plans only at the last moment.

For one brief, shining moment in the Axis partnership, in September 1938, the Duce seemed to transcend his second-fiddle status. The occasion was the Munich peace conference, the notorious exercise in "appeasement" that sacrificed portions of Czechoslovakia to the Nazis in an effort by Mussolini and the West to avoid all-out war. Though the multilingual Duce appeared to occupy center stage at the four-power summit, conversing with the participating statesmen in their native languages, it was Hitler who pulled the strings and reaped all the benefits from the final agreement.

But Mussolini enjoyed his moment in the sun. When he returned to Italy in triumph, he announced that he had saved Europe from the maelstrom—and much of Europe seemed to agree.

Having lulled the world into thinking that peace was at hand, Hitler returned to his plans for future war. Shortly after the peace conference, Ribbentrop, Hitler's foreign minister, descended on Rome and informed the Duce and his son-in-law, Ciano, that, regardless of what had transpired at Munich, a world war was inevitable within three or four years.[60] Ribbentrop wanted to put Mussolini's signature on a military alliance between Germany, Italy, and Japan. But the Duce stalled for time. Having taken a measure of the Great Powers at Munich, Mussolini thought that he might be able to wring a few more concessions out of the West by playing the peace card.[61]

A few days before Ribbentrop arrived in Rome, the Duce and Ciano mocked him behind his back. "He is vain, fickle, and talkative," Ciano noted in his diary. "The Duce says that all you have to do is look at his head to see that he has a small brain."[62]

By 1939, the storm clouds were gathering ominously over Europe. In March of that year Hitler surprised Mussolini (and much of the world) when he occupied what remained of Czechoslovakia, thus tearing to shreds the very Munich agreement that had reflected so well on the Duce. Shocked and insulted, Mussolini referred to Hitler as untrustworthy and considered aligning himself with the Western powers against Germany.[63]

Jealous over Hitler's mounting successes, the Duce manufactured a victory of his own by pouncing on the small state of Albania in April 1939.[64] Albania was more or less under Italy's thumb before the attack, and the so-called invasion was actually a bumbling and meaningless adventure designed, at least in part, to soothe Mussolini's bruised ego.[65]

The Duce was well aware in the spring of 1939 that Hitler was planning to make Poland his next target and that such a move could easily ignite a world war for which Italy was unprepared.[66] He had repeatedly told the Nazis that Italy would not be strong enough militarily to wage war against England and France for several more years. But Hitler's hold on Mussolini was strong—stronger even than he was ready to admit. Instead of distancing himself from Hitler, the Duce simply put his faith in the empty promises of Ribbentrop, who assured the Italians in May that the climactic battle between the Axis and the West would not take place for another four years or so.[67]

Thus soothed, Mussolini agreed to sign a formal military alliance with Germany. (The king of Italy disapproved, but the Duce brushed off his reservations.)[68] He dubbed it the Pact of Steel, and Ciano signed it on May 22 in Berlin.[69] (Mussolini had considered calling it the *Patto di Sangue,* or Pact of Blood, but then thought better of it.)[70] The preamble of the treaty included this statement: "[T]he German and Italian nations are resolved in future also to act side by side and with united forces to secure their living-space and to maintain peace."[71] The "living space" phrase was a thinly veiled euphemism for territorial expansion.

But most important, the agreement required Italy to come to Germany's aid in the event of war.* To avoid misunderstandings on this last point, the Duce sent a secret memo to Hitler on May 30 reiterating his position that Italy could not be ready for war until 1943. "Italy requires a period of preparation," wrote Mussolini, who added that his country "does not wish to hasten a European war, although she is convinced of the inevitability of such a war."[72]

But Hitler was in a hurry. Three months later, he would plunge Europe into World War II.

The Pact of Steel put the official stamp on the Rome-Berlin Axis. But although it involved the fates of millions of Italians and Germans, the alliance was based almost exclusively on the personal relationship between the two dictators, many of whose own advisors expressed indifference or outright hostility over the new partnership.

Hitler and Mussolini paid them no mind. Indeed, the two leaders found plenty of common ground. For one thing, they were both essentially self-educated men who had risen from humble beginnings (Hitler's father was a civil servant, Mussolini's a blacksmith).[73] Having been underestimated by the opposition, they had skillfully exploited the explosive political atmosphere following World War I (in which both men had served as corporals) by playing on fears of communism, making deals with big business, and preaching a sermon of nationalism in which both men genuinely believed.[74] Despite some public comments to the contrary, both reveled in the idea of aggressive war and sought to expand their power and prestige at the expense of other nations. Neither knew much about such practical affairs of state as economics.[75]

To varying degrees, Hitler and the Duce both employed violence for the purpose of silencing potential enemies and achieving their

---

*In case of war, Article Five of the Pact forbade either country from concluding an armistice without the agreement of the other. This article took on special significance during the summer of 1943.

political ends. Admittedly, Mussolini never sank to the depths of villainy occupied by Hitler or Stalin, and he had a well-known habit of making threats that he never dreamed of carrying out. "Except occasionally in the years after 1943," observed Paolo Monelli, an Italian historian who worked as a journalist during the Fascist era, "Mussolini was never characterized by the cruelty and callousness of the typical tyrant; he was insensitive rather than cruel, mischievous rather than evil, cynical rather than wicked, and chiefly with the people whom he had decided were his enemies."[76]

On the other hand, though he occasionally tried to distance himself from the criminal acts carried out on his behalf, the Duce was not the benevolent blowhard that some of his defenders made him out to be. Opponents of the Fascist regime, for instance, were often beaten with cudgels, sometimes severely, forced to drink castor oil, or sentenced to years of exile. The Duce also made it known that he wanted certain men killed.[77] If his crimes paled in comparison to those of his German counterpart, this was slim consolation to thousands of Italians, Jews, Ethiopians, and Greeks who found themselves on the wrong side of Mussolini's domestic policies or unprovoked foreign wars.

Both dictators also understood the value of propaganda and the importance of politics as theater. Both had studied and praised a book by Gustave Le Bon called *The Crowd,* which discusses the nature of mass psychology, and compelling oratory was given a central place in their respective bids for power.[78] They also believed that the very personality of a charismatic leader could be a crucial factor in the success of a political movement. This point was brought home dramatically during the summer of 1943 when the Fascist Party collapsed overnight in the absence of the Duce. It can even be argued that Hitler's attempt to rescue his fallen Italian partner was, at least in part, an effort to resurrect what both men viewed as the sacrosanct idea of the absolute ruler.

■ ■ ■

Some of the more incidental details of their lives coincided as well. Both men were approximately the same height. Mussolini stood five feet six inches, and Hitler was only slightly taller.[79] They also suffered from mysterious, possibly stress-related health problems during the last few years of their lives. The Duce was plagued by a recurring duodenal ulcer for much of his adult life (it first surfaced in 1925), but the dramatic decline in his health during 1942 and 1943 has never been fully explained and may have been a severe case of nervous strain.[80]

Hitler's health, which had been good for most of his life, began to fail in 1943 just as the tide turned in the war.[81] The cause of Hitler's trembling extremities and foot dragging may well have been stress, as some of his doctors at the time believed. Undiagnosed Parkinson's disease could also help to explain some of his symptoms.

Each man carried on a long-term affair with a much younger woman. Hitler enjoyed the company of the innocuous but steadfastly loyal Eva Braun, although the relationship was kept hidden from the public until after Hitler's death. Mussolini, who was married and had fathered several children, carried on a stormy affair with the more flamboyant Claretta Petacci. Both men later died in the company of their mistresses, each of whom made a conscious decision to share the fate of her lover.

■ ■ ■

Hitler and the Duce were solitary souls who lived almost exclusively for the exercise of their personal power and the goal of national greatness, as they defined it. During their careers, the personalities of the two dictators were lost in and obscured by the outrageous propaganda that they employed to gain and hold power.

Over time, Hitler succeeded in convincing himself that he was the human embodiment of the German state, the infallible Messiah without whom Germany could not achieve true greatness. "Supported by his excellent propaganda," wrote Marshal Albert Kesselring, Hitler's top commander in Italy during the summer of 1943, "he really did become the idol of the masses. Small wonder that he gradually came to believe that he was unique and irreplaceable, that his destiny was to devote himself to Germany's greatness and her security for all time to come."[82]

In similar fashion, Mussolini was billed as a modern incarnation of the ancient Caesars, an all-knowing scholar-warrior who worked tirelessly to elevate Italy's position in the world at the expense of his personal comforts.*[83] The Duce liked to perpetuate the notion that he was a man of culture and learning, and had a tendency to exaggerate his own erudition.[84] When the University of Rome gave Mussolini an *honorary* law degree in 1924, for instance, he insisted on writing a thesis paper, titled "Introduction to Machiavelli."[85] As was true of Hitler, the Duce's infallibility was a cornerstone of his personality cult.

But once the layers of myth were stripped away—and perhaps they never could be—it was surprisingly difficult to get a grip on the two human beings hidden behind the elaborately constructed personas. Each man was known to wax eloquently about his concern for the "masses," the destiny of which he controlled by fiat, but neither had close friends or exhibited the ability to connect with those around him. Each was essentially unknowable.

Though he was a one-dimensional personality, Hitler remained an enigma to the men who worked with him. General Alfred Jodl, one of Hitler's key advisors, spoke for many in the Fuehrer's entourage when he tackled this subject after the war. "To this very day," Jodl wrote on March 10, 1946, about seven months before his execution at Nuremberg, "I do not know what he thought or knew or really wanted."[86] Ribbentrop sounded a similar note: "His whole character was indescribably aloof. . . . Although millions adored Adolf Hitler, he was a lonely man. Just as I never made close contact with him, so it was with others; I met no one who was close to him—perhaps Göring was the sole exception."[87]

---

*Mussolini was known to keep the lights on in his office (even when he was not there) to create the impression of ceaseless activity.

"With the madman's knowledge of how to excite," wrote Eliza-beth Wiskemann, author of one of the few book-length studies of the two Axis dictators, "Hitler combined the madman's—or the superman's—inability to communicate normally with others as in-dividuals: he either mesmerized or frightened them or perhaps did both these things."[88]

■ ■ ■

The inscrutability of Mussolini was also well known. "No one un-derstands him," wrote fellow Fascist Fernando Mezzasoma, attempt-ing to describe the paradoxical nature of Il Duce. "By turns shrewd and innocent, brutal and gentle, vindictive and forgiving, great and petty, he is the most complicated and contradictory man I have ever known. He cannot be explained."[89]

As Ciano himself was once forced to admit: "[E]ven I, who am constantly at his side, often find it extremely difficult, and sometimes impossible, to tell what he is really thinking and feeling."[90] The Ital-ian dictator openly admitted that he had never had any real friends (he seems to have considered this fact a virtue), and may have even encouraged the perception of his own aloofness in the belief that great men can never be fully comprehended by inferior minds.[91]

In contrast to the rigid figure of Hitler, who stuck stubbornly to his own views and pursued a fairly consistent, though repellent, set of goals for twenty years, Mussolini was more chameleon-like and could shift his allegiances and positions as the circumstances war-ranted. The real man, Denis Mack Smith believed, "was hidden by a succession of poses, many or all of which reveal aspects of his char-acter. The frequent changes of opinion do not necessarily mean that he was an intellectual light-weight, but rather that he placed little value on ideas. He appeared to adopt opinions merely because they fitted some new attitude or would help his career."[92]

■ ■ ■

The bond between Hitler and Mussolini, which both men referred to as a "friendship," was yet another enigma that even insiders found difficult to unravel. Though the association may have defied explanation, almost no one close to either dictator could deny the existence of an unusual and somewhat dysfunctional relationship between the two men. It is true that Hitler occasionally made fun of the Duce behind his back, entertaining his cronies with an imitation of Mussolini's flamboyant gestures; the Duce, for his part, thought that Hitler used rouge to make his cheeks look more lifelike.[93]

But though Hitler had little regard for the Italians as a whole, whom he considered lazy and incompetent, there was general agreement among the Fuehrer's entourage that he maintained a strange and enduring affection for Mussolini.[94] This steadfast loyalty, which seemed to increase when Mussolini was overthrown in July 1943, was all the more surprising considering the Duce's mixed feelings about Hitler and Italy's dubious value as a military ally.

To some extent, Hitler's bond with Mussolini may have been rooted in nostalgia and historical precedent. The Duce's Fascist revolution had made a powerful impact on Hitler during the *Kampfzeit,* the early years of struggle when his own prospects seemed less than brilliant.[95] Hitler considered Mussolini a political pioneer, and he made numerous comments during his career, often in private, that reflected the importance of the Duce's movement and the indebtedness that Hitler felt towards him.

"Don't suppose that events in Italy had no influence on us," Hitler remarked to his cronies one evening in July 1941. "The brown shirt would probably not have existed without the black shirt. The march on Rome, in 1922, was one of the turning-points of history. The mere fact that anything of the sort could be attempted, and could succeed, gave us an impetus."[96] Mussolini's rise to power was nothing less than a "heroic epic," Hitler said on another occasion: "It always warms my heart to think of it."[97]

Mussolini's having beaten out the Communists for political control of Italy also made Hitler warm all over. "We ought to be grateful to the Duce for having dispelled this danger from Europe," he reflected in 1941, shortly after launching Operation Barbarossa, his massive invasion of Stalinist Russia. "That's a service he has rendered that must never be forgotten. Mussolini is a man made to the measure of the centuries. His place in history is reserved for him."[98] The Duce had started his political career as a socialist—and then abandoned this position when it became untenable—but this was a sin for which Hitler could forgive him.*[99]

To Hitler, Mussolini was that rarest of birds: a world leader on his own level. He viewed him as "the only man to whom he could talk on something like equal terms," according to Denis Mack Smith, "and, perhaps for that reason, as one of the few people whom he genuinely liked."[100] In other words, Hitler viewed the Duce as a fellow Nietzschean Superman. "This is a curious thing: Mussolini, with such few resources, was yet the one man whom Hitler genuinely accepted as an equal," wrote the historian A.J.P. Taylor. "And the only one whom Hitler genuinely took seriously."[101]

Hitler, who had a tendency to romanticize the classical world, believed that the Duce was just the man to bridge the gap between a mediocre modern Italy and the glory of the ancient Roman Empire. "As I walked with him in the gardens of the Villa Borghese," Hitler once confided to his intimates, "I could easily compare his profile with that of the Roman busts, and I realised he was one of the Caesars. There's no doubt at all that Mussolini is the heir of the great men of that period."[102] As for Italian Fascism itself, it was "a spontaneous return to the traditions of ancient Rome."[103]

Yet there was always an intangible element in Hitler's feelings toward the Duce—a depth of emotion—that exceeded political calculations and seemed to puzzle just about everyone. "The Führer actually adored my husband," observed Rachele Mussolini, not without justification, "and when he spoke of Benito, to either his own sup-

---

*The younger, more left-wing Mussolini kept a picture of Marx in his office.

porters or the Duce's, the tears welled in his eyes. Ciano noticed this during a conversation. My husband noticed, too, that Hitler was on the brink of weeping when he left Italy [after a visit] in May, 1938."[104]

At times, even Mussolini seemed perplexed and embarrassed by Hitler's weepy effusiveness. "The man is hysterical," the Duce complained to one of his ministers during an Axis summit in 1941 after one of Italy's misguided military adventures. "When he told me that no one had lived through and shared my anguish more intensely than he had there were tears in his eyes. All that is an exaggeration."[105]

But Hitler was nonetheless aware that his alliance with Italy was more of a burden than an asset.[106] "The Axis must face the fact that it is saddled with Italy," Hitler admitted in May 1943, a few months before the Italian coup.[107] Near the end of his life, Hitler even reckoned that his partnership with Mussolini had helped bring about the defeat of the Third Reich.

"Judging events coldly," Hitler reflected early in 1945, "leaving aside all sentimentality, I have to admit that my unyielding friendship for Italy, and for the Duce, could be added to the list of my mistakes. It is visible that the Italian alliance rendered more service to the enemy than to ourselves. . . . It will have contributed, if we do not win in spite of everything, to making us lose the war. . . . My attachment to the person of the Duce has not changed . . . but I regrèt not having listened to reason which imposed on me a brutal friendship in regard to Italy."[108]

Yet through it all, Hitler generally spoke of Mussolini with admiration and warmth, even when the newsreel cameras and microphones were turned off. "The Duce himself is my equal," Hitler said just a few months before his death. "He may perhaps even be my superior from the point of view of his ambitions for his people."[109]

■ ■ ■

Mussolini's feelings toward Hitler were more complicated; they tended to evolve over time and to reflect the Duce's political aims and the changing fortunes of the two dictators. During the early part of the 1930s, for instance, Mussolini expressed his contempt for the upstart Hitler and the harebrained racial policies he espoused. But the Duce also believed that he could exploit the German dictator (and his admiration for his Italian counterpart), either by manipulating the West's fear of Germany or by forging an outright alliance with Hitler.

Over time, Mussolini became impressed with Germany's military might and what he viewed as the powerful personality of the Fuehrer. The Duce, who was wont to say that Italy had too many guitar players and not enough warriors, was instinctively drawn to strength, which Hitler exuded in spades.[110]

"Nothing about Hitler aroused his Italian co-dictator's envy more than his soldiers," observed Eugen Dollmann, who as an interpreter had observed the two men together on numerous occasions, "and this was the fatal origin of their curious friendship, which was based on a truly Freudian mixture of love and hatred. Everything the Fuhrer had—Stukas, tanks, submarines, countless divisions, paratroops, elite corps—the Duce wanted too, heedless of his limited resources and the total lack of interest and enthusiasm evinced by the overwhelming majority of his people."[111] Once World War II had broken out, Mussolini was also fascinated by Hitler's military successes, "the only successes that Mussolini really values and desires," according to Ciano.[112]

For the Duce, this political love affair, which he viewed as a "marriage of convenience" according to Rachele, began to turn sour fairly quickly.[113] Mussolini naturally considered himself the senior of the two statesmen, the "dean of dictators," as Ciano put it.[114] He was willing to concede Germany's superiority in military affairs but believed that his experience and opinions were also an important asset of the Rome-Berlin alliance.

"A number of people who knew them both," wrote Denis Mack Smith, "including some Germans, have testified that they thought Mussolini the more interesting personality—the more intelligent, even—and certainly less unattractive; so his conceit was not entirely unfounded."*[115]

But it was Hitler who dominated the policy of the Axis, just as he dominated the proceedings at the numerous summit meetings held between the two men. "We were never treated like partners, but always as slaves," remembered Ciano. "Every move took place without our knowledge; even the most fundamental decisions were communicated to us after they had been carried out."[116] The Duce was continually irritated by Hitler's failure to consult him on important matters concerning the Axis; indeed, he notified the Italian dictator of his plans only when it was too late for Mussolini to influence them.

"Hitler showed surprising loyalty to Mussolini," wrote Alan Bullock, an expert on Hitler, "but it never extended to trusting him."[117] Hitler was constantly worried that the Duce and Ciano, the latter of whom Hitler detested, would inform the enemy of his intentions—as they sometimes did. In this regard, Hitler once exhibited a rare display of humor: "[E]very memorandum I wrote to the Duce immediately reached England. Therefore I only wrote things I absolutely wanted to get to England. That was the best way to get something through to England quickly."**[118]

But even when it became clear that Hitler was "dragging us into an adventure," as Ciano phrased it, Mussolini found it impossible to break away.[119] There was an irrational element in his attraction to Hitler that even the Italian dictator's son-in-law had difficulty understanding. The Duce was "fascinated by Hitler," Ciano confided to his diary in 1940, "a fascination which involves something deeply rooted in his nature: action."[120]

---

*Dollmann, for instance, admits that he found Mussolini "so much the more intelligent, human and fascinating of the two men." Dollmann, *Interpreter,* 182.

**Hitler was not blaming Mussolini personally for these leaks, but rather the so-called traitorous clique that surrounded him.

This strange fascination—a potent mixture of envy, respect, and fear—helps to explain the docility that Mussolini exhibited in Hitler's presence: a docility that was all the more surprising in light of the respect that the Duce commanded among the Italians. When in his own element, Mussolini could be a forceful personality, exhibiting the same sort of magnetism for which Hitler was famous. He could dominate his own Fascist subordinates at will, and was known to make his ministers *run* from the door of his office, the *Sala del Mappamondo,* to his desk, a distance of some twenty yards.[121]

According to Monelli, the Duce "was capable of intimidating the people around him, even the most courageous and more sure of themselves, in the most extraordinary way. They would go to see him firmly intending to talk frankly, and to make him listen, and end by stuttering out a few words, unnerved by his fierce expression. Usually he received his visitors sitting straight up at his writing-table at the end of the huge, empty Mappamondo room in Palazzo Venezia; any courage the visitor possessed was spent in that endless walk from the door to the desk under those dominating eyes."[122]

But although Mussolini frequently disagreed with Hitler on vital points and spoke bitterly about the German dictator behind his back, he never quite mustered the courage to assert himself during their face-to-face meetings; indeed, at these times the Duce often remained inexplicably mum.

"As the Italian gradually declined to the status of a vassal of Hitler's," observed Paul Schmidt, Hitler's interpreter, "he became more and more silent. When I now look back at the gradual change in his demeanor during their many conversations, I am inclined to think that Mussolini realised before many others did whither the journey was taking them, and that he certainly foresaw the catastrophe looming ahead long before his German partner did."[123]

4

A DANGEROUS GAME

Although the events in Italy made a deep impression upon him [Hitler], they in nowise succeeded in throwing him off his equilibrium. On the contrary, his brain was already at work feverishly formulating and preparing new decisions.[1]
—Joseph Goebbels, from a diary entry dated July 27, 1943

UNBEKNOWNST TO THE WORLD AT LARGE, THE COUP OF JULY 25 HAD set the stage for a dramatic showdown between the Nazis and the Italians, even though their Axis alliance remained formally intact.

When news of the coup reached the Wolf's Lair on the evening of July 25, Hitler reacted with shock and outrage. Badoglio, the new Head of the Government, immediately tried to soothe him with pledges of Axis loyalty and assurances that Mussolini had resigned of his own accord; but Hitler would have none of it. He was certain that Badoglio was intent on switching sides in the war. In the secrecy of his headquarters in East Prussia, Hitler railed against Italian "treachery" and vowed to deliver swift retaliation against Rome's fledging government within days, and maybe hours.

With one quick, improvised stroke, he intended to arrest the Duce's usurpers and reinstate the fallen dictator before the new government in Italy could consolidate its hold on the country or throw open its ancient gates to the enemy. It was no secret that the Allies, who were already having their way in Sicily, were sharpening their spears in the Mediterranean in preparation for a massive sea-borne invasion of the Italian peninsula.

Though the coup was certainly a personal affront to Hitler, whose bond with Mussolini was well known, there was much more at stake than a bruised ego. If the power play in Rome was being closely coordinated with Churchill and Roosevelt—and Hitler strongly suspected this—it posed a threat of truly major proportions for the Third Reich and warranted an immediate response. In the nightmare scenario envisaged by the Nazis, the Duce's downfall would quickly be followed by an Allied landing on the Italian mainland, sanctioned by Badoglio and probably occurring near the Gulf of Genoa.[2]

An Anglo-American thrust in this region, located in northwestern Italy about two hundred miles or so north of Rome, would most likely split the peninsula in two and allow the Allies to gain control of most of the country with minimum effort. It would seal the fate of tens of thousands of German soldiers in Sicily and southern Italy by cutting their supply lifeline to the homeland and endangering their rear. It would also bring the war in Europe that much closer to Germany by opening up a new front on the doorstep of the Third Reich overnight and threatening Hitler's vital reserves of oil and other raw materials in the nearby Balkans. Indeed, Hitler and many of his commanders were haunted by the fear that the Allies would use Italy *primarily* as a springboard for an invasion of the Balkans.

The only forces available to meet this threat were the Italian armed forces; but they would offer no resistance should Badoglio decide to welcome the invaders. As for the Germans, who were caught wrong-footed by the coup, they simply did not have enough troops and armor in Italy to repel such a bold move on the part of the Allies. On July 25, the day Mussolini fell, the Nazis had only three divisions on the mainland: the Third Panzergrenadier Division in central Italy near Rome, and two more divisions in the south. The Germans did have about 60,000 troops fighting in Sicily, but it would be a relatively easy matter for the enemy to cut off and trap these island-bound forces.

Hitler therefore believed that the Italian coup signaled the beginning of a desperate race against time. To foil the plans of Badoglio and the Allies, he said, it was crucial that the Nazis engineer a speedy countercoup in the Eternal City because they must "reckon on the Allies attacking straight away."[3] By using force to restore the Fascists to power, Hitler hoped to prevent an Italian surrender and its inevitable consequences on the military front. Finding the Duce and placing him at the head of this Fascist resurrection was an essential part of his scheme.

Hitler's sense of urgency in the days right after the coup was palpable and infectious. It radiated through the Wolf's Lair and added fuel to the general feeling among Hitler's lieutenants that the situation in Italy would change radically in the near future—either for the better or the worse.

"In spite of the King's and Badoglio's proclamation," Erwin Rommel noted in his diary on July 26, "we can expect Italy to get out of the war, or at the very least, the British to undertake further major landings in northern Italy . . . at Genoa and Leghorn."[4] That same day, Martin Bormann dashed off a letter to his wife in which he expressed his fears: "[I]f the British were to land anywhere today, all Italy would fall into their laps, and all the Italians round their necks!"[5] Goebbels prophesied that the Allies would strike within a week unless the Nazis seized Rome at once.[6]

And yet, defying the apparent momentum of events, the nail-biting suspense brought about by Mussolini's abrupt disappearance remained unbroken by the passage of the next several days. As that anxious July crawled to a close, the precipitous German action promised by Hitler never materialized: No German tanks thundered through the sweltering piazzas of the Italian capital, no paratroopers fell silently from its cloudless skies.

But Hitler's enemies were also slow to act. At month's end, the newly minted Badoglio regime still had not surrendered Italy to the Allies, as Hitler had first anticipated. Though the war in Sicily continued to rage, with Germans and Italians fighting together in a losing effort (oblivious, no doubt, to the Machiavellian intrigues going on at the highest levels of their respective governments), the Anglo-American invasion force destined for mainland Italy remained coiled in its enclaves on the coast of North Africa, unwilling to strike.

Indeed, a week after the Italian coup, an uneasy modus vivendi seemed to prevail between the European Axis powers. This despite the conspicuous absence of Il Duce, whose whereabouts and fate were still a matter of speculation among Hitler and his cronies.

So what accounted for this almost eerie calm that had descended over Axis relations? Though Hitler and Badoglio seemed poised to turn on each other during this period, a closer look behind the scenes reveals how a series of unexpected complications and second thoughts forced both leaders to step back from the brink of open hostility, though for how long remained to be seen.

■ ■ ■

"When I reached my home I was immediately called by telephone from the Fuehrer's GHQ," Goebbels reported in his diary on July 26, one day after the coup. "The news from there sounds almost unbelievable. It is to the effect that the Duce has resigned, and that Badoglio has taken over in Italy in his place. The whole situation, I was informed, was still very obscure; such news as we received had come over the radio and was given out by Reuter. At GHQ nobody can figure out just what has really happened. The Fuehrer wants me to proceed immediately to his headquarters. He wishes there to evaluate the situation with his closest collaborators."[7]

These two themes touched on by Goebbels—namely, disbelief and confusion in regard to the events of July 25—would dominate the scene at Fuehrer Headquarters in the days to follow. Though the situation in Italy had been deteriorating for several months before the summer of 1943, the palace revolution engineered by King Victor Emmanuel was greeted with shock and surprise at the highest levels of the Nazi hierarchy, many of its members having overestimated the Duce's ability to keep afloat the sinking ship of Fascism. More to the point, the crisis also sparked a prolonged debate between Hitler and his top lieutenants concerning the significance of the coup and how Germany should respond.

The gravity of the situation was reflected in the hasty summons of Nazi VIPs to the Wolf's Lair for the intense, almost unceasing series of meetings that occurred in the days after Mussolini's fall. Among the dozens of Party bigwigs and lesser lights nervously pacing the hallways at GHQ during this chaotic time were Goebbels; Hermann Goering, the chief of the Luftwaffe; Marshal Rommel, the Desert Fox, who had flown in from Greece; the SS chief, Heinrich Himmler; Joachim von Ribbentrop, the German foreign minister, who was suffering from the flu; and Hitler's favorite architect, Albert Speer, who was Minister for Armaments.

"Everyone is deeply depressed," observed the young Rudolf Semmler, who worked under Goebbels and had accompanied his chief. "Everywhere [there are] strict precautions against entry and exceptional security measures. The dictatorship smells danger."[8]

Hitler *did* sense danger, and had reacted energetically to the crisis. By the time his war chiefs and other advisors had arrived at the Wolf's Lair, he had already cooked up four main plans with which to deal the Italians a counter blow.[9] Taken as a whole, this ambitious program was intended to accomplish several goals: to overthrow the Badoglio government in Rome by force, to rescue the Duce and reinstate him as the captain of the Italian state, and to secure the southern front of the Third Reich against the Allies. The lattermost objective, which was naturally considered paramount, was to be achieved by occupying Italy with German troops and establishing a solid line of defense.

Two of Hitler's plans were being improvised on the spot, namely, Operation Oak, the mission to find and rescue Mussolini; and Operation Student, the armed takeover of the Italian capital and the restoration of the Fascist regime, which also involved arresting the king, Badoglio, and various other Italian notables.*[10] The other two operations had been conceived at an earlier date—such was the sorry state

---

*Hitler had also threatened to seize the Vatican in the process, but Goebbels and Ribbentrop, among others, apparently talked him out of this rash move.

of Axis relations—and were now being revisited in light of current events. One of these, Operation Black, was the blueprint for Hitler's military occupation of the Italian peninsula.[11] Operation Axis, the last of the four plans, was designed to achieve the capture or destruction of the Italian fleet lest it fall into enemy hands and be used against the Germans.[12]

Needless to say, executing any of the four operations would constitute a flagrant violation of the fragile alliance that still existed in name between the Nazis and the Badoglio regime; indeed, Badoglio's control of the Italian armed forces could potentially jeopardize any one of these Nazi maneuvers. But, then again, risky moves were nothing new for Hitler. Had he not conquered most of Europe by single handedly taking a series of political and military high-stakes gambles? Even if he did not possess hard evidence to support his suspicions, the man who had swept the strongest armies of the Western world from the Continent was loath to sit on his hands while the Italians connived with his enemies to destroy him.

Problems, however, arose immediately. For one thing, Hitler's strident call to action ignited stiff opposition from most of his generals, who doubted the feasibility of a quick solution. "At night there was another conference with the Fuehrer," Goebbels noted in his diary on July 27, referring to one of the major brainstorming sessions. "He once more developed his view that action against Italy or against the rebellious camarilla must be undertaken as quickly as possible." But as the propaganda guru quickly noted, one of Hitler's best commanders advised caution: "Rommel thinks this action should be prepared adequately and upon mature reflection. The debate lasted until far after midnight. Unfortunately it led to no final result as the number of participants was too large; about thirty-five persons took part."[13]

■ ■ ■

Rommel's was not a lone voice. Though men such as Goebbels, Goering, and Ribbentrop adopted Hitler's point of view, most of the Fuehrer's top soldiers contended that Germany did not have enough forces on the ground in Italy to carry out his grandiose schemes.[14] At this precarious stage of the war, with German armies hard-pressed in the East and in Sicily, the Fuehrer's weary, practical-minded generals had no enthusiasm for risky adventures on mainland Italy; after all, that nation's army and an unfriendly populace could join ranks and foil Nazi improvisations. These points were driven home that same day by Admiral Karl Doenitz, chief of the German navy, who argued hotly with Hitler during another meeting.

"A removal of the present [Italian] leaders by us might . . . have an undesirable effect . . . if it is not skillfully engineered," warned Doenitz, who was skeptical of Hitler's plan to cart off the new Italian government by force and resurrect the Fascist regime. "I doubt that Fascism still means anything either to those who favor continuing the war on our side or to the Italian people themselves. It is not to be expected that we can superimpose conditions on the Italian people. . . . All will depend on the correct timing of any contemplated action against the present Italian government."[15]

Doenitz was deeply concerned about the risks of acting prematurely. He suggested that Hitler maintain the alliance with Italy long enough to increase the number of German troops on the peninsula. "I believe there is still time, and that it can be used by us for further strengthening our position in the Italian area by bringing in several more divisions."[16]

Hitler bridled with impatience. "We must act at once," he told Doenitz. "Otherwise the Anglo-Saxons will steal a march on us by occupying the airports. The Fascist Party is at the present only stunned and will rise up again behind our lines. The Fascist Party is the only one that is willed to fight on our side. We must therefore restore it. All reasons advocating further delays are wrong; thereby we run the danger of losing Italy to the Anglo-Saxons." He arrogantly brushed off the sailor's nagging reservations: "These are matters which a soldier cannot comprehend. Only a man with political insight can see his way clear."[17]

Yet, to Hitler's annoyance, other high-ranking military advisors, such as Keitel, Jodl, and Rommel, also voiced their hesitations about

Operation Student during this conference and advocated a gradual infiltration.

Hitler received more novel advice from Marshal Albert Kesselring, the overall commander of German forces in Italy. Kesselring, nicknamed "Smiling Albert" by his troops, was an optimist by nature and, what was rarer among Hitler's soldiers, had a reputation for being an Italophile.[18] He went so far as to suggest that Badoglio should be taken at his word.

"Kesselring believes that the present [Italian] government is trustworthy," Doenitz noted, "and he is therefore against any interference on our part."[19] Hitler could only roll his eyes. "Kesselring is a terrific optimist," Hitler had remarked two months earlier, "and we must be careful that in his optimism, shall we say, he doesn't misjudge the hour when optimism must give way to severity."[20] To Hitler's mind, Kesselring's faith in the Italians reflected an incredible and dangerous naïveté. Hitler was irritated to learn that most of the German diplomats based in Rome also put stock in Badoglio's repeated pledges of friendship.

The endless debates at the Wolf's Lair in the days following the coup boiled down to one overriding question: Should the Germans risk taking strong action against the new Italian government *immediately*—by invading Rome and restoring the Fascists to power—or should they take a more conservative, wait-and-see attitude? If carried out effectively, the first option just might prevent the Italians from switching sides in the war (but it could also result in disaster). On the other hand, choosing the latter course would provide the German army with time to build up its forces on the ground in Italy, which in turn would increase Hitler's odds of success should the Nazis be forced to fight the combined armies of the Italians and the Allies in the not-too-distant future.

Aside from the pressing military concerns, Hitler had a variety of other reasons for strenuously opposing the Italian coup, some of which were less obvious than others. For one thing, it was shaping up as a far-reaching public relations dilemma for the Nazis: The loss of a major ally at this stage of the war could send German morale spiraling. As the able spin-doctor of the Third Reich, Goebbels had the unfortunate job of interpreting the Italian crisis for the puzzled German *Volk*. Not knowing what else to do, he decided simply to print the news of Mussolini's resignation without any hint of the feverish deliberations going on at the Wolf's Lair.

But the ripples could spread far beyond the borders of Germany. A defection by Italy, Hitler feared, might embolden other German allies (such as Rumania and Hungary) to jump ship, further weakening Hitler's ability to wage war and threatening his access to essential raw materials. "If the Italians collapse," declared Martin Bormann in a letter to his wife on July 23, two days before the coup, "it cannot remain without repercussions among the Hungarians, who are anyhow a treacherous lot, and among the Croats, the Rumanians and the rest."[21]

Far more ominous was the possibility that the Italian revolt might prove a tempting example for would-be plotters in Germany.* The coup, Goebbels noted, "might conceivably encourage some subversive elements in Germany to think they could put over the same thing here that Badoglio and his henchmen accomplished in Rome. The Fuehrer ordered Himmler to see to it that most severe police measures be applied in case such a danger seemed imminent here."[22]

It was also clear that Hitler had personal motives for rescuing Mussolini and restoring him to his former grandeur, or what was left of it. In 1938, Hitler had made a dramatic promise regarding the Duce: "If he should ever need any help or be in any danger, he can be convinced that I shall stick to him whatever may happen, even if the whole world gangs up on him."[23] Now, in the summer of 1943,

---

*Though Hitler did not know it, he had narrowly escaped an assassination attempt just four months earlier in March 1943. A German general and his accomplice had hidden a timebomb on Hitler's plane during a flight from Smolensk to the Wolf's Lair. The bomb failed to explode.

Hitler seemed determined to keep that promise, though he certainly had plenty of other, more self-serving reasons for doing so.

■ ■ ■

Unfortunately for Hitler, from a practical standpoint there were many factors that seemed to argue against a quick fix in Italy. As Doenitz and others had suggested, Hitler's heady scheme to turn back the clock in Rome naturally depended on the viability of the Fascist Party. Without its active participation, any heavy-handed intrusion into Italian politics by the now-unpopular Nazis was likely to trigger unrest among the people and within the Italian army. Hitler thus looked eagerly for signs of life in what remained of the decapitated regime.

He was dismayed by what he found. With the Duce gone, the Fascist Party had practically disintegrated overnight. Indeed, Badoglio's new cabinet dissolved the Party altogether on July 27.[24] It was inconceivable to Hitler that the political system dominating Italy for the last twenty years could evaporate so completely. Yet the news from Rome seemed unanimous in proclaiming the speedy and unlamented demise of Fascism. The husk, it seemed, had collapsed.

Cables from Ambassador Mackensen, who was on the scene in the Italian capital, read like a coroner's report. On July 26, he caught up with Dino Alfieri, until recently the Italian ambassador to Berlin under the Duce's regime, who informed him that the Fascist Party had "disappeared from the stage unsung and unheard."[25] (Alfieri eventually fled to Switzerland.)[26] The next day, Mackensen offered his own prognosis: "The Fascist Party in Italy stood and fell, as events have shown, with Mussolini. The majority of the Fascist leadership had delivered a political death-blow to Mussolini, and without wanting to, at the same time committed suicide."*[27]

---

*This is a reference to the Grand Council meeting of July 24–25. By giving Mussolini a vote of no confidence, the Fascists paved the way for the Italian coup, which was engineered by the king of Italy in conjunction with the military.

Yet Hitler professed to be undeterred by such dispiriting news. "At noon I had another long talk with the Fuehrer," Goebbels wrote on July 28. "He is firmly determined to act, no matter what the cost, preferably by clever improvisation rather than by too systematic preparations that begin late and allow things to become consolidated in Italy. . . . Today he is still entertaining illusions about the Duce and the possibilities of a Fascist comeback."[28]

Illusions indeed. Mussolini's mysterious disappearance represented yet another major wrinkle in Hitler's plans. Surely he would be a pivotal factor in a Fascist revival in Italy as a figure whom the Party and country at large could rally around, at least in theory. Yet the Germans had no idea where the Duce was or what had really happened on July 25. Had the ailing dictator really stepped down of his own accord? Or had he been physically removed from power as Hitler believed? German intelligence was unable to provide conclusive answers.

When it came to Mussolini, the Italians were giving the Nazis the run-around. Kesselring, for one, had already made an attempt to find out where the Duce was. On Monday, July 26, one day after the coup, he met with Badoglio and the king separately, but was unable to learn anything. Badoglio told him that Mussolini was in protective custody but did not know where—only King Victor Emmanuel had detailed information. The king, in turn, feigned ignorance of the Duce's whereabouts and suggested that Kesselring ask Badoglio.

With the Axis alliance still intact for the moment, Hitler sought to probe the new Italian leaders for clues regarding his fellow dictator's fate. Mussolini's birthday provided the perfect opportunity for Ambassador Mackensen to seek an audience with the king. Their meeting took place in Rome on July 29—the Duce's sixtieth birthday. Having created a fictional "back story" for the occasion, the nervous monarch was well prepared for this polite interrogation.

When asked by Mackensen why Mussolini had not informed Hitler of his intentions to resign, Victor Emmanuel answered that the omission was probably a result of "the Duce's state of mind."[29] The king then elaborated by spinning the deceptive tale of a twentieth-century Caesar who was betrayed by his friends. By giving Mussolini a vote of no-confidence in the Grand Council of Fascism on the evening of July 24–25, Emmanuel said, the Duce's colleagues had broken the dictator's heart as well as his will to rule.

"In the quite long conversation which had passed as warmly and trustingly as untold others in the course of more than twenty years' work together," the king told Mackensen, referring to his meeting with Mussolini at the Villa Savoia on July 25, "he gave the impression of a man struck to the heart, who was faced with the to him inconceivable fact of being rejected by the Party 'faithful.' The Duce was at that moment in the same position as the Fuehrer would be if he were suddenly abandoned by Reichsmarshal Goering or Dr. Goebbels. The Duce was broken by his own Party."[30]

The king's account was a complete fabrication, yet the gullible Mackensen had no evidence to the contrary. When asked, Victor Emmanuel refused to disclose the whereabouts of Mussolini, but told Mackensen that certain arrangements had been made for the protection of his person. Mackensen promptly countered with a ruse of his own. Taking advantage of the date, the German ambassador slyly suggested that he personally deliver Hitler's birthday present to the Duce.[31] The king rejected this proposal but told Mackensen that he would accept the gift on Mussolini's behalf and make certain that the dictator received it.[32]

To further confuse the Germans, Badoglio had given them a copy of a letter allegedly from the pen of the Duce himself.[33] They had no way of knowing whether the letter was a fake, but its deferential tone did seem to lend credence to the king's claim that Mussolini had gone gently into the good night. It was addressed to Badoglio, and dated July 26, 1943 (one day after the coup). Part of it read: "I wish to thank Marshal Badoglio for the attention he is according my person . . . I wish to assure Marshal Badoglio . . . that not only will I raise no difficulties of any sort but I will co-operate in every possible way."[34]

As Goebbels noted, the curious document displayed a conspicuous lack of protest. "The decisive thing, of course," he wrote in his diary, "is whether Fascism or the Duce has any intention whatever of doing anything about the situation that has now developed. . . . It is hard to tell whether this letter is forged or genuine. If genuine, it would be an eloquent indication that the Duce no longer has any intention of interfering with developments." However: "Should a German coup create an entirely new set of circumstances in Italy, the Duce would surely be ready to take an active hand again."[35] Or so the Nazis hoped.

■ ■ ■

When all was said and done, after feverish consultations and ringing declarations, a frustrated Hitler did not give the order to swoop down upon Rome and ensnare the Badoglio regime. At the crucial moment, he backed down.

The reasons were many. The utter collapse of the Fascist Party, the unknown whereabouts of Mussolini, and the lack of German forces on the ground in Italy had all conspired to stay the itchy trigger finger of the German dictator. To be sure, Hitler's hesitation to act did not reflect a sudden change of heart or lack of determination. He deferred his promised attack on Rome only to give himself sufficient time.*

Hitler would use this peaceful interlude in Axis relations to locate and rescue the Duce, and if possible rally the remaining elements of Mussolini's Fascist Party. But just as important, Hitler would also use the extra time to race as many German troops as possible into northern Italy—passing them off to Badoglio, somewhat improbably, as reinforcements in the fight against the Allies—in expectation of an open break between the two Axis partners. To accomplish this and amass the necessary forces, it would be necessary to

---

*In essence, Hitler put all four of his main plans for Italy on hold except for the initial phase of Operation Oak, which concerned the search for Mussolini. Preparations for the remaining three plans were allowed to continue. Hitler decided, at least for the moment, to allow the German troops fighting in Sicily to remain on the island.

pull units from other theaters, including France and the all-important eastern front.[36] This new strike force in the making was dubbed Army Group B and put under the command of Rommel, one of Hitler's favorites.*

The flexible strategy that Hitler adopted allowed him to keep his options open. He also hoped that the insertion of Army Group B might intimidate the Badoglio regime and discourage it from seriously contemplating the notion of surrender. But even this approach, which was relatively conservative when compared to the alternative of an immediate body blow against the Italians, was not without its risks. Specifically, none of the Germans knew how Badoglio, who was in firm control of the Italian armed forces, would react to the appearance of these uninvited guests from the north—to this virtual invasion of Nazi men and machines cloaked in the transparent guise of friendship.

"Undoubtedly the English and the Americans sponsored this crisis," Goebbels wrote in his diary on July 27, reflecting Hitler's initial fears that the Italian coup had been closely coordinated with the Allies. "The Fuehrer was firmly convinced that Badoglio had already negotiated with the enemy before he took these decisive steps. . . . The English would certainly try to land at the most opportune moment, possibly in Genoa, in order to cut off the German troops stationed in southern Italy."[37]

These were certainly reasonable enough assumptions, and they rightly filled many of the Nazi leaders with alarm. Fortunately for the Germans, there was no truth to them. (The Allies had also been caught off guard by the Italian coup.)[38]

---

*The creation of Army Group B meant that the command of German forces in Italy was divided between Kesselring and Rommel. Kesselring maintained command over the German forces in central and southern Italy. Rommel retained operational control only of his Army Group B divisions, which eventually were concentrated in the northern part of the country.

With the Duce out of the picture, the fate of Italy abruptly descended on the somewhat creaky shoulders of the seventy-three-year-old Victor Emmanuel III and his obedient *Capo del Governo* (Head of the Government), Marshal Pietro Badoglio. Though he had held the throne for more than forty years, Victor Emmanuel had taken a backseat to his more charismatic partner Mussolini during the twenty years of Fascist rule and was therefore a bit rusty when it came to actually wielding power.

The diminutive king had a well-earned reputation for being cautious (some said overly so) and playing his cards close to the vest. He had the maddening habit, his visitors often observed, of allowing others to express their views on a subject without disclosing a hint of his own thoughts until he believed the time was ripe. The king's natural aversion for resolute action led Galeazzo Ciano to remark that he was "more of a Hamlet than Hamlet."[39]

At seventy-two, Badoglio had enjoyed a long (though often checkered) career as a soldier but lacked any real experience as a politician.[40] As a former chief of *Comando Supremo* (the Italian High Command), he had led the Italians to a brutal victory in Ethiopia in 1936, becoming a national hero in the process. He was equally successful, cynics observed, at amassing a small fortune during the Fascist years.

His star began to fade in 1940 when Mussolini's invasion of Greece turned into a debacle and the dictator sacked him in a fit of frustration.[41] Since that time, he had watched Italy's decline from the sidelines, consoling himself with drink—he downed a pint of champagne daily—and passing the time with card games and frequent naps.[42] Though ambitious and not averse to power, Badoglio was deferential to the king and rarely made a move without the monarch's approval.[43]

As a team, the two men proved to be vacillating and indecisive. Though both desperately wished to break free of the Axis, neither had developed a clear-cut strategy for getting out of the war as quickly and cleanly as possible.[44] For better or worse, the king and

Badoglio had made no serious efforts to secretly surrender their country to the Allies before the Italian coup and coordinate military plans with General Dwight D. Eisenhower.

This omission was not entirely their fault. They had made several covert attempts to contact the West while the Duce was still in power but found that the Allies were not interested in making compromise peace deals with an Axis Power: "Unconditional surrender" was the only offer on the table.[45] And though no one on either side of the war seemed to know exactly what this ominous phrase meant, the king and Badoglio were inclined to reject such a harsh and inflexible stance.[46]

Even after they had arrested Mussolini, Italy's new decision-makers hesitated from contacting the Allies right away and sounding them out on the possibility of making a separate peace. This was because they still held out hope that they could come to an understanding with Hitler and thereby exit the war without incurring any Nazi reprisals.[47]

"There was a considerable body of opinion [among leading Italians] that thought it possible that the Germans might allow Italy to withdraw into neutrality," recalled Friedrich von Plehwe, a member of the German embassy in Rome, "and envisaged an agreement with them about the withdrawal of German troops from Italy."[48] The Duce, who understood Hitler better than most of his countrymen, had never put much stock in such naïve fantasies, which helped to explain the paralyzing predicament he faced in the weeks and months before his fall.

But the king and Badoglio did cling to such illusions, or at least felt a responsibility to entertain them. Toward the end of July, Badoglio contacted Hitler and requested a summit meeting in northern Italy between Hitler and the king or Badoglio.[49] "I was convinced," Badoglio recalled, "that the German Government would have to be told that Italy must make peace. This was the step that Mussolini had not dared to take at Feltre on 19 July and though it was not likely that the Germans would agree, I still wished to tell them that we could not continue the war."[50]

The Italians were willing only to hold such a conference on their own soil, fearing (correctly) that if they set foot in Germany they would be clapped in irons. But Hitler, who spent much of this week ranting and raving about treachery, promptly rejected the notion of sitting across the table from the Duce's captors and having a civil conversation.

If Hitler's first reactions to the coup had been icy, those of the Allies were not much warmer. That the Italians had publicly proclaimed their fidelity to the Axis had not helped matters. This was made abundantly clear in a speech delivered by Winston Churchill.

"A decision by the Italian Government and people to continue under the German yoke," Churchill told the House of Commons on July 27, "will not affect seriously the general course of the war. . . . The only consequence will be that in the next few months Italy will be seared and scarred and blackened from one end to the other. . . . We should let the Italians, to use a homely phrase, stew in their own juice for a bit, and hot up the fire to the utmost in order to accelerate the process [of capitulation]."[51] These vivid culinary metaphors were hardly encouraging to the Italians, who in their attempts to dupe the Nazis had created uncertainty in the minds of the Allies.*[52]

By midweek, therefore, Italy found herself in an awkward and dangerous position. Having provoked the ire of the Nazis and the apparent indifference of the Western powers, the king and Badoglio suddenly found themselves isolated and alone. It was clear that they would be on their own in their dealings with the Germans for several weeks to come at the very least. And to complicate matters, the one Italian who had a rapport with Hitler—namely, Mussolini—had been removed from the equation by their own hand.

But the Italian duumvirate did have a few things to be grateful for. The coup had been carried off without a hitch, the Duce had

---

*The uncompromising attitude of Western leaders, which seemed to cast doubt on a collaboration between the Allies and the Italians, was yet another reason why Hitler decided to defer his more aggressive plans for Italy; for without the aid of foreign powers, Italy did not pose an immediate threat.

been stashed away in a secret location, and most of the other leading Fascists were either in custody or keeping a low profile; indeed,
dozens of them were too busy writing ingratiating letters to Badoglio to contemplate a possible insurrection.[53]

"The King struck one resolute blow at their leader," Badoglio remembered, "and without any resistance or violence the whole Fascist structure collapsed. On 26 July one did not see a single person
in Rome wearing the Fascist badge. Fascism fell, as was fitting, like
a rotten pear."[54] Just as important, the change of government also
seemed to have the blessing of the Italian people, many of whom
had identified Mussolini and his corrupt henchmen as the cause of
the nation's ills.

But there was something almost unsettling about the success
with which the king and Badoglio had achieved their immediate
aims. Much like Hitler, they found it difficult to believe that the Fascist Party, with its 4 million members, would lay down without a
fight.[55] Badoglio, who had prudently instituted martial law shortly
after the coup, worried constantly about an organized response to
the fall of Fascism—either in the form of a Fascist counterstrike, a
Nazi intervention, or some combination of both. These fears only
deepened toward the end of July when the Italians learned that German army units (elements of Rommel's Army Group B) were beginning to mass near Italy's northern frontier.[56] The tension got so
thick that on July 28 the king made arrangements to leave Rome if
necessary.

But a lot more than Victor Emmanuel's personal security was at
stake. It was obvious by this time that the Allies, already fighting
their way across Sicily, and the Nazis, who were about to pour into
northern Italy, were destined to meet in a head-on collision on the
southern border of the Third Reich; and Italy would provide the
stage for the clash that threatened to ravage the peninsula.

Avoiding this scenario was the top priority of the king and the
Italian people in general, therefore it was necessary to keep one of
the opponents off the field. There was no chance of stopping the Allies, whom the Italians would soon welcome as their protectors.

The only other option was to prevent the influx of German troops and armor that Hitler was planning to send into the country. This could only be accomplished by diplomacy or by force (and considering Hitler's belligerent attitude, the former did not seem to be a viable strategy).

In the critical days following the coup, however, Victor Emmanuel and Badoglio did nothing to sabotage the progress of Army Group B into northern Italy. Though some of Badoglio's own generals were advising him to make a clean break with the Nazis at once, before German reinforcements had time to get a foothold, the cautious marshal and his king apparently never gave this idea serious consideration.[57] They took great pains, in fact, to avoid action that might conceivably provoke the Nazis, preferring to keep them off balance with pledges of Axis loyalty until the Italian duo could come to an understanding with Hitler or, failing that, secure military support from the West.

In his own defense, Badoglio later claimed that in the summer of 1943 the Italian military was simply too weak and demoralized to survive a showdown with Hitler. And there was some truth in this. Even on a good day, the Italian armed forces were no match for the dreaded German *Wehrmacht,* which was far superior in training, equipment, and leadership. To make matters worse, much of the Italian army was stationed in France and the Balkans.

Although no one can say for certain what would have happened if Badoglio had resisted the Germans by force of arms, one thing soon became clear: By failing to make the attempt, he allowed the Nazis to seize control of the vital alpine passes—the main points of entry on Italy's mountainous northern borders—and use them to funnel their troops into the peninsula during the crucial month of August and beyond.

■ ■ ■

Having been rebuffed by Hitler, the king and Badoglio thought it wise to make their first tentative approach to the Allies near the end of July. The new Italian foreign minister was a seasoned diplomat named Raffaele Guariglia. He arrived in Rome on July 29 from Turkey, where he had formerly served as ambassador, and quickly assumed the initiative in contacting the West. The next day, he went to the Vatican and met with the British minister to the Holy See, Sir D'Arcy Osborne. (As a political entity unto itself, the Vatican possessed its own foreign diplomatic core.) Osborne was sympathetic to Guariglia's position but replied that he could not be of any help because his security codes were out of date.

"The British Minister," Badoglio recalled, "informed us that unfortunately his secret code was very old and almost certainly known to the Germans and that he could not advise us to use it for a secret communication to his Government. The American Chargé d'Affaires replied that he had not got a secret code."[58]

Though not apparent at the time, this incident was an early omen of the tortuous and confused path that Italian negotiations would assume in the tense weeks to follow.

As July of 1943 passed into history, the European Axis powers settled into what would become an elaborate and dangerous game, the broad outlines of which were established during the week following the Italian coup. Both Hitler and Badoglio recognized the necessary expedient of maintaining their fragile alliance, disguising their mutual antagonism of one another in an effort to buy time. The Germans would use this opportunity to fortify Italy with German troops and to probe further the intentions of their reluctant ally; indeed, some in the Nazi camp still believed that Italy could be seduced or bullied into submission.

The Italians, meanwhile, would try to exploit this unpredictable interim by negotiating a favorable agreement with the Allies, never knowing whether their covert activities would suddenly be cut short by German intervention or a violent resurgence of the Fascist regime they had so recently banished with the imprisonment of Benito Mussolini.

Their fear of Hitler was well justified. Though he had been dissuaded from pouncing on the Badoglio government immediately, he still harbored hopes of resurrecting the Fascist regime in Italy and restoring Mussolini to his former glory—that is, if Il Duce could be found and rescued before being handed over to the Allies and vaunted as the war's most famous POW. This task was in the hands of General Student and Otto Skorzeny, whose progress was monitored closely in the ensuing weeks by an impatient Hitler.

5

TONIGHT NO
SLEEP FOR ANYBODY

*At Berlin . . . they had meanwhile mobilized even clairvoy-
ants and astrologers. It was Himmler himself, it would seem,
who was inspired to appeal to such "savants."* [1]
— Otto Skorzeny, *Skorzeny's Secret Missions*

LATE ON THE EVENING OF MONDAY, JULY 26, AS HITLER AND HIS
lieutenants debated their next move and the new Italian leaders in
Rome tried to steady their nerves, Otto Skorzeny and General Kurt
Student were huddled in a small office of the Wolf's Lair trying to
work out the preliminaries of Operation Oak, as the Mussolini
search-and-rescue mission was code named. To complicate matters,
the two men were also responsible for launching a small *Blitzkrieg*
against Rome and arresting members of the Badoglio regime as well
as prominent anti-Fascists in the Italian army. At the time, Hitler
was threatening to carry out the latter scheme (dubbed Operation
Student) within a matter of days, though he later decided to put it
on hold before canceling it altogether. [2]

On July 26, Student, who was in Nîmes in southern France, responded to an urgent summons to the Wolf's Lair, where he met with
Hitler that evening. "I chose you and your paratroopers for a very important assignment," Hitler told Student, the fifty-three-year-old

commander of Germany's airborne forces. "The Duce was dismissed and arrested by the Italian king." Badoglio would soon turn traitor, he said, and the German divisions in Sicily and southern Italy would be cut off and trapped by enemy forces as a result. To thwart Badoglio's plans, Student must immediately transfer a large contingent of para-troopers to Rome and prepare to take over the city. "One of your spe-cial assignments," Hitler added, "will be to find and free my friend Mussolini. He shall of course be handed over to the Americans."[3]

For a strike force, Student had at his disposal the Second Para-chute Division—an elite force of about 20,000 highly-trained crack troops—which he was planning to transfer to Rome from southern France as soon as possible.[4] He intended to use these daredevil sol-diers, who were considered among the best in the Third Reich, to capture the Eternal City in the event that Hitler gave the final order for Operation Student (he could also call upon the Third Panzer-grenadier Division, a motorized unit that was already in central Italy).

The paratroopers could also be used, in concert with the Ger-man navy if necessary, to snatch Mussolini from captivity on land or at sea, assuming the Duce could be found. Skorzeny persuaded Student to supplement this force with a few dozen men from the Friedenthal Battalion, Skorzeny's fledgling SS commando outfit in Berlin. The two men decided to fly to Rome early the next morning to begin the search. "As for the rest," Student added, "we shall see when we get there."[5]

After taking leave of Student, Skorzeny telephoned his second-in-command at the Friedenthal Battalion, thirty-one-year-old Lieu-tenant Karl Radl, sometime after 11:00 P.M.[6] "We are charged with an important mission," Skorzeny told him. "We leave tomorrow morning. I cannot give you more exact details over the telephone. Besides, I myself must think the thing over. I will call you later. For the moment, here are the earliest orders: tonight no sleep for any-body . . . have all the trucks ready because we must pick up equip-ment . . . I am taking along fifty men with me, our best men, that is all those who can more or less speak Italian . . . everything must be done by five in the morning . . . as soon as I have more details, I will call you back."[7]

Hunkered down in the Tea House of the Wolf's Lair, Skorzeny spent the next several hours drinking black coffee and brainstorming what supplies and equipment he thought might be required for the nebulous assignment, which was still little more than wishful thinking on the part of Hitler. As the night wore on, Skorzeny relayed his frequent last-minute requests to an increasingly frantic Radl, who was responsible for organizing the effort in Berlin and making certain that the men and equipment lifted off at dawn.

It was a tall order for Radl, who still had no idea what the mission was really about. All he knew was that Skorzeny was sending him instructions every half an hour and he was having difficulty keeping up.[8] Aside from gathering a mountain of equipment—guns, explosives, and such—he was told to select forty commandos from Friedenthal.[9] In addition, he was instructed to bring ten intelligence officers from Amt VI (Department Six) of the Reich Security Main Office (RSHA), the Third Reich's mammoth police and spy organization.[10] Amt VI was the foreign intelligence branch of the RSHA—roughly equivalent to the American CIA, though the latter did not exist by that name at the time—and these ten men had been assigned to Skorzeny to aid in the search for the Duce.[11]

To conceal the fact that a special SS unit was being sent to Rome, which would be sure to arouse the suspicions of the Italians, Skorzeny told Radl to dress the men in German paratrooper garb and make sure that they carried bogus IDs.[12] This device would allow Skorzeny's men to blend in with Student's parachute troops, who would be arriving in Rome at the same time (and whose presence would not be kept secret from the Italians). Each of the Friedenthalers was also required to bring a set of civilian clothes.[13]

Some of Skorzeny's requests were stranger than others. For one thing, he told Radl to order all the commandos and other SS men to dye their hair black before departing Berlin.[14] Presumably, this odd instruction was designed to allow Skorzeny's agents to move

around Rome in their civilian clothes and pass themselves off as
Romans. Skorzeny later chalked up the idea to Himmler.[15] Radl
thought the hair-dye order was ridiculous and decided to ignore it
on his own responsibility, though he did bring the dye with him on
the plane, just to be on the safe side.[16] For unknown reasons, Radl
was also asked to scrounge up a couple of monk's robes and pack
them with the other gear.[17]

■ ■ ■

Early on the morning of July 27, Skorzeny and Student boarded a
twin-engine Heinkel 111 for the flight to Rome.[18] At the helm was
flying ace Captain Heinrich Gerlach, Student's personal pilot.*[19]
Skorzeny had also donned a disguise for the duration of the mission: He was planning to pose as Student's aide-de-camp. As the latter was a general in the air force and Skorzeny was a captain in the
Waffen SS, this decision necessitated an impromptu wardrobe
change. They were unable to find the proper Luftwaffe uniform on
such short notice, so Skorzeny squeezed into a badly fitting flight
suit. "I was forced to don a flier's suit which was much too small for
me," recalled Skorzeny, who was six feet four inches tall, "and a
Luftwaffe cap was crammed down on my head."[20]

After flying for several hours, the Heinkel crossed the majestic
Apennine Mountains in central Italy—an area that would take on
special significance for the duo in the weeks to come—then
dropped down to an altitude of nine hundred feet to avoid detection by Allied planes (another poignant reminder of how the balance of military power in the region was beginning to change in
favor of the Western powers). At 1:30 P.M. on Tuesday, the Heinkel
touched down at an airport on the outskirts of the city, having made
the 1,000-mile trip in about five and a half hours.

---

*Though no one knew it at the time, Gerlach would later play a pivotal role in the
Nazis' last-ditch, all-or-nothing effort to rescue Mussolini.

It was another oppressively hot day in Rome. When Skorzeny stepped out of the plane, the blast of Mediterranean heat that greeted him prompted him to reconsider his tight-fitting costume. "As I alighted from the plane," he remembered, "I wanted to take off my fur-lined flying suit; but at the last moment I recalled that I was a Luftwaffe officer as yet without a uniform. A Waffen SS as aide-de-camp to a general in command of airborne troops would certainly have puzzled everybody."[21]

After landing, he and Student made the short drive to Frascati, an ancient hill town lying on the northern slopes of the Alban Hills about ten miles southeast of Rome.[22] Throughout the centuries, this small and picturesque suburb, famous for its vineyards and locally produced white wine as well as for the beautiful patrician villas scattered on its hillsides, had attracted Roman emperors, popes, and medieval princes. In the summer of 1943 it was home to Marshal Albert Kesselring's command center, the GHQ for German troops in Italy: *Oberbefehlshaber Sued* (Headquarters, Commander in Chief South), or *OB SUED*. For the next six weeks it would also serve as a sort of covert headquarters for Operation Oak.

That night, Student and his new "adjutant" probed Kesselring and his staff to determine whether they had heard any rumors regarding the whereabouts of the missing dictator.

Kesselring, who generally had a good relationship with the Italians (he had worked closely with them for more than a year and a half), professed to have no inside knowledge of the events of July 25 or the fate of Mussolini.[23] Skorzeny was interested to learn that one of the marshal's officers had recently broached the subject of Il Duce with a general in the Italian army. The latter had claimed, on his word of honor no less, that neither he nor any other Italian commander had knowledge of Mussolini's location.

For Skorzeny, this was an assertion that stretched the boundaries of plausibility. "It remains to be seen whether this statement is reliable," he said, unaware that Kesselring was standing directly behind him.[24]

"As for me," Kesselring said angrily, "I trust in it implicitly. I have no reason to doubt the word of honor of an Italian general. You would do better, Captain Skorzeny, to maintain a like attitude in the future."[25]

Skorzeny could feel his face grow red with embarrassment. "From then on to the end of the evening," he later wrote, "I scarcely opened my mouth."[26]

Like other Nazi VIPs, Kesselring had made an appearance at the Wolf's Lair in the aftermath of the coup. But as noted earlier, the fifty-seven-year-old Luftwaffe commander did not share the Fuehrer's deep concern over the turn of events in Italy. "Kesselring was favorably impressed," Goebbels had huffed in his diary. "He believes Badoglio actually intends to continue the war with all the military means at Italy's disposal. Very evidently Kesselring fell for a well-staged show."[27]

Hitler concurred. Frustrated by the naïveté of his key men in Italy, he ordered Skorzeny to keep his mission secret from Kesselring as well as the German diplomats in Rome. "You must consider this the most absolute of secrets," Hitler had said, referring to Operation Oak. "As for the military command of our troops in Italy [i.e., Kesselring] and the German Embassy in Rome, both must remain in ignorance of everything; they have a completely false conception of the situation and they would only act counter to our interests."[28] Hitler gave Student a similar lecture about the importance of secrecy.[29]

As it happened, Hitler's pessimism on this subject was largely justified. Practically all of the Fuehrer's "point men" in the Italian capital—from Marshal Kesselring to Ambassador Mackensen and his military attaché, General Enno von Rintelen (the military liaison at the embassy)—believed Badoglio's claim that Italy would remain loyal to the Axis. Hitler's secrecy order reflected yet another layer of deception. He was not only trying to keep his diabolical plans for Italy a secret from Badoglio but also attempting to withhold knowledge of these schemes from some of his men on the spot in Rome, whom he did not fully trust.

But the secret was not a well-kept one. By the end of July, just about every German of note in Rome knew of Hitler's plans, at least in general terms. In fact, Kesselring and Rintelen had been brought into Operation Student almost from the beginning because General Student needed their help in carrying out Hitler's ambitious plan to arrest Victor Emmanuel and other ringleaders of the Italian coup. Both men were opposed to the kidnapping plot and did whatever they could, using various indirect methods, to throw obstacles in Student's way.*

Kesselring was also aware that Hitler was trying to locate his friend the Duce, but apparently Student and Skorzeny tried to keep him out of the loop as much as possible.[30] "Even though this hare-brained scheme was kept secret from me," Kesselring later wrote, "naturally I could not fail to get wind of it as all the threads ran together through my hands."[31]

If Kesselring's faith in the new Italian government was misplaced, it also served to show how the dissimulations of the Badoglio regime had managed to divide the German mind. Though the depth of his gullibility was rare among senior commanders, other important Nazis in their turn would also come to harbor illusions about Italian intentions. Even the gloomy Rommel had momentary bursts of optimism. "It is not impossible," he wrote to his wife on July 30, "that the new Italian Government will continue the fight on our side."[32]

■ ■ ■

The Nazi "cavalry" soon arrived on the scene in the form of the Luftwaffe's Second Parachute Division, which landed in Rome over the next several days.[33] It arrived, incidentally, without the consent of the Italians, who were fobbed off with the assurance that it would soon be transferred to Sicily or southern Italy (an outright lie).[34]

---

*Hitler's obsession with secrecy during this period sometimes led to bizarre episodes. On August 2, for instance, Rintelen went to see Hitler at the Wolf's Lair with the intention of dissuading him from carrying out Operation Student. But before he had a chance to see the Fuehrer he was told by Wilhelm Keitel that Rintelen was forbidden from mentioning the subject. Hitler would have a fit, Keitel informed him, if he found out that Rintelen had been let in on the secret! See Plehwe, 100.

On the evening of July 28, Radl and the Friedenthal commandos touched down at the small airfield at Pratica di Mare, located
about twenty miles south of the capital.[35] (They had made a detour
to France on July 27 and then flown to Italy the following day.)[36]
The Friedenthalers, dressed in paratrooper garb or the nearest
equivalent, were quartered near the airport for the time being.[37]
Skorzeny showed up on July 29 and, without going into much detail, informed his men that they would be called upon in the near
future to carry out an important operation—an oblique reference to
Operation Oak as well as Operation Student.[38]

As they listened to Skorzeny, the SS men were sweating heavily.
"The men are standing in the blazing summer heat of the south,"
Radl remembered. "It is hardly bearable. Skorzeny has a swollen
lip: a fever blister."[39] The speech was interrupted when one of the
commandos fainted.[40] Skorzeny became annoyed at this. "If any of
you thinks that he cannot participate in this assignment, that he'd
rather go home, he should tell me," he said. "I will send him home
right away; we can only use the best, most robust men, who are
ready to put their lives at stake. That's what it's about."[41]

After this pep talk, Skorzeny and Radl drove to Frascati, where
they had quarters in one of the villas comprising Kesselring's GHQ
(Student also established his Eleventh Air Corps headquarters
there). During the drive, Radl was struck by the pastoral nature of
the images passing by his window: trotting donkeys, children playing by the side of the road, women carrying jugs on their shoulders,
the colorful wares of the fruit peddlers, and always vineyards—to
the left and to the right.

It was only after arriving in Frascati that Radl learned of the existence of Operation Oak. He was stunned. After discussing the
matter, both he and Skorzeny agreed that it would be no easy task
to discover where Mussolini was being held prisoner. "As for our action," Skorzeny recalled, "in other words his actual liberation, we
did not even dream about it because Zero Hour still seemed to us to
be very far off."[42]

In the coming days and weeks, the focus of the investigation into the Duce's disappearance would revolve around Skorzeny and his intelligence-gathering effort in Rome, which is where Mussolini had last been seen. Contrary to later Nazi propaganda, Skorzeny did not single-handedly carry out the mission; instead, it was a group effort from its inception. In addition to General Student, who was technically in charge of Operation Oak, Skorzeny and Radl worked with the general's intelligence officer (Ic), Captain Gerhard Langguth.*[43] On the advice of Himmler, Skorzeny also sought assistance from two local SS Nazis who called the Eternal City their home, namely, Herbert Kappler and Eugen Dollmann.

Kappler was the police attaché at the German embassy. Though basically a liaison, the blue-eyed, thirty-six-year-old SS major, whose face still showed the dueling scars of his youth, had a background that included training in espionage and security.[44] In fact, a large part of his job involved spying on the Italian police.[45] His more innocuous interests reportedly included dogs, roses, and Etruscan vases, the last of which he collected.[46] He also claimed to have a special fondness for Rome, to which he had been posted in 1939.[47] As noted by Skorzeny, who tended to minimize the roles played by others in Operation Oak, Kappler "commanded an organization which would seem able to do us many favors."[48]

Dollmann was harder to categorize. The forty-two-year-old was an officer of the *Allgemeine* (General) SS who had lived in the Italian capital for many years and served as Himmler's personal spy among Roman high society.[49] With his excellent knowledge of Italian, the blond, dapper expatriate was often called upon to act as an interpreter for members of the Axis hierarchy and was present at various

---

*Every large unit of the German army—division, corps, army, and army group—had its own general staff. The third general staff officer, known as the "Ic," handled local intelligence matters, assisted by a team of varying size. The job of the Ic was to gather up-to-the-minute information about the enemy: He monitored the positions of hostile forces, identified targets for reconnaissance, and so forth.

important meetings between Hitler and the Duce. He was also reputed to be a confidant of Eva Braun's.[50] What distinguished Dollmann from most of his SS brethren—superficially at least—were his
elegant manners, gratuitous literary references, and knowledge and
appreciation of culture, Italian and otherwise.[51] By all accounts he
enjoyed his comfortable life in Rome, had a flair for intrigue, and
had cultivated contacts among the politicians and aristocrats of the
Eternal City.[52]

■ ■ ■

Skorzeny first made contact with Kappler and Dollmann at Frascati
on the night of July 27 (the same night that Kesselring had up-
braided Skorzeny). "Kesselring had established himself at Frascati,
once the summer retreat of Roman princes and cardinals," Dollmann recalled. "On 27 July, as far as I can remember, I was invited
to dine there. I had barely arrived before the Field Marshal [Kessel-
ring] introduced me, with a look of unwonted gravity, to a mountainous man in a fur-lined flying jacket which seemed strangely out
of place on such a warm summer evening. The giant with the sabre-
scarred visage extended a giant hand."[53]

At some point that night, Skorzeny closeted Dollmann and Kappler and revealed to his fellow SS men the ambitious plans being
dreamed up at the Wolf's Lair. "After a few preliminaries," remembered Dollmann, "Skorzeny solemnly enjoined me and Kappler,
whose own duelling scars glowed red with joyful anticipation, not
to inform anyone of what he was about to tell us, Mackensen and
the embassy staff included . . . Skorzeny soon came to the point: he
was there to find the Duce and set him free."[54]

Skorzeny also told them about the blitz against Rome (which
had not yet been cancelled). Hitler was determined, he explained,
to arrest the king of Italy, Badoglio, various officers of the Italian
armed forces, and the so-called Fascist turncoats who had voted
against Mussolini in the Grand Council of Fascism. The fifty or so
intended victims would be rounded up in a complicated series of

commando raids, carted off to a nearby airport, and flown back to Germany to meet an uncertain fate.*

Kappler and Dollmann could not have been too shocked by this revelation. Just one day earlier, on July 26, a hysterical Ribbentrop—Hitler's foreign minister—had contacted the German embassy to demand the immediate arrest of the "wire-pullers" who had orchestrated the Italian coup.[55] Kappler, whose entire office at that time consisted of three men and one female secretary, reportedly reacted to Ribbentrop's instructions with bitter amusement.[56]

Though they may have kept mum in the presence of Skorzeny, who was acting as an agent and emissary of Hitler, the two SS men were less than happy to learn of Hitler's big plans. Though Kappler and Dollmann had a natural dislike of one another, they were in agreement that rescuing the Duce and resuscitating the Fascist cause by force was a bad idea.[57] In Dollmann's eyes, Mussolini was merely a political "living corpse."[58]

As for Kappler, he was convinced that Fascism was finished and could not be foisted back on the Italian people.[59] "He compared the Italians to a child who had been sick after eating some nasty soup," remembered Friedrich von Plehwe, an official at the embassy, "and so could not be persuaded to swallow the same soup again."[60] But after a few attempts to sway their superiors—Kappler, for instance, flew to see Himmler himself to voice his objections personally—Kappler and Dollmann reluctantly fell in line with their orders from above and gave what help they could to the burly Austrian.[61]

Dollmann soon met up with Skorzeny again in Kappler's office, which the commando chief had practically commandeered. "Once again," Dollmann later wrote, "it would have been heroic of me if I had told the State Security Bureau's agent flatly what I thought of his plans for Rome, but I naturally refrained from doing so. I even showed him the location of various ministries and royal palaces on

---

*According to several reports, Skorzeny's commandos spent much of that week driving all around Rome acquainting themselves with the layout of the city and casing the various houses and ministries being targeted for Operation Student.

a street map, and pointed out an ill-guarded entrance to the royal
palace at the foot of the Quirinal with a tremendous show of secrecy."[62] According to one member of the German embassy, it was
Dollmann and Mackensen who, under pressure from Hitler, actually
drew up the list of victims for kidnapping.[63]

Though Kappler resented Skorzeny's presence in Rome (which
he viewed as an intrusion into his territory) and doubted the wisdom of the latter's dual mission, he was also a good Nazi and
a stickler for orders.[64] The shrewd Gestapo sleuth, aided by his
Italian-speaking second-in-command, thirty-year-old Erich Priebke,
would come to play an important role in the hunt for the Duce.[65]
Though Kappler did not have a large police force at his disposal, he
had made connections among the Italians over the years and presumably knew a few who might be sympathetic to Skorzeny's cause;
and he may also have had Italian operatives on his payroll.[66] From
the early days of the investigation, he was actively involved in attempting to track down the missing dictator.[67] General Student later
commented that "throughout the entire course of the search operation Kappler and his efficient intelligence service rendered the best
and most valuable help."[68]

Such was the motley cast of characters making up the Mussolini
task force in Rome. Elsewhere, Hitler was marshaling just about
every other resource in the Third Reich's spy and police agencies. In
1943, a unified Nazi intelligence service did not yet exist. The responsibility for information gathering was divided primarily between
two competing organizations: German Military Intelligence, also
known as the Abwehr and run by Admiral Wilhelm Canaris, and the
foreign intelligence wing of the RSHA. Both these agencies vied with
each other for Hitler's favor, and that was the way the Fuehrer preferred it.

With the Duce's life possibly hanging in the balance, it seems
that no methods of inquiry were off-limits—even those of the more
mystical variety. In their desperation to produce results for Hitler,
the Nazis began rounding up psychics, astrologers, and other experts
in the supernatural arts. "At Berlin . . . they had meanwhile mobi-

lized even clairvoyants and astrologers," Skorzeny remembered. "It was Himmler himself, it would seem, who was inspired to appeal to such 'savants.'"[69]

There was only one problem: Many of these experts had been arrested and thrown into concentration camps by Hitler years earlier for practicing their craft! The crackdown occurred in 1941 shortly after a bizarre incident involving Rudolf Hess, the deputy leader of the Nazi Party. In May that year, Hess had made a mysterious and unauthorized solo flight to Britain (he bailed out over Scotland), presumably to broker a peace between Germany and England. The effort failed and Hess was subsequently arrested.

The Nazis believed that he had made the ill-advised flight on the advice of an astrologer. "After the Hess affair," remembered SS intelligence officer Wilhelm Hoettl, "a nation-wide witch hunt had been carried out on Hitler's orders and most of the soothsayers, clairvoyants and fortune tellers in the country had been incarcerated in concentration camps. Himmler therefore had to comb his own camps [after the Italian coup] before he could gather together his team of astrologers and magicians."[70]

Walter Schellenberg, who was chief of foreign intelligence for the SS during the summer of 1943, later described the Nazis' dilemma. "At the beginning of August," he recalled, "Hitler gave instructions for the liberation of Mussolini from his place of internment. But we had not the faintest inkling of where he was. Therefore, Himmler summoned some of the practitioners of the 'occult sciences' arrested after the flight of Hess to Great Britain, and had them closeted in a Wannsee country house. These quacks were given orders to find out the whereabouts of Mussolini. (This, incidentally, cost my department a considerable amount of money, for the 'scientists' had an insatiable appetite for good food, good drinks and good tobacco.)"[71]

In addition to the so-called Wannsee group, the German astrologer Wilhelm Wulff was also tapped for detective duty. According to Wulff, who was a free man at the time, two officials from the Gestapo came knocking on his door on July 28. "Thank God I've found you," one of them exclaimed. "I've been looking for you for days." Wulff was then whisked off to Berlin and presented to SS General Arthur Nebe, the head of the Criminal Police. The astrologer thought he was being placed under arrest (yet again), but it turned out that Nebe "was chiefly interested in discovering where Mussolini was being kept." Wulff was unfazed. "Indian astrology," he later wrote, "offers a method for making calculations of this kind. I myself had used it in a previous case in my practice."[72]

The psychics were thus set to work on the case. As shall be seen later, the information they conjured up turned out to be remarkably, if improbably, accurate.

■ ■ ■

Meanwhile, back in Rome, Skorzeny and his agents were forced to rely on more down-to-earth methods of investigation. Their options, however, were limited by the unusual nature of their enterprise. "This search," Student later wrote, "turned out to be very difficult."[73] Because Operation Oak was ostensibly a covert mission, and diplomatic relations between the two Axis powers being precarious at best, strong-arm tactics were largely forbidden.

Rome was not yet hostile territory, and Hitler meant to keep it that way for as long as it served his interests. Therefore, despite the high importance attached to their task, Skorzeny and his men did not have the luxury of resorting to the uglier methods associated with the SS. They could not, for instance, barge into government offices, rifle through filing cabinets, and rough up officials to extract the necessary information.

A variety of more subtle techniques were required. One approach involved playing upon old loyalties. Surely, Skorzeny believed, there were some individuals in the Italian army or civil administration who still harbored sympathy for the Duce. These men—soldiers, officials, and bureaucrats—had to be surreptitiously contacted and gently probed for information. If fidelity to the Fascist cause failed as an incentive, bribery could also be used to loosen lips. Skorzeny brought about 5,000 pounds in forged British banknotes to Rome for the purpose of paying informers.[74] These phony bills were no doubt viewed as the real thing by those who received them in exchange for useful scraps of information. The Nazis also monitored Italian radio transmissions, listening for unusual messages or a revealing slip of the tongue.

As Skorzeny and his men hunted for clues in Rome, they had ample opportunity to gauge the mood of the city. What they observed there was enough to give Hitler, who still harbored dreams of a Fascist revival, a severe case of heartburn. Within days of the Italian coup, nearly all traces of Fascism had been eradicated.

Back on July 25, the day of Mussolini's arrest, the king of Italy and Badoglio had both taken to the airwaves to break the news of the regime change to the Italian people. At around 11:00 P.M. (Rome time), Victor Emmanuel electrified the nation by announcing that he had accepted the resignation of the Duce and his entire cabinet. About twenty minutes later, Badoglio's voice crackled over the radio: "Italians! On the demand of His Majesty the King-Emperor, I have assumed the military government of the country with full powers. The war will continue. Italy, bruised, her provinces invaded, and her cities ruined, will retain her faith in her given word [i.e., her word to the Nazis], jealous of her ancient traditions."[75]

That evening a wave of popular feeling rippled through Rome and the country at large.[76] People sang songs in the streets and wept openly with joy, declaring that the end of Fascism had come and cursing the name of Mussolini.[77] Much like Hitler, most Italians believed that the coup was a prelude to peace. Though Badoglio had said that Italy would remain loyal to Hitler and continue to make war against the Allies, the ebullient Romans did not seem to take notice.

Next day, people poured through the streets of the capital to rejoice, ransacking the offices of Fascist organizations and, in some isolated incidents, roughing up former Party officials who were not wise enough to steer clear of the celebrations. "A car went down the Via Nazionale dragging a bust of Mussolini on a chain behind it," recalled Friedrich von Plehwe, "and boys battered it with sticks to the accompaniment of shouts of joy. A tram bore the legend *E finito il carnevale tragico* ('The tragic carnival is over')."[78]

"The streets in the centre of the city milled with excited, jubilant crowds," remembered an Italian journalist, "there was a feeling of relief, almost of light-headedness, at finding a life they had forgotten, and an ingenuous hope that better times would be here almost at once. People tried the experiment of shouting curses at Mussolini and Fascism out loud and found to their satisfaction that nothing happened to them."[79] Similar scenes took place in other cities throughout the country.

There was little physical violence.[80] Much of the people's anger was directed towards the symbols of the old regime. Literally thousands of busts and photographs of the Duce were torn down and destroyed in the wake of the coup, as were Fascist ensigns and other physical reminders of Mussolini's reign. By the time Skorzeny and Radl arrived on the scene, many shop windows already bore photographs of the new heroes of the moment, King Victor Emmanuel and Badoglio.[81]

But the people's jubilation began to fade almost as quickly. When Badoglio took over the government, many ordinary Italians expected a quick end to the war. "How peace could be achieved," Badoglio recalled, "was never considered, nobody stopped to consider; people did not argue about it; they took it for granted."[82] To their deep disappointment, the new regime, which worried constantly about threats from within and without, continued to emphasize its commitment to Hitler during the month of August and occasionally outdid the Fascists when it came to using repressive measures.[83]

On taking office, Badoglio instituted martial law in Rome and took other steps designed to intimidate possible subversives.* A 9:00 P.M. curfew kept people off the streets, and meetings involving

---

*The king and Badoglio were just as fearful of left-wing radicals as they were of the (right wing) Fascists. The former group, they believed, posed a grave threat to the very institution of monarchy, and Victor Emmanuel was obsessively concerned with preserving the authority of the Royal House.

more than three people were outlawed.[84] Harsh prison terms were doled out for what many Italians viewed as minor offenses or even God-given rights.

The complex web of deceit woven by the king and Badoglio seems to have left almost everyone guessing about the real nature of the new government, whether it be the Nazis, the Allies, or the Italian people. Within days of assuming power, Victor Emmanuel and his new *Capo del Governo* managed to alienate just about everyone who had a stake in Italy's future.

Wary as Badoglio was, it was not long before he got wind of Hitler's plans to overthrow his government and rescue the Duce. But although he took these threats seriously—the Badoglio regime took almost every threat seriously—he did not dare risk an open break with the dreaded Nazis. Instead of confronting Hitler on this score, Badoglio chose to take preventive measures on the sly. For one thing, he decided to beef up the security of the new regime and so make it more difficult for Skorzeny's commandos to arrest the Italians on Hitler's blacklist. In the coming weeks he also took covert action to lead the Mussolini task force astray.

His strategy in the latter regard was twofold. To stay one step ahead of the Germans, Badoglio repeatedly moved the Duce from one location to another. He also tried to throw the Nazis off the scent by surreptitiously feeding them a variety of false clues and rumors via the good offices of the Italian Military Intelligence Service— *Servizio Informazione Militare* (SIM)—one of the best organizations of its kind in the world.[85] Although these red herrings could not be expected to derail the rescue mission entirely, it was hoped that they might slow it down long enough to buy the Italians more time in which to negotiate a surrender. No one, it seems, be it Hitler or Badoglio, had really believed that the precarious Axis alliance would stay intact for as long as it did.

Sure enough, Skorzeny soon discovered that rumors concerning Mussolini were flying all over the capital. Some informers, for example, told the Germans that he was locked up in a mental hospital in

Switzerland. Others said that he had killed himself or was seriously ill. The Germans usually had little choice but to waste precious time by following up these and other specious and contradictory leads, some of which were reportedly planted by Italian agents.[86] "However," Skorzeny recalled, "we did manage to establish that the Duce had called upon the King on the afternoon of July 25. From that moment on, no one had laid eyes on him."[87]

As General Student dramatically put it, "It was as if Mussolini had disappeared from the face of the earth."[88]

6

THE ODYSSEY OF BENITO MUSSOLINI

And it was then, as I sat thinking in my room, that for the first time a doubt began to trouble my mind—was this protection or captivity?[1]

—Mussolini, recalling his thoughts on
the evening of July 25, 1943

BENITO MUSSOLINI WAS ONLY DIMLY AWARE OF THE ELABORATE AND top-secret machinations set in motion by Hitler and the Badoglio regime in the days immediately following the Italian coup. He was, understandably enough, preoccupied with his own troubles.

They began in earnest back on July 25, when the king of Italy gave the Duce the shock of his life by informing him that the Italian people were no longer in need of his services. Just after this meeting, at around 5:20 P.M., Mussolini staggered down the steps of the Villa Savoia in Rome and began walking towards his car, a black Alfa Romeo, which was parked some distance away on the other side of the drive. His head was probably still spinning from the news that the king had abolished the dictatorship with a wave of his tiny hand and tapped Marshal Badoglio to be the new Head of the Government.

But whatever thoughts were racing through the Duce's mind at this moment were interrupted by the sudden appearance of a figure in uniform. It was an officer of the carabinieri, a Captain Paolo Vigneri.[2]

"His Majesty has charged me with the protection of your person," Vigneri said to Mussolini, who registered the remark and then continued walking in the direction of his Alfa Romeo.[3]

"No," the captain said, "We must get in there."[4] As the Duce turned, he was surprised to see Vigneri pointing in the direction of a nearby ambulance.

After some mild protest—he preferred to take his own car and dispense with the theatrics—Mussolini did as he was told. He hesitated for a moment when he spied several armed guards waiting for him in the belly of the vehicle. But then he obligingly stepped inside (taking a seat on a stretcher), and the ambulance sped off at high speed through the streets of Rome.[5] "Strictly guarded by two plain clothes policemen armed with machine pistols," the Duce recalled, "we drove a long and uncomfortable way with such bumps that the car all but overturned."[6]

While he was being jostled around in the back of the stuffy ambulance, it never occurred to him that he had been arrested. Despite the heavy security, or perhaps because of it, Mussolini was under the vague impression that such extreme measures were considered necessary for his own good. "I still thought that all this was being done, as the King had said, in order to protect my person."[7]

Half an hour later, at around 6:00 P.M., he found himself in the courtyard of the Podgora carabinieri barracks in Via Quintino Sella.[8] Despite the rude awakening he had experienced at the Villa Savoia, the Duce was still clinging to the role of the stern dictator, old habits being difficult to break. When he stepped out of the vehicle, he thrust out his chin and placed his hands on his hips in a characteristic pose; indeed, he looked as if he had appeared on the scene to carry out a surprise inspection.[9] He was shown to the officers' mess, where he sat quietly biding his time for forty-five minutes or so.[10] Then he was led back to the ambulance and whisked away to another barracks (this one for carabinieri cadets) in Via Legnano, arriving at 7:00 P.M.[11]

He was promptly escorted to the second floor, installed in the office of the commandant, and placed under guard. As the hours passed and Mussolini took stock of his situation, he began to grow suspicious. "And it was then," he recalled, "as I sat thinking in my room, that for the first time a doubt began to trouble my mind—was this protection or captivity?"[12] He took note of a popular Fascist slogan written in large white letters on the wall of the barracks square: "Believe, Fight, and Obey."[13] It must have had a mocking ring to it.

Later that evening, at around 1:00 A.M. on July 26, the Duce received a visitor in the person of General Ernesto Ferone, who arrived at the compound bearing a message for the ex-dictator. Mussolini fingered the green envelope, which had the words "War Office" inscribed on it, and pulled out a handwritten note.[14] It was from Badoglio.

"The undersigned Head of Government," it read, "wishes to inform Your Excellency that what has been done in your regard has been done solely in your personal interest, detailed information having reached us from several quarters of a serious plot against your person. He much regrets this, and wishes to inform you that he is prepared to give orders for your safe accompanying, with all proper respect, to whatever place you may choose."[15]

Ah, now things were beginning to make more sense, the Duce must have thought to himself. Under the soothing influence of Badoglio's letter, which seemed to promise him a larger degree of freedom, he immediately dictated a reply to his old nemesis. In his message he thanked Badoglio for his trouble and said that he would like to be taken to Rocca delle Caminate, his country house (which was more like a medieval fortress) in the Romagna region, not far from Forli.

"I wish to assure Marshal Badoglio," he said to Ferone, who was scribbling down his words verbatim, "if only in remembrance of the work we have done together in the past, that not only will I raise no difficulties of any sort but I will co-operate in every possible way."[16] He said that he approved of Badoglio's declaration to continue the war at Germany's side, and then wrapped up the note: "I express my earnest hope that success will crown the grave task which Marshal

Badoglio is assuming by order and in the name of His Majesty the King, whose loyal servant I have been for twenty-one years and shall continue to be."[17]

It was a most conciliatory message. Mussolini did not voice outrage about the coup of July 25—not yet one day old—nor did he express concern about finding himself confined to a barracks. The letter was so passive, in fact, that Badoglio happily sent a copy of it to the Nazis in the days after the coup as evidence that the Duce had accepted his fate. This was the same letter that had left Goebbels scratching his head on July 27. "He would like to be taken to Rocca della Camminata to do nothing but rest," a puzzled Goebbels noted in his diary, adding that if the letter was genuine "it would be an eloquent indication that the Duce no longer has any intention of interfering with developments."[18]

Mussolini later tried to explain away his defeatist attitude by claiming that Badoglio's letter had misled him. "That letter, of a perfidy unique in history," he wrote, "was designed to convince me that the King's word concerning my personal safety would be respected and that the crisis would be dealt with within the framework of the Régime—i.e., of Fascism."[19]

As he sat idling away the hours at the cadet barracks, where he had little news of the outside world, the Duce apparently still held out hope that the Party he had created would survive the regime change. He found it hard to fathom that the old field marshal would seek to destroy Fascism, he later wrote with bitterness, "for Badoglio had too often explicitly and solemnly declared his allegiance to the Party . . . he had accepted too many honors and too much cash; anything was possible rather than that he should have prepared this betrayal and intrigued for it for months."[20]

On the evening of July 27, while Student and Skorzeny were meeting with Kesselring at Frascati, Mussolini learned that he was about to be transferred yet again, and he assumed that the destination was the Romagna. "I asked no questions," he recalled, "convinced that the goal of this nocturnal journey was Rocca delle Caminate."[21] But during the drive he peered through a slit in the lowered blinds and realized that they were traveling in the wrong direction. When he questioned one of his escorts, he was informed that there had been a change in plans. As the Duce soon learned, they were on their way to Gaeta, a small port on the western coast of Italy, about eighty miles southeast of Rome.[22]

■ ■ ■

Waiting for Mussolini at the Costanzo Ciano Wharf in Gaeta—it was named after the father of the Duce's son-in-law, Galeazzo Ciano—was Admiral Franco Maugeri, the forty-five-year-old Italian chief of Naval Intelligence.*[23] A veteran of both world wars, the wiry, gray-haired Maugeri had been informed earlier in the day that he had been selected to perform "a little escort job."[24] He quickly guessed the true identity of his mysterious charge. The destination, he was told, was the small island of Ventotene, located opposite Naples a few dozen miles off the western coast of Italy. A corvette called the *Persefone* and its eighty-man crew were detailed for the assignment.

Around 2:00 A.M. on July 28, Mussolini's six-vehicle convoy pulled up to the Ciano Wharf, where Maugeri and several other officers were chain smoking and making small talk in the stifling heat as they awaited their infamous captive. The convoy was two hours late, and Maugeri was anxious. This was quickly forgotten, however, when he laid eyes on the dictator, whose almost unearthly appearance gave the sailor pause.

"Mussolini's face was green and sallow even in the dimmed-out light of the dock," wrote Maugeri, who had jotted down the details of his adventure shortly after it occurred. "His huge, hypnotic, snakelike eyes shone out of the darkness startlingly. A three-day growth of beard masked his face."[25] The Duce was still wearing the

---

*Maugeri later distinguished himself in the resistance movement during the German occupation of Rome and in 1946 was elevated to chief of the Naval Staff, the highest post in the Italian navy.

same blue suit, now wrinkled, that he had donned during his audience with the king, a short-sleeved white shirt with a black tie, and a felt hat.

"A far cry from the arrogant, bloodthirsty bully on the Balcony," Maugeri thought to himself as he took the measure of the man.[26] He hated Mussolini for what he had done to Italy, but could not help feeling a tinge of sympathy for the pathetic figure standing before him.

Maugeri saluted the Duce respectfully before leading him below decks to the empty cabin of the *Persefone*'s commanding officer, Lieutenant-Commander Tazzari. The corvette got underway shortly afterward, sailing through the Tyrrhenian Sea and dropping anchor off Ventotene at around 5:15 A.M. Two of Mussolini's escorts, General Saverio Polito and a Colonel Pelaghi, then went ashore to find appropriate accommodations for their prisoner. Amazingly, it seems that no one had reconnoitered the island in advance to determine whether Ventotene was an appropriate place to keep the Duce under wraps.

While waiting for them to return, Maugeri decided to venture below and check up on Mussolini, with whom he had had no contact since the vessel departed Gaeta. Though he did not have explicit authority to fraternize with the Duce, his curiosity had gotten the better of him.

When he entered the cabin, he discovered the guard sound asleep in a corner of the room. Mussolini, who was awake, lifted up his large eyes as the door opened. Maugeri greeted him and asked whether he wanted a cup of coffee, but the Duce said he would rather have some information. Did the admiral, he wondered, know the approximate size of Ventotene?

Maugeri tried to recall the modest proportions of the island from memory. As he did so, he saw Mussolini break into a smile for the first time.

"Ah!" said the Duce, his voice sounding gravelly and tired. "A small island."[27]

As Maugeri well knew, Mussolini was drawing a parallel between Ventotene and another, more famous island by the name of

St. Helena. Napoleon Bonaparte had been exiled to this small tropical island in the South Atlantic after his legendary defeat at Waterloo and his second fall from power in 1815. It was no secret that Napoleon was one of the Duce's idols.*

Then another question.

"This is a corvette, isn't it?" Mussolini asked in a demanding tone.[28]

"Yes," Maugeri replied.[29] It seemed like a silly question, he thought to himself, considering that the Duce had been chief of the navy for so many years. During his long reign as dictator, Mussolini had simultaneously occupied a mind-boggling number of other positions in the regime, including the top posts of the three military services.

The two men proceeded to talk at length, mostly about the Italian navy and naval warfare in general, until Polito and Pelaghi returned. They told Maugeri that their scouting expedition had been a bust. The presence of a German garrison on the island, among other reasons, rendered Ventotene unsuitable for their purposes. At Pelaghi's suggestion, the *Persefone* continued on to Ponza, another small island located about twenty-five miles to the northwest.[30] (The Pontine islands, which include Ponza and Ventotene, were the traditional home of Circe, the sorceress immortalized in Homer's *Odyssey*).

While Polito and Pelaghi went ashore again, Maugeri returned to the captain's cabin. This time the Duce jumped to his feet.

"Admiral, what is the meaning of these useless irritations?" Mussolini demanded, staring intensely into Maugeri's eyes. It was obvious that he was highly agitated, but that he was also trying hard to keep his cool. "Why must I be persecuted in this way? Since last Sunday I've been completely cut off from everyone. I've had no news of my family. I'm without a penny. All the clothes I have are the ones I'm wearing. Why should I be treated this way—like a common

---

*Mussolini may also have been thinking of Elba, another small island on which Napoleon had spent time as an exile.

criminal? According to the letter Badoglio wrote me, I wasn't arrested, but only placed in protective custody to guard me against a plot against my life."[31]

The Duce then produced a crumpled sheet of paper—what was left of the Badoglio letter—and read it to Maugeri. The admiral was slightly amused by Mussolini's naïveté. "It was a euphemism, of course," Maugeri thought to himself, "and no one should have known that better than Mussolini. He had put enough men in similar 'protective custody' in his time."[32]

Mussolini continued to vent. He had ruled Italy for two decades, he reminded Maugeri, and had already lost one son in the war. He had been promised safe passage to Rocca delle Caminate, and now his captors seemed to be reneging on the deal.

"It's not generous to treat me this way," he said, "it's not wise, either. It will displease Hitler; he has the strongest feelings of friendship toward me. This business can cause much damage. What are they scared of, anyway? I'm all through politically. I've been betrayed. I know now that my political career is finished."[33]

Mussolini eventually simmered down and the two men began to talk. At one point, Maugeri told him that Allied propaganda was advising the Italians that if they wanted the best surrender terms they should expel the Nazis from the peninsula. The Duce seemed to agree. "We must unshackle ourselves from them," he concurred, nodding. "We're entitled to tell them that we've waged three years of war, that we've lost our entire merchant marine and almost all our Navy, that any number of our cities have been completely or partially destroyed. We should tell them they can't help us now. There is no other course for us."[34] Though Maugeri may not have known it, this was precisely what Mussolini was supposed to have told Hitler face-to-face at the Feltre conference on July 19.

"Germany is a steel cable," the Duce explained with a characteristic metaphor, "we Italians are a hemp rope—more elastic, more tensile under pressure. The steel cable snaps with one good pull."[35]

"Perhaps, Excellency, we in Italy have attempted things bigger than ourselves," said Maugeri.[36]

"Yes, with the Italians it's all a question of character," replied Mussolini, repeating one of his pet themes. "All the other qualities—stamina, sobriety, intelligence—they possess. Character, alone, they lack. It will take years and years of education and these terrible trials they are enduring now."[37] He had long criticized the Italian people for being too soft and artistic, for their lack of the martial qualities their German neighbors to the north possessed.[38]

Polito and Pelaghi returned from Ponza—a small, crescent-shaped island only about five miles long—and announced that they had finally found a suitable place to stash Mussolini: a modest dwelling in the village of Santa Maria known to the locals as the House of the Ras.[39] It was an ironic choice. In recent times it had served as the prison of the Ras Immiru, an African prince who had been captured by the Italians in 1936 during the Ethiopian war. He had been imprisoned on the island by the Duce.*

At around 10:00 A.M., Mussolini was taken to Ponza aboard a launch and led to a small, gray-colored house with green shutters.[40] "Polito approached me," he recalled, "and, pointing out a greenish-coloured house half-hidden by big, laid-up fishing boats, said: 'That is your temporary home.' Meanwhile, through some unexplained impulse, all the windows and balconies [of the houses in Santa Maria] were suddenly filled with men and women armed with binoculars who were watching the boat as it came ashore. In a flash the whole island knew of our arrival."[41]

Aside from its security risks, the House of the Ras was a far cry from the luxurious villas to which the Duce had become accustomed. According to one report, the furnishings amounted to little more than an iron bedstead (sans bedding), one well-worn and greasy table, and a chair.

"We didn't know you were coming to Ponza, Excellency," explained Sergeant-Major Marini, one of the local carabinieri assigned to keep an eye on the dictator. "I was told barely half an hour ago."[42]

---

*Ponza had a long history as a penal colony, as did Ventotene.

"Don't worry, sergeant," Mussolini told the man, who subsequently left on a mission to scrounge up a mattress, sheets, and pillows.[43]

It was in these Spartan accommodations that the Duce celebrated his sixtieth birthday on July 29, one day after his arrival on Ponza. He experienced it profoundly alone, if one excludes the presence of guards and other strangers. In honor of the occasion, the great man received a gift of four peaches from the carabinieri. Mussolini agreed to accept the fruit only after receiving assurances from Marini that the inhabitants of the island could spare it.

"The days were long at Ponza," remembered the Duce, who was cut off from the outside world and prohibited from reading newspapers or listening to the radio. "At Ponza, I realised the miserable conspiracy which had got rid of me, and I was convinced that all this would lead to capitulation and to my being handed over to the enemy."[44]

7

HITLER TAKES CONTROL

*Again and again in the situation conferences he insisted that
everything must be done to locate the missing Duce. He declared that Mussolini's fate was a nightmare that weighed on
him day and night.*[1]
—Albert Speer on Hitler's obsession with finding Mussolini

DURING EARLY AUGUST, AS THE NOT-SO-SECRET SEARCH FOR MUSSOLINI
was getting underway in Rome, the two Axis powers continued to
eye one another warily from their respective bases in Rome and
East Prussia. The challenge for each side lay in pursuing its own
clandestine agenda without provoking the open hostility of the
other. Neither the Nazis nor the Italians were ready to throw off
their masks and reveal their true intentions. Whether they liked it
or not, the two estranged allies were stuck with each other.

But their relationship had been transformed. The once-dreaded
Rome-Berlin Axis, which at its height seemed tantalizingly close to
vanquishing its powerful foes, was beginning to deteriorate into a
complicated game of mutual deception and Machiavellian intrigue
that neither country could afford to lose.

The Badoglio regime was beginning to worry that the endgame
was already upon them. In Rome, Hitler's agents were sniffing around
under the very walls of the capital in an effort to find out what had
really happened to Mussolini. In northern Italy, large numbers of

German troops were swarming into the country through the Brenner Pass without the formal authorization of the new government,
which did its best to look the other way; indeed, by the end of the
first week of August, approximately 30,000 German soldiers had
crossed into Italy.[2]

These soldiers arrived ostensibly as comrades, of course, and for
the most part did not take aggressive action toward their Italian
counterparts. Nevertheless, in a provocative touch of propaganda,
some of the Germans had the words "Viva il Duce" brazenly
scrawled across their helmets.[3] The current administration, actively
engaged as it was in erasing Mussolini's legacy, could hardly have
viewed the Germans' defiance as an encouraging sign.

Having failed to make contact with the Allies through the Vatican in late July, Raffaele Guariglia, the Italian foreign minister, took
another step on the long road toward peace. On August 2, he sent
an envoy named Lanza D'Ajeta, a member of the Italian embassy to
the Holy See, to Lisbon in neutral Portugal to make contact with the
Allies via their representatives in the city. Despite Italy's poor bar-
gaining position, Badoglio (as well as the king) remained confident
that he or his diplomatic emissaries could talk the Anglo-Americans
down from their rigid "unconditional surrender" stance.*[4]

His optimism was misplaced. This fact, coupled with the regime's
natural tendency to vacillate, threatened to drag out the peace process for a lot longer than anyone could have imagined. For one thing,
when D'Ajeta left for Lisbon he was not given the authority to conduct negotiations with the Allies; he could merely inform them of
Italy's desire to detach itself from the Nazis. "D'Ayeta [sic] never from
start to finish made any mention of peace terms," Churchill informed

---

*Just for good measure, the Italians also took a scattershot approach by dispatch-
ing two additional emissaries in early August. One of these, Alberto Berio, headed
for Tangier in North Africa to establish contact with British. The other, the mil-
lionaire industrialist Alberto Pirelli, hastened to Switzerland to see whether that
neutral country would agree to facilitate talks between Italy and the Allies.

Roosevelt after this contact, "and his whole story . . . was no more than a plea that we should save Italy from the Germans as well as from herself, and do it as quickly as possible."[5]

With Hitler's troops breathing down their necks, the king and Badoglio were apparently in no hurry to switch sides in the war. Though the truth of the matter is not entirely clear, it seems that the two men were stalling for time in the vain hope that Hitler would have a change of heart and allow Italy to withdraw peaceably from the Axis.[6]

Churchill, for one, was prepared to cut the Italians a little slack. "Badoglio admits he is going to double-cross someone," Churchill wrote on August 7 to Anthony Eden, his foreign secretary, "but his interests and the mood of the Italian people make it more likely Hitler will be the one to be tricked. Allowance should be made for the difficulties of his position."[7]

■ ■ ■

Meanwhile, halfway across Europe, Hitler continued to pace the hallways of the Wolf's Lair in East Prussia. Playing the waiting game was proving almost as difficult for him as it was for the Italians. The restless dictator had not entirely given up the idea of kidnapping Badoglio and the royal family and then occupying Rome by force, thereby engineering a political revolution that would ensure Italy's loyalty. He clearly relished the idea—partly for personal reasons and partly because he believed it could work—and almost seemed to find therapeutic value in repeatedly threatening to carry it out.

If nothing else, a turnabout in Italy might help to lift the sagging spirits of the German people. Some of them, Goebbels noted around this time, were "almost in a state of panic."[8] But despite the PR guru's pleas, Hitler refused to console them: The crisis in Italy had presented him with a riddle.

"It is hardly possible for me to speak to the German people now," Hitler confided to one of his top military men. "I am not in a position to express my views on the Italian question. If I should do so in an approving manner, I would lend support to the circles who are even now preparing for treachery. Nor can I speak out against the present Government of Italy, for well-known military reasons. However, I cannot ignore the problem of Italy either, since that would be interpreted as a sign of internal and external weakness. As soon as the Italian question has been clarified one way or the other, I shall be in a much better position to address the German people."[9]

But "clarification" was no simple matter. Throughout August, the so-called Italian question and the rescue of Mussolini continued to dominate Hitler's psyche during his regular military conferences at the Wolf's Lair. "After the Italian Chief of State was overthrown and vanished without a trace," Albert Speer recalled, "Hitler seemed to be inspired with a kind of Nibelungen loyalty. Again and again in the situation conferences he insisted that everything must be done to locate the missing Duce. He declared that Mussolini's fate was a nightmare that weighed on him day and night."*[10]

■ ■ ■

Fortunately for him, the Mussolini task force in Rome had already begun to make progress. After reaching out to one of his Italian contacts, Herbert Kappler, the Gestapo man at the German embassy, learned that the Duce had been taken to the carabinieri cadet barracks in Via Legnano on the evening of July 25.

"Among the Italian officials whom our police attaché frequented," Skorzeny explained, "was a captain of Carabinieri or militarized police who in the depths of his heart was perhaps still a supporter of the Fascist regime. In the course of a conversation, this man dropped a valuable hint: apparently the Duce had been conveyed by ambulance . . . to the Carabinieri barracks. Checking this information, we found it to be correct; we actually contrived to

---

* "Nibelungen loyalty" is a reference to German mythology.

learn in what part of the building and on what floor the prisoner had been interned."[11] The bad news was that Mussolini had already been moved by the time they received the tip.

But even before this revelation, chance had come to their rescue. Within days of the Duce's disappearance, the Nazis had managed to turn up two German eyewitnesses with corroborating stories. One man, a Luftwaffe engineer named Dessauer, had apparently spotted a heavily guarded convoy of cars passing through Gaeta on the evening Mussolini was handed over to Admiral Maugeri and placed aboard the corvette *Persefone*. This bit of news was consistent with the testimony of a petty officer in the German navy who said that he had seen the Duce boarding a vessel in Gaeta.[12]

According to notes made by Admiral Doenitz, who was a frequent visitor at the Wolf's Lair during the period of Mussolini's captivity, after learning of these promising developments Hitler began to take an active hand in the investigation. (He had already demanded that he be kept personally informed of all the latest leads.)[13] When Doenitz arrived at Fuehrer Headquarters in early August for conferences, he found that Hitler had temporarily put aside other pressing matters of state so that he could interrogate potential witnesses. The first of these was Dessauer, whom General Student had flown all the way to Rastenburg so that the Fuehrer could examine him personally.

"In the afternoon, Aviation-Engineer Dessauer has a conference with the Fuehrer," Doenitz noted on August 2.* "He reports that a column of cars, heavily guarded by Carabinieri, was sighted but the Duce himself was not seen." This was presumably the same convoy that bore Mussolini from the carabinieri cadet barracks in Rome to the Costanzo Ciano Wharf in Gaeta on the night of July 27–28. By the end of the day Hitler ordered the appearance of the navy witness. "During the evening session, the order is given to immediately bring Petty Officer Laurich unobtrusively from Gaeta to Headquarters via

---

*For the sake of simplicity, certain German naval records have been ascribed to the person of Doenitz. In some instances, Doenitz really did take down the notes in question.

Berlin. He was mentioned by Dessauer as an additional witness." Hitler had even zeroed in on a potential target. "Furthermore, it is directed that operation 'Eiche' [Oak] be limited to Ventotene Island."[14]

Ventotene. This was the point at which the search for the Duce began to veer off target. At the same moment that Hitler was interviewing Dessauer, Mussolini was idling away the hours at the House of the Ras on Ponza (about twenty-five miles from Ventotene). The ultimate source of the Ventotene lead—as Hitler must have been told—was Petty Officer Laurich.[15] The latter, who worked at a German navy signals base at Gaeta, had received the tip from an Italian naval officer with whom he had become friendly.[16] Laurich himself did not meet with Hitler until several days later.

Soon Heinrich Himmler, chief of the SS, jumped on the Ventotene bandwagon. On August 5, Doenitz got word from the Wolf's Lair that "according to additional information from the Reichsfuehrer SS [Himmler], only the island V. needs to be considered for operation 'Eiche.'"[17] It is not clear what led Himmler to this conclusion.

Oddly enough, though, Ventotene and Ponza were both roughly consistent with the information produced by Himmler's psychics. The German astrologer Wilhelm Wulff declared in late July that the Duce was located somewhere southeast of Rome and within seventy-five miles of the capital. The Wannsee group, according to Walter Schellenberg, was even more precise: a so-called Master of the Sidereal Pendulum determined that Mussolini was being held on an island to the west of Naples, but did not, of course, specify *which* island.

Though Ventotene was essentially a red herring—and may well have been a plant by SIM, the Italian Military Intelligence Service—the island continued to capture the Nazi imagination for days to come.[18]

■ ■ ■

Even as he was chasing the Duce's shadow, Hitler continued to spar with his subordinates regarding the reliability of the Badoglio regime, the intentions of which were still the subject of some debate among the Nazis. To his credit, Hitler never seriously doubted his instinctive belief that Badoglio was planning to double-cross him, even though close advisors such as Jodl and Doenitz occasionally softened their views on the new government.

"At the [afternoon] Fuehrer conference Lt. General Jodl reports that the Italians have completely ceased resistance to our measures," Doenitz noted on August 3. Jodl was apparently noting that the Italians were not doing much to impede the German infiltration of northern Italy. Hitler seemed unmoved: "During the discussion of the possible reasons for this, the Fuehrer advances the theory that they may just be biding their time in order to come to terms with the Anglo-Saxons before an open break with Germany. Jodl and [Doenitz] suggest that the Italians may feel helpless and therefore want to rely more on us again. It remains to be seen what the actual situation is."[19]

But Hitler, who at the moment had no solid evidence either of Mussolini's whereabouts or of Badoglio's treachery, was not yet ready to strike. "Operations 'Achse,' 'Eiche' and 'Schwarz' are not to be undertaken yet," wrote Doenitz.[20] This meant that the rescue of the Duce was put on hold for the moment, as well as Hitler's plans to take over Italy by force, though preparations for both of these operations were allowed to continue.[21]

The Nazis' paralyzing predicament around this time was summed up concisely by Marshal Wilhelm Keitel, the chief of OKW (German High Command), in a letter to his wife. Aside from the devastating Hamburg bombing, Keitel wrote on August 3, "there is not much to report: there is a state of flux and we can only wait and see what will happen with the new developments in Italy. Badoglio has reassured us that they will go on fighting, and that it was only on this condition that he accepted office. Nobody knows where Mussolini is."[22]

■ ■ ■

Keitel's last sentence was not entirely true, of course. The Nazis thought they had a pretty good idea of where the Duce was: namely, Ventotene Island. In fact, on August 6, Himmler caused a minor panic at the Wolf's Lair by announcing that the Italians were preparing to evacuate Mussolini from Ventotene aboard a destroyer. The news sent Hitler into a tizzy and immediately sparked a long-distance debate between himself and Doenitz about how to prevent such a move without coming to blows with their Italian allies and breaking the Axis wide open.

Doenitz, who spent much of August shuttling back and forth between Berlin and the Wolf's Lair, was at his office in Berlin when he learned of the development at 1:45 P.M. on August 6. "The Admiral at the Fuehrer's Headquarters," he noted, "reports that the Reichsfuehrer SS [Himmler] has sent information that the Italians are holding a destroyer in readiness for removal of the 'valuable object' in case of an emergency."[23] The "valuable object" was a codename for the Duce.

"The destroyer is said to be stationed at Gaeta. The Fuehrer wishes to have [Doenitz] informed at once asking him to re-examine the distribution of the Italian destroyers. Preventive measures must be taken at once; he suggests the use of submarines." Fifteen minutes later, Hitler sent Doenitz a more specific proposal. "The Admiral at the Fuehrer's Headquarters telephones that the Fuehrer has no objection to a blockade of V. harbor by submarines."[24]

This suggestion posed a problem for Doenitz. The Germany navy could certainly try to blockade the harbor at Ventotene if Hitler so desired, but such a clumsy measure was sure to be noticed by the Italians. Doenitz sent Hitler a reply at 4:30 P.M.: "An inconspicuous blockade of the harbor, even by submarine, is impossible since it would have to stand right off the harbor entrance. Likewise, he knows of no inconspicuous means with which to render the destroyer at its present anchorage harmless. [Doenitz] therefore advises against a blockade, not because of its impossibility, but in order to prevent our intentions from being recognized prematurely. If the Italians become aware of our plans, they will certainly remove the 'valuable object' secretly, e.g., by motorboat, to a different place."[25]

Doenitz also pointed out the obvious by reminding Hitler that attempts to prevent the transfer of Mussolini would be likely to cause an open break with the Italians. "The only possible military solution exists in forestalling the Italians, but such a step will have serious consequences. It is not within the province of [Doenitz] to make decisions in such matters."[26] It was, in fact, a political matter, and only Hitler had the authority to decide.

Doenitz waited for Hitler's response. It finally arrived at 6:30 P.M. "Answer from the Admiral at the Fuehrer's Headquarters: 'The Fuehrer will reconsider the matter.'"[27]

As it turned out, Himmler was close to the mark.

On the afternoon of August 6, the same day that Hitler and Doenitz were debating the possibility of blockading the harbor at Ventotene, Admiral Maugeri received word that he would be supervising yet another transfer of the Duce. "We've got to stow Mussolini away somewhere that's safer than Ponza," he was informed by Admiral Raffaele De Courten, the portly new Minister of Marine, "somewhere where the Germans can't lay hands on him."[28] The Italians had selected the island of La Maddalena, located off the northeastern tip of the much larger island of Sardinia. A carabinieri officer had flown to La Maddalena that very morning to lay the groundwork.

Badoglio later claimed that Ponza had become untenable as a hideout for the Duce because of the rumors running rampant in Rome. "He was transferred to the Island of Ponza," Badoglio remembered, running through the sequence of events, "but after a few days we had to remove him to La Maddalena because everyone in Rome knew where he was and talked openly of his whereabouts, so it was to be expected that the Germans would rescue him by a *coup de main*."[29]

On the evening of August 7, Maugeri drove back to Gaeta on the west coast of Italy and boarded the F.R. 22, a twenty-year-old destroyer that in a former life had gone by the more colorful name of the *Panthère* (when she belonged to the French).* The ship dropped

---

*The *Panthère* had a turbulent history. She had been scuttled by the French at Toulon in November 1942 to prevent her capture by the Nazis. She was then raised by the Italians in March 1943, towed to Italy, and renamed F.R. 22. Her luck finally ran out on September 9, 1943, at La Spezia, when she was scuttled again to prevent her seizure by the Germans. On this occasion, it was the Italians who sank her.

anchor off Ponza at 11:30 P.M., and Mussolini was brought aboard shortly afterward along with his armed escort, which had increased to about eighty carabinieri and policemen. As the *Panthère* carved its way through the Tyrrhenian Sea—La Maddalena was located a little less than two hundred miles northwest of Ponza—Maugeri once again found himself face to face with the Duce.

He thought the dictator looked a little better. His eyes even had a trace of their "old sparkle."[30] He could not say the same about Mussolini's wrinkled blue suit, which he was still wearing. The lonely despot seemed hungry for conversation (or for an audience), and held forth for hours on a wide variety of topics.

When Maugeri revealed that the Italians were worried about the prospect of a German rescue operation, the Duce said that the very idea was anathema to him. "That's the biggest humiliation they [the Nazis] could ever inflict upon me," said Mussolini, who assumed that the next logical step would be a new Fascist government-in-exile. "To think that I would ever go to Germany and set up a government there with the support of the Germans! Ah, no! Never! Never that!"[31]

At one point, Maugeri expressed his surprise that the Fascist regime had collapsed so quickly and completely, "that it should have been possible to overthrow it in a few hours without anyone lifting a finger or making the slightest effort to defend it, without anyone dying on the barricades with Mussolini's name on his lips, waving the Fascist banner."[32] The Duce, who knew that Maugeri was speaking the truth, was quick to provide an explanation.

"It's just another example of the Italians' fundamental lack of character," said Mussolini. "Nonetheless, the things Fascism accomplished have been worthwhile; many things can never be destroyed, much less denied or disowned. . . . As time passes, Fascism will be missed more and more. But it will never really die." As the Duce spoke of the enduring power of Fascism, Maugeri noted how his expression intensified and his face became "the famous Roman mask with outthrust jaw and hard, glittering eyes that had scowled down from the Balcony."[33]

The failures of the Fascist regime, its founder explained, were ultimately the fault of the Italian people themselves. They simply did not measure up. "Italians are too individualistic," he complained to Maugeri, "too cynical. They're not serious enough. . . . It's different with the Germans; they submit readily to Nazism and any kind of discipline. That sort of thing comes naturally to them. . . . They don't even begin to understand what individualism means. That's why Hitler has had an easier time than I. Germans are born Nazis; Italians had to be made into Fascists."[34]

■ ■ ■

Mussolini's newest prison was an attractive Moorish-Italian-style villa overlooking the sea and located just outside of the town of Maddalena, on the southern coast of the island of the same name. Constructed in the mid-1800s by a British expatriate named James Webber, the small two-story Mediterranean mansion was nestled snugly among low-lying hills and surrounded by a small forest of pine trees. About a hundred men, a mixed force comprised of carabinieri and policemen, guarded the compound twenty-four hours a day once their prisoner arrived.

"The house destined for my use," the Duce recalled, "was situated outside the town, on a height surrounded by a park thickly studded with pine trees. The villa had been built by an Englishman called Webber who, strangely enough, of all the places in the world where he could have settled, chose just the most stark and lonely island of all those to the north of Sardinia. The Secret Service? Possibly."*[35]

---

*The island's inhabitants apparently took a different view of the villa's namesake. At the turn of the century, the Municipal Council of Maddalena decided to name a street after Webber (he had died in 1877). In the council's minutes, Webber is described as "a man who valued his own honesty, son of the celebrated General Webber, like Byron's Harold he loved solitude, loved this island, in his beautiful dwelling he established a library of which any town could be proud."

It was even more stark and lonely by the time Mussolini arrived. Most of the civilians living on the island—which was also home to an Italian naval base—had been evacuated after a heavy Allied bombing raid.[36] The population was now composed mainly of sailors and fishermen.[37]

"The scorching days went monotonously by without the slightest news of the world outside," recalled Mussolini, who passed much of the time standing on the terrace of the villa and staring across the harbor at the mountains of Sardinia or taking short walks among the pine trees with one of his guards.[38] He also continued to write down his thoughts in a sort of journal that he had kept since his fall from power: a disjointed smattering of observations and pseudo-philosophical ruminations. He called his journal the *Pontine and Sardinian Musings*.[39] A few excerpts:

> As far as gratitude is concerned, animals are superior to human beings perhaps because they have instincts and not reason.[40]

> This morning the sun is striving to pierce a grey bank of cloud which is coming up from the east. The sea is like lead.[41]

> [T]he masses are always ready to cast down the Gods of yesterday, even though they rue it to-morrow. But for me there is no return. My blood, the infallible voice of the blood, tells me that my star has set for ever.[42]

> In all my life I have never had any "friends," and I have often asked myself whether this is an advantage or a handicap? Now I am sure that it is a good thing, for now there is no one called upon to suffer with me.[43]

The Duce also received a special delivery from the mainland. "The only surprise was a gift from the Führer," Mussolini remembered, "a splendid complete edition of Nietzsche's works in twenty-four volumes with a signed dedication. A real marvel of German book-production."[44] Nietzsche, who among other things was the originator of such Fascist mottos as "Live dangerously," was a favorite of both Axis dictators.[45] The belated birthday present arrived in an enormous case and was accompanied by a letter from Kesselring.[46] Part of it read, "The Führer will consider himself happy if this great work of German literature gives you a little pleasure, Duce, and if you will consider it as an expression of the Führer's personal attachment to you."[47]

This was the same gift that Mackensen, the German ambassador to Rome, had attempted to deliver personally on July 29, Mussolini's sixtieth birthday, during his meeting with the king of Italy.[48] Not wishing to provoke the Nazis, the Italian authorities had agreed to deliver it on Hitler's behalf. "He incessantly inquired about this present," Badoglio recalled wearily, "until he had received a personal acknowledgement from Mussolini."[49]

During his stay at La Maddalena, the Duce asked General Saverio Polito, his senior jailer of the moment, why his request to go to Rocca delle Caminate had been ignored.[50] Polito explained that his country house in the Romagna had been considered too risky from a security standpoint. The prefect of Forli, one of the officials who would have been responsible for the Duce's safety at his country estate, had informed Badoglio that he was not certain he could prevent the dictator from being seized by angry mobs.*[51]

When Mussolini scoffed at this explanation, Polito attempted to give him a reality check by describing the depth of anti-Fascist feeling among the people. "The demonstrations of hatred against you are innumerable," Polito said. "I have myself seen a bust of you in a lavatory in Ancona."[52]

---

*This explanation apparently contained an element of truth. However, the fact that the Nazis were desperately searching for Mussolini was another important reason for rejecting the Duce's request.

8

THE RAID ON SANTO STEFANO

An early execution of the operation "Eiche" [Oak] appears necessary. The general conviction is that Mussolini is on [Santo] Stefano.[1]

—German navy records, August 9, 1943

EVEN AS THEY ENGAGED IN A BIZARRE GAME OF HIDE AND SEEK WITH Mussolini in the Tyrrhenian Sea, the Nazis and the Italians did their best to keep up appearances on the diplomatic front. On August 6, the Rome-Berlin alliance held its first Axis conference since the Italian coup. Though Hitler and Badoglio did not take part, the day-long meeting in Tarvisio, in northern Italy, gave both sides an important opportunity to probe each other's agenda. Needless to say, the atmosphere was frosty.

One sign of this was the intimidating "grand entrance" made by the German delegation—including Joachim von Ribbentrop and Marshal Wilhelm Keitel, chief of OKW—which rumbled into town aboard a heavily armored train so ostentatiously adorned with machine guns, antiaircraft weapons, and armed SS men that some may have thought the Nazis were preparing to do battle. The Italians at Tarvisio were represented by Raffaele Guariglia, Badoglio's foreign minister, and General Vittorio Ambrosio, who was Keitel's opposite number.*

---

*Ambrosio and Guariglia, incidentally, were on the list of Italian notables to be arrested during Operation Student.

According to several eyewitnesses, German paranoia was running high. "We must leave all our secret papers and cipher keys on German soil," Ribbentrop had announced before leaving for Tarvisio, according to his interpreter, Paul Schmidt. "It's by no means impossible that these brigands intend, on British and American instructions, to kidnap us on Italian territory."[2]

"A few SS men sat by us in the train with loaded tommy-guns," Schmidt remembered, "and when we arrived at Tarvisio they immediately threw a protective cordon round Ribbentrop's saloon coach in which the negotiations were carried on."[3] General Walter Warlimont, who was at Tarvisio, noted Hitler's decree: "[U]nder no circumstances were we to eat or drink anything which had not previously been tasted by our hosts."[4] Indeed, for most of the summer, Hitler was preoccupied by the fear that the Italians would attempt to poison his top envoys.

Ribbentrop, declaring at the outset that his purpose was "to discuss the situation resulting from the change which has taken place in Italy and which has had political and psychological repercussions," did nothing to ease the tension once the conference started.[5] He then asked Guariglia for a "clarification" of recent events.[6] This was a polite and restrained way of demanding an explanation from the Italians for the disappearance of Mussolini and the dissolution of the Fascist Party.

But Guariglia did not stray from the official script, which maintained that the regime change of July 25 was merely a domestic matter and had no bearing on Axis relations. "It would not have been wise," added the crafty Neapolitan, alluding to the demise of the Fascist Party, "to entrust the government of Italy to those very men who overthrew the Duce."[7]

Here again was the same myth—all the more plausible because it contained an element of truth—that was fed to the Germans several days earlier during the meeting between Mackensen and the king of Italy: namely, that Mussolini had fallen from power as the result of a betrayal by his own subordinates in the Fascist Grand

Council. Such men as this, Guariglia suggested slyly, were not worthy to wield power.

At one point, Ribbentrop, who had been instructed by Hitler to gauge Badoglio's real intentions, asked point-blank whether the Italians had begun peace talks with the Allies.[8] Guariglia, who was actively working toward this end, told Ribbentrop with a straight face that they had not. The Germans did not pursue the matter.

As it happened, Ribbentrop was not the only one seeking clarification. Ambrosio, who was chief of *Comando Supremo* (the Italian High Command), began probing Keitel for the reason so many German troops were suddenly descending upon his country.

"Ambrosio demanded to know why an endless stream of German reinforcements was pouring southwards across the Brenner," recalled SS man Eugen Dollmann, who acted as an interpreter for the two soldiers, "and his German opposite number countered by asking why the Italians were withdrawing their men from Greece and the Balkans. Mutual distrust grew and voices rose in volume. Before long, Keitel and Ambrosio were bellowing orders at each other on an imaginary parade-ground, and I half expected to hear the fatal words 'Duce', 'treason' and 'loyalty to the Axis' burst in the air like shrapnel shells at any moment."[9]

The irony of Ambrosio's position was rich, but grim. When they pleaded for German arms and assistance in the days after the invasion of Sicily, the Italians were disappointed by Hitler's thrift. But now that they had secretly decided to sue for peace, and it being crucial to keep German troops off Italian soil, they were being overwhelmed by Hitler's newfound generosity. Though they were helpless to stem the tide of German reinforcements, the Italians did manage to broach another potentially touchy subject at Tarvisio.

The issue at hand was the return of Italian troops fighting in foreign lands.[10] As mentioned earlier, the Italians had numerous divisions stationed on other fronts. In light of Italy's decision to switch sides in the war, it made sense to recall these soldiers to the homeland—where they might very well be needed in fighting their soon-to-be enemy, the Nazis. The Italians, of course, could not explain their request in these terms; instead, they justified the return of their troops as necessary for the defense of Italy. After hearing their case, Keitel said that he would refer the matter to Hitler for consideration.[11]

■ ■ ■

All in all the conference was a bust.[12] The only thing the two sides had in common, it seems, was that each had become "positively intoxicated by its own lies and treachery" by the time the meeting had ended.[13] But Ribbentrop had not yet finished with his intrigues. As if to heighten the air of unreality surrounding the proceedings at Tarvisio, the German foreign minister dropped a bombshell on his Italian audience by suggesting an Axis summit between Hitler and the king of Italy—to take place in Germany!

"The rulers of the two countries were to meet on German soil," Dollmann recalled sarcastically, "like lambs grazing peacefully in green pastures, to eliminate all suspicions and misunderstandings once and for all."[14] The implication was that Hitler had accepted the demise of the Fascist system and was now ready to accept the Badoglio regime as the legitimate administration of Italy.

From the Italian point of view, this new proposition, though sensible enough on its face, was unexpected and sinister. Badoglio had requested just such a meeting shortly after the coup, but Hitler had rebuffed him. Was it in the Fuehrer's nature, the Italians must have wondered, to experience a true change of heart during the intervening days? It hardly seemed likely. In light of Hitler's increasingly aggressive behavior, the idea of sitting across the table from Germany's top Nazi was probably enough to send shivers down the collective spine of the Italian regime.

And with good reason. The offer may have been the first step in a German ploy to kidnap the king as well as Badoglio, the latter of whom was also invited to attend. "Whatever it was," recalled Dollmann, "Guariglia retained his composure with Machiavellian skill and referred the matter to Rome, well knowing that current negotiations with the West ruled out any possibility of agreement."[15]

Before leaving Tarvisio, Ribbentrop took care of one bit of unfinished business that had nothing to do with the Italians directly. It concerned Mackensen, the German ambassador to Rome. As was seen earlier, Mackensen had been surprisingly oblivious to the warning signs preceding the Italian coup. But now it was time for a reckoning. Once the business of the conference had ended, Ribbentrop summoned Mackensen, who was also at Tarvisio, and gave him the bad news: He was being recalled to Germany, effective immediately.

Mackensen had received no advance warning. When he boarded the train with Ribbentrop, he carried only a single bag.

On August 3, Hitler had expressed hesitations about snatching Mussolini right away. However, after Tarvisio, the operation to find and free the Duce was viewed with a greater sense of urgency. The Nazis, of course, had no inkling that Mussolini had been put aboard a destroyer right under their noses and transferred to the island of La Maddalena, near Sardinia. Hitler was still putting his money on Ventotene, the small island west of Naples.

On August 8, Admiral Doenitz finally vetted Petty Officer Laurich—the navy witness that Hitler had summoned several days earlier—and made him promise to "observe absolute secrecy" in the matter of the missing Duce.[16] The following morning, the two men flew to the Wolf's Lair in East Prussia. There, Doenitz sat in on the afternoon Fuehrer Conference (sans Laurich) and listened to Hitler berate the Italians.

"A report was made on the general war situation," noted Doenitz, "which was followed by a discussion of the situation in Italy. The entry of our troops into Italy has been marked by an ever increasing number of incidents still of minor importance. Distrust is mounting. The Fuehrer is convinced that both the King of Italy and the Badoglio Government are planning treachery."[17]

But the main event took place that evening. It was then that the unassuming Laurich, petty officer second class, found himself standing before Adolf Hitler and a veritable A-list of the Nazi elite. "After the general war situation has been discussed," noted Doenitz, "Laurich, PO/2c, makes his report before a select few."[18] Aside from Hitler, the "select few" included Doenitz, Ribbentrop, Goering, Himmler, and an assortment of other diplomats and military officers. General Student may also have been in attendance because earlier in the day Hitler had ordered that he be summoned at once to GHQ.

Hitler was impressed by Laurich's presentation. (As was seen earlier, Laurich had spotted Mussolini boarding a corvette in Gaeta and was subsequently informed by his friend, an Italian naval officer, that the ex-dictator had been conveyed to Ventotene.) "The Fuehrer dismisses him," wrote Doenitz, "with the words 'Well done, my boy'. Then follows a long discussion concerning the operation 'Eiche' [Oak] and Italy."[19]

The focus of the search had now shifted slightly to the tiny islet of Santo Stefano, a small, rocky, volcanic protrusion located less than one mile to the east of its larger neighbor, Ventotene. Resembling a large boulder tossed into the sea, Santo Stefano was practically barren aside from the presence of an odd-looking, horseshoe-shaped prison dating back to the eighteenth century. This prison was apparently what had captured Hitler's interest.

He was moving closer to giving the go-ahead for a rescue attempt. "An early execution of the operation 'Eiche' appears necessary," Doenitz noted in his summary of the August 9 evening conference. "The general conviction is that Mussolini is on Santo Stefano. Therefore the action will be confined to this island. An aerial photograph shows that the only possible access to the island, by means of steps and a road cut into the rocks, can easily be secured. The rest of the coast is practically inaccessible because of cliffs over 150 feet high."[20]

The next step was to devise a rescue plan. "The question, whether the use of parachutists is preferable to a landing along the coast, is debated at length. [Doenitz] considers a sea landing, at an unguarded spot at night, the only possibility that promises success.

An alternative, in case the landing party cannot get through, the use of parachutists and support by the Air Force might be planned [sic]. The Fuehrer points out the necessity of covering the operation with several submarines."[21]

The operation was growing more complicated by the minute: Hitler was beginning to toy with the idea of snatching the Duce *without* shattering the Axis—a delicate proposition. To avoid an open break, he was apparently thinking of denying responsibility for the rescue and placing the blame on Italian Fascists. "Under given circumstances it may become necessary to deny, at least temporarily, any part played by the Navy and Air Force in order to give the impression that the deed was accomplished by local Fascists."[22]

Hitler, the same man who had threatened to send German tanks into Rome on July 25, or soon thereafter, had become a bit more cautious in the intervening days. The relationship between the Axis powers was now a "game," after all, and he was determined to play his cards carefully.[23]

After discussing the rescue plan in broad outline, Hitler began once again to editorialize. "He calls it shameful the way the Duce has been treated after he had directed the destinies of Italy for twenty years and had been hailed by all of Italy during this time," wrote Doenitz. "The Fuehrer feels the predicament of the Duce all the more due to the close ties of friendship which exist between them. The Fuehrer still considers the Italian Government as being extremely unreliable and, on the basis of recent events, believes it capable of most any kind of treason."[24]

■ ■ ■

Two days later, on August 11, Hitler was ready to review a more detailed plan for grabbing Mussolini. During the afternoon Fuehrer Conference, he continued to rail at the Badoglio regime: "The Italians will not show their true colors," he said, "until the presumed trip of Grandi to Lisbon or the meeting of Churchill and Roosevelt in Canada has produced results. The Italians are going ahead with their negotiations at full speed. They will be taken in by any promise of the Anglo-Saxons if only the continued rule of the Royal House is guaranteed. Their negotiations are treasonable. They go along with us in order to gain time."*[25]

Hitler was referring to Dino Grandi, the sponsor of the so-called Grandi resolution and one of the key figures responsible for engineering the no-confidence vote against the Duce in the Grand Council of Fascism. The Nazis believed that Grandi was preparing to travel to Portugal on behalf of Badoglio in an effort to obtain a separate peace from the Western powers. As shall be seen later, Hitler's suspicions concerning Grandi were not far from the truth.

The disastrous meeting at Tarvisio, which both Axis partners had viewed as unproductive, had also increased Hitler's suspicions. "In contrast to former occasions," he said, "they have not appealed to us for military support in connection with the meeting at Tarvisio, but remained completely inactive."[26] More German soldiers in Italy were the last thing Badoglio wanted at this point!

That night, Hitler and his advisors discussed their plans for Operation Oak. Among those in attendance were Doenitz, Himmler, Ribbentrop, General Alfred Jodl (an important figure on the General Staff), General Student, and Captain Gerhard von Kamptz of the navy.

Erwin Rommel was also present for at least part of this conference, but apparently he managed to make his exit before the discussion turned to Mussolini's liberation. And that was how Rommel liked it. "During the evening conference," he wrote in his diary on August 11, "the Fuehrer kept studying air photographs of Ventotene [i.e., Santo Stefano], the island where Mussolini is held prisoner. He kept Doenitz and Student back to discuss the liberation of Mussolini. I hope this job won't be put on my plate. I can see no good in it."[27]

---

*Roosevelt and Churchill met in Canada for the Quebec conference (code-named Quadrant). Allied relations with Italy were not the only item on the agenda.

Once Rommel had departed, Hitler and his lieutenants discussed the concept for the Santo Stefano raid, which involved a combined air-sea operation involving several hundred paratroopers and sailors. "General Student is put in charge of the whole operation," said Hitler. Though the ostensible target was Santo Stefano, the flexible plan also made room for the possibility of multiple assaults. "The operation is to be limited to [Santo] Stefano," Hitler explained. "Only in case M. [Mussolini] is not found there and his actual whereabouts have become known, will a new action be undertaken immediately by parachutists against the new site. Participation of the naval forces will have to be improvised accordingly. For this purpose special code words are given for Ventotene [i.e., Santo Stefano] and Ponza."[28]

Now that it was too late, Ponza had finally made it onto Hitler's short list of targets. (It was on Ponza that the Italians had hidden the Duce during the ten days or so between July 28 and August 7.) The credit for this development goes to the Mussolini task force in Rome. However, it is not exactly clear how Skorzeny and the others managed to score this coup or why Hitler chose to give the island a secondary status. Years later, Student claimed that Herbert Kappler had traced the Duce to Ponza early in the investigation—probably after the German eyewitness sightings in Gaeta—but that Hitler did not believe it.[29] Karl Radl, Skorzeny's deputy, maintained that one of the "agents" working for the Mussolini task force got the information from an Italian grocer who supplied the island with his goods.*[30] According to Radl, this discovery was made sometime during the first ten days of August.[31]

But Hitler's gut told him that the Duce was on Santo Stefano, and he wanted Student's tough paratroopers to be in the vanguard

---

*Skorzeny also mentions an Italian merchant. But he says the man got the information from a female client on the mainland whose boyfriend was a member of the carabinieri stationed on Ponza (the latter had apparently written her a letter in which he hinted at Mussolini's presence on the island).

of the assault. "From 100 to 200 parachutists are to jump from troop-carrying gliders and small gliders and to land soon *after* dawn. These will be followed by additional forces coming in from the sea. If necessary, the way for the troops landed from the sea must be cleared by the parachutists."*[32]

Once Mussolini was freed, Student's soldiers would make their escape by sea aboard navy vessels under the command of Captain Kamptz who, according to Student, had "distinguished himself as a particularly smart daredevil by a series of operations in the Mediterranean."**[33] The Duce would leave Santo Stefano by seaplane, change planes at the airfield at Pratica di Mare near Rome, and fly off to Germany without delay. It is unclear what role Skorzeny and his commandos would play in the assault.

Hitler continued to stress the importance of pre-mission security. One example of this involved a German-manned radar station on Ventotene. Hitler ordered that, just prior to the rescue operation, some of its staff be evacuated and replaced with operatives who were in the know. "The 'Wuerzburg' radar station in Ventotene is to be given secret orders not to take radar-bearings of airplanes on this day. Part of the crew is therefore to be relieved by men who have received the new instructions. The relieved men shall be questioned about [Santo] Stefano, particularly about cables, wireless station, other observations made, and rumors among the population."[34] ("Wuerzburg" was a type of radar and not a place name.) Hitler also suggested that some undercover reconnaissance of the island might be in order.

Several more days would be needed to implement these measures and put the finishing touches on the rescue plan. "Further preparations and final instructions will follow later," Doenitz noted. "The final order will be given by the Fuehrer."[35]

---

*Italics in original.

**Kamptz had received a Knight's Cross in 1940.

But certain questions remained unanswered. For instance, what would happen if the raid were executed and Mussolini could not be found? Would the botched rescue mission shatter the Axis and trigger large-scale battles between Italian and German soldiers on the mainland, where Hitler's military preparations were far from complete?

In the mind of Admiral Doenitz, who was fast becoming one of Hitler's closest advisors, these concerns were somewhat beside the point.[36] The important thing was that Germany had Adolf Hitler at the helm. In fact, Doenitz was so impressed by Hitler's handling of the so-called Italian question that he added a personal note in the records of the German navy.

"The enormous strength which the Fuehrer radiates," he gushed around this time, "his unwavering confidence, and his far-sighted appraisal of the Italian situation have made it very clear in these days that we are all very insignificant in comparison with the Fuehrer, and that our knowledge and the picture we get from our limited vantage [point] are fragmentary. Anyone who believes that he can do better than the Fuehrer is silly."[37]

While Hitler fretted over Mussolini, the relentless march of the Allied armies continued to put additional pressure on what was left of the fragile Axis alliance. By early August, it was already apparent that Hitler's major offensive in the East, launched just several weeks earlier, had failed. In dramatic fashion, the Russians had turned the tables on the German Wehrmacht and were now advancing westward (in the general direction of Germany), wiping out Hitler's past gains as they went.

In Sicily, where Germans and Italians were nominally working together to throw back the invaders, Axis forces were gradually losing ground to British and American troops. Hitler's advisors were still debating whether the Germans should stand and fight in Sicily or pack up and get out. The tenuous nature of the Rome-Berlin alliance greatly complicated Nazi calculations. When they were not mulling over plans for rescuing Mussolini, Doenitz and General Jodl continued to argue over Sicily. Jodl was in favor of evacuating the island. He believed that the German position on Sicily was becoming increasingly untenable and would only worsen if Hitler broke relations with Italy or if the Italians suddenly switched sides in the war.

Doenitz vehemently disagreed. He wanted to contest every inch of Sicilian soil to keep the Allies out of Italy and away from the all-important Balkans. "The evacuation," argued Doenitz on August 11, "means an irreparable loss of this strategically important position which should not be undertaken while present developments are obscure but only when we have no alternative."[38] Rommel sided with Doenitz. Hitler listened to these debates but continued to defer his decision. "In regard to Sicily and the southern tip of Italy he [Hitler] makes no definite decision but wishes to have the various solutions considered as possible choices," Doenitz noted.[39]

When it came to defending Italy against the Allies, Hitler wished to keep his options open. He put off the evacuation of Sicily, General Walter Warlimont later argued, because he was afraid that it might give the Italians an excuse to break the Axis. Hitler "continued to postpone the evacuation of Sicily in order that this should not be an excuse for the Italians to renounce the alliance," Warlimont wrote, "and in this Dönitz agreed with him for reasons of maritime strategy."[40]

■ ■ ■

Meanwhile, in Germany, which remained untouched by the ground wars raging in distance lands, the Nazis were still coming to grips with the devastating aftermath of the Hamburg bombing. They feared that Berlin would be next.

On August 3, Wilhelm Keitel wrote to his wife and advised her in graphic terms to flee Berlin, which he feared would soon be the victim of major air attacks. "Hamburg has been a catastrophe for us," he wrote, "and last night there was yet another very heavy air raid on it. The same must be expected for Berlin. . . . That is why I want you to leave Berlin as soon as possible. . . . I am afraid of vast *conflagrations* consuming whole districts, streams of burning oil flowing into the basements and shelters, phosphorus, and the like."*[41]

The mighty Third Reich, it seemed, was incapable of protecting its own capital from Allied wrath. For this reason, the Nazis organized a mass exodus from Berlin during August.[42] One million civilians were eventually evacuated from the city, many of them women and children.[43]

In the face of these and other setbacks, even an able spin-doctor such as Joseph Goebbels was finding it increasingly difficult to rally Germany's spirits. It was all the more important to avoid the loss of Italy, the Nazis' strongest European ally.

---

*Italics in original.

9

THE MYSTERY OF
MADDALENA ISLAND

Skorzeny had imagination and good ideas. He was able to smuggle one of his SS officers, who spoke fluent Italian, onto the island disguised as a sailor.[1]

—General Student, *Memoirs*

THE GERMANS NEVER CARRIED OUT HITLER'S PARATROOPER DROP ON Santo Stefano. Sometime around mid-August, while they were still finalizing their plans to pounce on this small rock near the island of Ventotene, new intelligence emerged suggesting that Mussolini had already flown the coop. It was fortunate for Hitler that the raid did not materialize, for the Duce had never set foot on Santo Stefano.

The latest tip was apparently provided courtesy of Captain Gerhard von Kamptz, the officer who was assigned the command of the naval forces for the Santo Stefano *Blitz*. By pure chance, according to General Student, Kamptz had run across an old navy buddy in Rome who was then serving as the German liaison officer to the Italian naval base at Maddalena Island.[2] To Kamptz's surprise, his friend, Commander Helmut Hunaeus, passed on a juicy bit of gossip. There was a rumor going around the island, he reported, that La Maddalena was currently playing host to a very famous guest—none other than Benito Mussolini.[3]

Captain von Kamptz promptly went to La Maddalena to do some detective work of his own. When he returned to Rome and informed Student of what he had discovered, the general put Kamptz on a plane and the two men flew to the Wolf's Lair, where they arrived on August 16.[4] Admiral Doenitz later summarized the story that Kamptz presented to Hitler.

"During one of his visits to Maddalena," Doenitz noted, "Captain von Kamptz heard persistent rumors that cruisers which arrived at Maddalena some time ago brought the Duce with them. He is now quartered in a villa in Maddalena in the immediate vicinity of the naval air base and is under guard there. Von Kamptz requested an automobile under some pretext and intended to check the veracity of the rumor."[5]

What Kamptz heard next must have shocked him: "The Italian in charge replied that, in view of the presence of the Duce, the only naval car available in Maddalena is being reserved for the exclusive use of the Chief of the Carabinieri." *The presence of the Duce?* The loose-lipped Italian had inadvertently revealed the secret of Mussolini's hideout. "Von Kamptz reported these observations immediately to General Student who in turn boarded a plane with him and flew to the Fuehrer Headquarters."[6]

Hitler was intrigued. "The Fuehrer ordered that a raid on the villa in Maddalena is to be included in operation 'Eiche' [Oak]. Execution of such a raid is considered an easy matter. German ships are constantly steaming in and out of the harbor; that would make possible an inconspicuous transfer of German troops from [the nearby island of] Corsica and a surprise raid."[7] The words "included in" are interesting because they seem to imply that Operation Oak was taking on the shape of a blanket operation that might hit several targets simultaneously just to ensure that the Duce was found in one of them.

■ ■ ■

But the notion of mounting a rescue mission at this stage was premature. In fact, when Student and Kamptz arrived at the Wolf's Lair on August 16, Student discovered that Hitler had another theory regarding the dictator's whereabouts, namely, that he was being held captive aboard an Italian warship in the port of La Spezia on the northwestern coast of Italy.[8] The information had supposedly come from, of all people, Erwin Rommel, who had recently visited northern Italy; there, a "reliable source" revealed to him Mussolini's secret location.*[9] (Skorzeny maintained that the ultimate source of the La Spezia tip was an Italian naval officer, but neither he nor his deputy Radl mentioned Rommel's role in the affair.)[10]

"He [Hitler] was convinced that Mussolini was in La Spezia," Student remembered. "He was sure that the Italian government intended to hand him over to the enemy as a war criminal."[11] According to Student, there were two main reasons why Hitler was inclined to view Rommel's information as credible. For one thing, the notion that the Duce had been stowed away on a warship seemed consistent with Hitler's belief that the Italians were preparing to turn him over to the enemy (by sea) in the near future. The second factor was Rommel himself. In those days, Hitler held the Desert Fox in high esteem and was planning to give him the command of the entire Italian theater when the time was ripe. Rommel had already been given command of Army Group B, which was pouring into Italy through the Alpine passes, but Kesselring retained control of German forces in the south.

At this point, Student did not know what to believe.[12] La Spezia, after all, was not totally inconsistent with other intelligence the Nazis had gathered. According to Radl, one of the agents working for the Mussolini task force in Rome had determined that the Duce had left the Pontine Islands aboard an Italian warship (destination unknown) prior to mid-August.[13] The Italians had also reportedly thrown a cordon around the harbor at La Spezia, making it look as if the port had something to hide.[14] Student, for one, began to wonder whether the Italian Military Intelligence Service (SIM) was getting the better of the Nazis.

---

*Rommel was in Bologna on August 15 for an Axis conference with the Italians.

"It could not be excluded," he later wrote, "that the rumors that Mussolini was in La Spezia or on Maddalena were spread by Italian intelligence to confuse [us]."[15] Even so, Student and his new SS partner (and subordinate) Otto Skorzeny had no choice but to examine the unattractive possibility of snatching the Duce from his prison-on-the-sea at La Spezia. "For twenty-four hours we battled feverishly with the problem," Skorzeny recalled. "No doubt at G.H.Q. they imagined nothing was easier than to make a man vanish from under the eyes of the crew of a cruiser on war footing."[16]

They did not lose much sleep over it. After a bit of long-distance snooping, Student was able to determine that Rommel's piece of intelligence was yet another red herring. According to the general, the Luftwaffe had some *Jaegerleitoffiziere* (fighter-control officers) based in La Spezia.[17] Some of these men were contacted on the sly, but they were unable to find evidence that Mussolini was being hidden in their midst. "It was quite apparent that Mussolini was not there," Student finally concluded.*[18] (The presence of Germans throughout Italy, even though they were scattered in relatively small numbers in some places, proved immensely helpful throughout the investigation.)

The island of La Maddalena, on the other hand, seemed to warrant further investigation. General Student was becoming increasingly bogged down in the detailed planning of Hitler's military occupation of Italy at this time, so he asked Skorzeny to see what he could find out. "He threw himself in this new assignment with fanaticism and astounding energy," Student recalled. "Soon he had results."[19]

■ ■ ■

Skorzeny did not require much coaxing. Indeed, the burly Austrian seemed to possess a measure of self-confidence proportional to his size. His trademark feature was a long and menacing-looking duel-

---

*Mussolini was never at La Spezia.

ing scar (dating from his University of Vienna days) that ran down the left side of his face. For Skorzeny, this old wound was a badge of honor. "My knowledge of pain, learned with the sabre," he once commented with a characteristic touch of melodrama, "taught me not to be afraid of fear. And just as in duelling you must fix your mind on striking at the enemy's head, so, too, in war. You cannot waste time on feinting and sidestepping. You must decide on your target and go in."[20]

But Skorzeny was also something of an amateur when it came to matters of intelligence gathering and special operations. He had spent much of the war as a Waffen SS engineering officer, fixing tanks and trucks on the battlefront.* After being wounded in Russia during the winter of 1941–1942, he was sidelined to a repair depot in Berlin, where he seemed destined to sit out the rest of the war. "They undoubtedly needed engineering officers in the reserve units," he later wrote. "But I found that I could be more useful. The thought of being no more than a conscientious working engineer did not please me."[21]

As luck would have it, while Skorzeny was growing restless in the Reich capital, the Nazis were casting about for a man to head up a new commando unit known as the Friedenthal Battalion, which took its name from the small town near Berlin in which it was based (Friedenthal means "valley of peace"). Created under the auspices of Himmler's SS, Friedenthal was set up as a rival to the famed British commandos, whose exploits during World War II were already the stuff of legend by 1943. The SS was looking for an officer with combat experience as well as technical expertise to lead the new unit. Skorzeny's name was reportedly suggested by Ernst Kaltenbrunner, who at the time was the head of the Reich Security Main Office

---

*The Waffen SS was the combat wing of the large and complicated organization known as the *Schutzstaffel* (SS). In general, many members of the Waffen SS fought on the frontlines in conventional military units during World War II, though Hitler did consider these so-called elite (and fanatical) troops more "politically reliable." See Keegan, *Waffen S.S.*, 130–155.

(RSHA)—the Third Reich's labyrinthine police and spy apparatus—
and who had known Skorzeny since their prewar Vienna days.

In April 1943, just a few months before Mussolini's overthrow,
Skorzeny assumed command of Friedenthal and met with his immediate supervisor, Major Walter Schellenberg, who was chief of
foreign intelligence for the SS (Amt VI of the RSHA).* "Frankly,"
Skorzeny later admitted, "I did not understand much of what he explained to me; after all I was only entering a realm which until now
had been a total mystery to me."[22] The purpose of the new organization, as he understood it, was to carry out commando missions
and acts of sabotage. Friedenthal already existed in embryonic
form. Skorzeny's task was to expand, reorganize, and inject new life
into it. His assignment was accompanied by a promotion, and Skorzeny was bumped up to the rank of captain.

Naturally, he assumed that Friedenthal would be used to strike at
targets behind enemy lines in the Soviet Union or in territory occupied by British and American forces. He never suspected that his first
real mission would pit him against the Italians, Germany's Axis ally.
But the unusual nature of Operation Oak did nothing to dampen his
zeal. As a fanatically loyal and ambitious SS man, Skorzeny was determined to carry out Hitler's order by finding the Duce and bringing
him back to Germany at any cost.

■ ■ ■

In mid-August or so, Skorzeny tried his hand at solving the mystery
of *Isola Maddalena*. As one of his first steps, he commandeered a German minesweeper and took a lap or two around the island, located a
few miles from the northeastern tip of Sardinia. As German ships
were common in the area, Skorzeny probably assumed that his little
cruise would not arouse undue suspicion on the part of the Italians.

---

*"Amt" is the equivalent of "Department." The Friedenthal Battalion was desig-
nated as Group S of Amt VI within the RSHA.

Situated in the Strait of Bonifacio, the narrow sea-lane between Corsica and Sardinia, La Maddalena was roughly triangular in shape and about eight square miles in size. As Skorzeny sailed round the jagged coastline, he found himself gazing up at the island's reddish-colored, rocky heights. He surreptitiously snapped a few photos of the harbor works and other items of interest, including the so-called Villa Webber, a small mansion on a hill overlooking the sea. Nestled among a tiny forest of pine trees, the villa was located about five hundred yards west of the small town of Maddalena on the southern coast of the island.[23]

The Villa Webber had figured in some of the rumors reaching German ears at this time—Commander Hunaeus, for one, had mentioned it—but Skorzeny did not know whether the information was credible or just another false clue being circulated by the Italians.[24] To complicate matters, La Maddalena was surrounded by numerous other islands and islets of all shapes and sizes. Though multiple leads pointed to the general area of Sardinia, some of them indicated that Mussolini was not on La Maddalena at all but was being hidden nearby.[25] For instance, when Skorzeny had paid a visit to Palau on the northeastern coast of Sardinia (opposite La Maddalena), the German commander of a flak unit stationed there said that he had heard that the Duce was convalescing in a monastery in the nearby Sardinian village of Santa Maria, which was apparently Santa Maria Navarrese on the eastern coast.[26]

All the leads would need to be checked out, but La Maddalena seemed to be the most promising. To figure out whether Mussolini was really on the island, Skorzeny proposed an undercover operation involving Lieutenant Robert Warger, the only man among his Friedenthal commandos who spoke perfect Italian.

"My scheme," Skorzeny later explained in the politically incorrect language of the time, "was based entirely on the fact that all Italians have a passion for betting."[27] To exploit this stereotypical proclivity, Warger was dispatched to La Maddalena in the guise of a German sailor and passed off as an interpreter working for Commander Hunaeus, the German naval liaison.[28] Warger's real job was to spend as much time as possible drinking and carousing in the small bars of Maddalena town. Whenever he overheard the Italian patrons discussing the Duce and his fate, Warger, pretending to be intoxicated, would join the conversation and put forward the view that Mussolini was dead or seriously ill. If any of the Italians disagreed, Warger would challenge him to put his money where his mouth was.

Skorzeny figured that at least some of the locals, civilians or sailors, were probably aware that the Duce was on the island, if indeed he was. Perhaps Warger could tempt one of them into accepting a wager.

There was one potentially fatal complication in Skorzeny's scheme: Warger was a teetotaler who never touched alcohol. In fact, he was the only Friedenthaler who did not drink. "It was only by insisting at great length on his duty as a soldier," Skorzeny recalled, "that I managed to persuade him to violate his principles."[29] Before leaving for La Maddalena, Warger was given an impromptu lesson on the art of imbibing that apparently left him feeling ill.

"Skorzeny had imagination and good ideas," Student later wrote. "He was able to smuggle one of his SS officers, who spoke fluent Italian, onto the island disguised as a sailor. . . . At the same time he investigated the conditions for the [rescue] operation on [my] instructions."[30]

■ ■ ■

Having set Operation Warger in motion, Skorzeny decided to take some aerial photos of the island. On August 18, his Heinkel 111 departed Practica di Mare airport near Rome, refueled at Pausania on Sardinia, then climbed to an altitude of 15,000 feet and completed a reconnaissance run. The He 111 was a twin-engined medium bomber with a large, transparent cockpit, which allowed for excellent visibility.

Skorzeny squeezed into the forward gun position and using a handheld camera began taking several pictures of La Maddalena. To do this, he had to lie face down in the space adjacent to the pilot's seat. (When the He 111 was fully manned, this position was normally occupied by the bombardier, who was also responsible for operating the manual 7.9-mm MG 15 machine gun that protruded from the tip of the cockpit.) Skorzeny had just taken a moment to admire the panoramic view of the sea below him when a sudden announcement from the rear gunner jolted him to attention.

"Look out behind us!" the gunner cried. "Two planes. British pursuit planes!"[31]

Skorzeny instinctively gripped the handle of the forward gun as the pilot began an evasive maneuver. The aircraft straightened out momentarily, but then went into a sickening dive. One look at the pilot and Skorzeny knew that he and the crew were in deep trouble. "Turning around," he remembered, "I saw the pilot's contorted face as he sought vainly to straighten out his ship. A glance through the window [of the cockpit] showed me that our left motor had failed. The plane was diving at a dizzying speed."[32]

Skorzeny grabbed hold of the gun once again—this time to brace himself for impact. He felt a violent jolt when the 20,000-pound airplane hit the water and began to plow across its surface, then everything went black.[33] The next thing he remembered was being dragged upwards by a member of the crew. Skorzeny and the others managed to scamper to safety through an emergency exit in the crumpled cockpit, which was quickly filling up with water. It dawned on him that he had left his camera and briefcase behind, so he climbed back into the plane through the cockpit, retrieved the items, and returned to the surface. He then hopped into an inflatable life raft with the plane's crew (all of whom had survived the crash) and watched the He 111 disappear into the waves.*

Skorzeny and his stranded comrades found refuge on a nearby reef until an Italian cruiser happened by and picked them up. "What luck," Skorzeny mused to himself, "that the skipper cannot

---

*It is not clear why the Heinkel's engine failed. In his memoirs, Skorzeny denies that the Heinkel was actually shot down by the enemy fighters.

guess the reason for our presence hereabouts."[34] He had escaped the crash without obvious injuries—or so it seemed at the time. A few days later, a doctor told Skorzeny that the nagging pain he felt in his chest was the result of three broken ribs.

Instead of returning to the mainland, Skorzeny made a detour to the island of Corsica to make contact with the Waffen SS unit that was stationed there. He thought that he might need its help if the Nazis decided to mount a rescue operation. When he arrived in Rome on August 20 and met with Radl, he learned that Herbert Kappler, the German police attaché, had made another discovery.[35]

According to Radl, Kappler had focused his attention on members of Mussolini's immediate family, most of whom were still in Italy at this time, though the Duce's son Vittorio had fled to the relative safety of Germany.[36] He hit pay dirt with Edda Ciano, the dictator's favorite daughter. Edda, it seems, had written a letter to her father, and Kappler had somehow managed to trace it to Maddalena Island.*[37] (It should be mentioned at this point that Badoglio had agreed to facilitate the exchange of mail between Mussolini and the outside world.)

A more dramatic breakthrough soon followed. When Skorzeny reestablished radio contact with Warger, he discovered that his Italian-speaking undercover agent had actually seen the Duce![38] Skorzeny wanted to speak to Warger face-to-face, so on August 23, having evidently shaken off the effects of his plane crash in the Tyrrhenian Sea, he flew back to La Maddalena with Radl.[39]

Warger explained to them that he had carried out his mission as instructed and eventually found an Italian merchant who took the bet. The man delivered fruit to the Villa Webber and claimed to have seen Mussolini there. He even offered to show Warger a good spot from which to view the estate. Warger decided to stake out the villa for a few days. At some point during his reconnaissance, he spied a bald, stocky man on the terrace of the building.[40] He could

---

*According to some reports, Kappler's discovery occurred earlier in the investigation. See Deakin, 544.

not see the man's face clearly because he was too far away, but Warger was almost certain that it was the Duce.[41]

Skorzeny and Radl returned to Rome on August 24 and conferred with General Student.[42] The three men agreed that they had finally tracked down the dictator, or so it appeared from their perspective. But not everyone in Nazi intelligence circles was inclined to agree. "Then suddenly," remembered Skorzeny, "like lightning blazing down from a clear blue sky, we received an order from the Führer's G.H.Q.: G.H.Q. has just received a report from Ausland Abwehr (Admiral Canaris) that Mussolini is on a small island near Elba."[43]

Skorzeny was dumbfounded. He knew that Elba was a mountainous island located off the northwestern coast of Italy about one hundred miles from La Maddalena. But the whole business was more than a little suspect because there was no credible evidence that placed the Duce anywhere near Elba.

■ ■ ■

If Skorzeny is to be believed, the Elba lead originated with the Abwehr, the spy network run by the German military and headed by Admiral Wilhelm Canaris. It was roughly analogous to the foreign intelligence wing (Amt VI) of the RSHA. The Abwehr and Amt VI were separate organizations with similar agendas, and the lines of demarcation between them had always been gray.[44] For years, the rival agencies had competed with each other for Hitler's favor.[45] Indeed, pitting his own subordinates against each other was almost a matter of policy for Hitler.[46] As wasteful and inefficient as it was, this philosophy of "divide and rule" had made it easier for the Fuehrer to control his henchmen: It was the totalitarian counterpart of a democracy's checks and balances.[47]

This ongoing struggle for power within Nazi intelligence circles—which pitted the regular German military against the SS— took a strange and unexpected turn when Canaris, who was a notoriously enigmatic figure, secretly began to turn against Hitler and Nazism. The spy chief had apparently come to see the evil of

Hitler's ways—or perhaps simply the inevitability of Germany's demise under the Fuehrer.

If Canaris really did try to thwart Operation Oak, as Skorzeny later implied, this effort may have been part of a broader campaign designed to shield the Badoglio regime from Hitler's wrath. According to Walter Schellenberg, Himmler's top SS spook in the RSHA, during the summer of 1943 Canaris was working in the shadows to aid Badoglio in his covert war against the Germans. Canaris accomplished this, allegedly, by reassuring the Nazi leadership that the loyalty of the new Italian regime was beyond reproach.[48]

Schellenberg—who was Canaris's rival and mortal enemy—soon got wind of this activity, which he deemed nothing less than treasonous. He had made it his life's mission to bring down Canaris, but the latter managed to escape the clutches of the dreaded SS for another year.

■ ■ ■

Whatever the reasons, during the last week of August Hitler was apparently convinced that Mussolini was hidden away either on Elba or somewhere close by.[49] In light of this development, General Student thought it best to meet with Hitler in person and argue the case for La Maddalena.[50] Student spent much of August, it seems, flying back and forth between Rome and the Wolf's Lair, often with witnesses in tow, to update Hitler on the search for the Duce. On this occasion, he brought along his SS partner because he wanted Hitler to hear the details of their La Maddalena reconnaissance "directly from Skorzeny."[51]

They arrived at Fuehrer Headquarters in late August. Skorzeny found himself in the same room in which he had met Hitler several weeks earlier, and the atmosphere was probably just as imposing. According to Skorzeny, some of the most prominent figures of the Third Reich were seated at a large table. Flanking Hitler on each side were Marshal Wilhelm Keitel; General Alfred Jodl; the foreign minister, Joachim von Ribbentrop; the SS chief, Heinrich Himmler; General Student; Admiral Doenitz; and the Luftwaffe chief, Hermann Goering. After some discussion, Skorzeny got the nod from Student to make his presentation.

He was intimidated at first, but managed to explain "in a simple and clear way" how he and his colleagues had concluded that Mussolini was on La Maddalena: "I also described the terrible adventure of our teetotaler Warger. Goering and Doenitz smiled. Himmler's gaze remained ice-cold, and Hitler wore a rather ironic look."[52] Skorzeny spoke for about thirty minutes, after which Hitler shook his hand and announced that he had been persuaded. "Hitler was now finally convinced," Student recalled. "He gave [me] freedom of action again."[53]

Student and Skorzeny also outlined their plans for a rescue operation, which had been developed in conjunction with Captain von Kamptz and Commander Max Schulz, the latter being in charge of the German motor torpedo boats in the Mediterranean. The assault was designed to exploit the all-important element of surprise and the fact that German ships were fairly common in the waters surrounding Sardinia.

On D-day, several German minesweepers, covered by motor torpedo boats with 20-mm cannon, would swoop into the harbor and disembark the assault force. These soldiers would then head for the Villa Webber, overwhelm the 150 or so carabinieri they believed were guarding the Duce, and storm the building.

Telephone lines at the villa would be cut to prevent Mussolini's guards from summoning reinforcements. Special squads would capture the guns guarding the exit of the port and disable a Red Cross seaplane, believed to be a getaway vehicle for the Duce, and its two fighter escorts, which were moored close to the shore. Once Mussolini was safely in German hands, he would be hustled away on board one of the escaping motor torpedo boats.*

---

*The raid may have been more complicated than Skorzeny made it out to be after the war. Mussolini later claimed that the Maddalena rescue operation was supposed to involve a bogus British submarine and German commandos dressed in English uniforms. Benito Mussolini, *Memoirs,* 132.

According to Skorzeny, Hitler approved the plan and authorized its execution.* He then drew Skorzeny aside to issue a private admonition. "Something else, [Captain] Skorzeny," Hitler said. "It's possible that at the time that you carry out your operation, the new Italian government will still, officially at least, be our ally. Therefore if the attack fails, or if Mussolini is not on Santa Maddalena, I might be forced to disapprove of your action publicly. In that case you will have acted on your own and not informed your superiors. I hope that you understand that I will have to punish you against my will in the event of failure?"[54] Skorzeny accepted the proviso.

■ ■ ■

After their meeting with Hitler, Student and Skorzeny hurried back to Rome to work out the details for the raid on La Maddalena, which was scheduled for sometime near the end of August. "All preparations were rushed forward," Student remembered.[55] Every passing day increased the risk of failure, for no one could be sure that the Duce would still be on La Maddalena at the moment the Germans came crashing through the doors of the Villa Webber. Worried about such a possibility, Skorzeny and Radl, accompanied by Lieutenant Warger, decided to visit the island and do some final checking just twenty-four hours prior to D-day.

Dressed as German sailors, Skorzeny and Warger grabbed a basket of dirty laundry and made their way into Maddalena town to the house of the local washerwoman. There, they struck up a conversation with another customer, a member of the Italian carabinieri. When Skorzeny steered the conversation toward the subject of Mussolini, the man seemed uninterested. Skorzeny got a rise out of

---

*It is worth mentioning that Hitler's military plans for the German occupation of Italy were fairly well advanced by this time. Thus, if the rescue mission led to an open break with the Badoglio regime, the Nazis were prepared to subdue the Italians by force.

the Italian only when he asserted that the Duce had gone the way of the ancient Caesars.

"No, no, signore, impossibile!" he protested. "I saw the Duce this very morning. I was one of the men who escorted him on board the white plane in which he left here."[56]

The words stung Skorzeny because his gut told him that the Italian was telling the truth. What was worse, the story seemed to check out. Skorzeny looked for the Red Cross seaplane and discovered that it was gone. There were still some carabinieri guarding the Villa Webber, but he could see that they were manning their posts in a noticeably casual manner. According to Radl, some of them were even drinking wine.[57] "So that explained their unmilitary attitude," Skorzeny thought to himself, "there was no longer a prisoner in this prison!"[58]

"Everything was almost ready," Student recalled, "when Skorzeny reported that Mussolini disappeared overnight, the country house on the shore of Maddalena was again abandoned and deserted and the white ambulance plane was gone as well."[59]

It was true: The Duce was gone. And the Nazis had absolutely no idea where to look next. "In point of fact," Skorzeny recalled, "we were back where we started from. . . . For a few days we were completely at a loss. There were rumors aplenty, to be sure; but as soon as we investigated them with the slightest care, they vanished into so much smoke."[60]

Though they were unaware of it at the time, Student and Skorzeny were having an easier time keeping track of Mussolini than were the Allies. During the summer of 1943, the Office of Strategic Services, or OSS, the forerunner of the American CIA, was also keeping tabs on the Duce and trying to monitor his movements. By August 16, for instance, the OSS learned from an Italian informant that Mussolini was on Ponza, though he had left that island on August 8. Ten days later on August 26, Allen Dulles, the head of the Bern office of the OSS, wired an intelligence update to Washington, D.C.: "Mussolini is now on the island of Maddalena, according to latest reports."[61] This information was accurate at the time, but was out of date within two days or so.

La Maddalena had been a close call for the Italians. As the month of August was drawing to a close, they had become increasingly nervous about the security of the island. Mussolini's presence there was apparently an open secret among the local population, and the Duce's captors feared that it was only a matter of time before the Nazis picked up the scent.[62] Believing that a German rescue attempt was in the making, they decided to move their prisoner yet again— just hours or days before Skorzeny was ready to nab him.*[63] It was an instance either of very good fortune or of inside information: No one can say for certain.

All Mussolini knew was that on August 28 at around 4:00 A.M., he was rustled from his bed in the Villa Webber and led to a seaplane with Red Cross markings that was waiting for him in the harbor below.[64] After a flight lasting about an hour and a half, the plane touched down on mainland Italy at a seaplane base, Vigna di Valle, on Lake Bracciano, a short distance northwest of Rome.[65] This was not far, incidentally, from the headquarters of the Third Panzergrenadier Division, the same German unit that Hitler had planned to use to capture Rome in the immediate aftermath of the coup.[66]

On exiting the aircraft, the Duce was greeted by his new senior jailer, Police Inspector Giuseppe Gueli, who had replaced Saverio Polito after the latter was injured in a car accident.[67] Mussolini was then shown to the "usual motor-ambulance" (as he later put it), which whisked him away in an easterly direction, beyond the towns of Rieti and Cittaducale.[68] The Duce and his convoy traveled into the heart of the Abruzzi region of central Italy, a rugged but beautiful area known for its mountains (the Apennines) as well as for the olive groves and vineyards adorning its rolling hills. After passing

---

*The date set by the Nazis for the Maddalena raid is a bit fuzzy. But by all accounts, they missed Mussolini by a matter of a few days at the most.

through L'Aquila, the regional capital, the convoy drove another fifteen miles or so before arriving at its destination: a small inn called La Villetta, located near the village of Assergi.[69]

La Villetta was merely a pit stop. Mussolini was scheduled to spend a few days there under the watchful eyes of his two primary guardians of the moment, namely Gueli and Lieutenant Alberto Faiola, before being transferred to a more secure location nearby.[70] The Italians were about to up the ante. The Duce's next prison, they assured themselves, would make the Nazis think twice before launching a rescue attempt.

La Villetta was a small, rustic-looking place, to be sure. But it stood in the shadow of the tallest mountain ridge in the Apennines: the majestic *Gran Sasso d'Italia* (Great Rock of Italy).

10

THE BADOGLIO SHUFFLE

However, no one at the present time dare predict the course of
future events, even for a day ahead.[1]

—Secret German memo on Axis relations, August 13, 1943

DURING THE SECOND HALF OF AUGUST, AS STUDENT AND SKORZENY
were zeroing in on Maddalena Island, Hitler and his archenemies in
the Italian regime edged ever closer to a final showdown. Though
the German dictator was reluctant to seize Italy by force, at least
until such time as Mussolini could be rescued, the king and Badoglio were not aware of this. They continued to worry that the
Fuehrer and his efficient soldiers would ruin all their plans by occupying the peninsula before the Italians were able to strike a bargain
with the Allies.

If the secret struggle between Hitler and Badoglio had all the
elements of high drama, one of the most fascinating (and surprising)
subplots involved the smaller skirmishes that Hitler had to fight in
his own backyard with subordinates who did not necessarily share
his cynical view of Italy's new leaders. General Walter Warlimont,
who worked under Jodl on the Operations staff, observed that the
"tension became all the greater when opinions within [Hitler's]
headquarters began to differ regarding the ultimate aims of the Italians. Only Hitler and Göring remained unshaken in their belief that
'treachery' was at work; in spite of this even Hitler felt that it was

better to try to keep Italy on our side, hoping for a new turn of events as a result of the liberation of Mussolini."[2]

To Hitler's endless frustration, most of his men on the spot in Italy continued to put their faith in the word of Badoglio. This group included Marshal Albert Kesselring, commander of German troops in the Italian theater, and most of Hitler's diplomats at the German embassy in Rome, such as Ambassador Mackensen (then in Germany) and the military liaison, General Rintelen. At mid-month, Erwin Rommel noted in his diary that Hitler had "sharply criticised the work of Mackensen, von Rintelen and Kesselring, on the grounds that they are still completely misreading the situation—especially Kesselring—and are putting their full confidence in the new Italian Government."[3] General Student, for one, wondered whether there was something in the Italian air that had "bewitched" Hitler's men in Rome.[4]

The confusion and diverging opinions sparked by the Italian coup were also reflected in a lengthy memo emanating from the office of the German foreign minister, Joachim von Ribbentrop, in mid-August. In his summary of recent events in Italy, Hitler's so-called foreign policy expert still seemed somewhat perplexed by the regime change and Badoglio's repeated pledges of Axis loyalty.

"The wealth of rumor circulating about the events which led to the overthrow of the Duce," read the memo, dated August 13, "has so far made it impossible to form a clear picture of the essentials. Later developments are equally obscure and unclarified."[5]

To Hitler's chagrin, the only thing the memo assumed for certain was the total collapse of Mussolini's Fascist Party. "It cannot, however, be doubted that the leadership of the Fascist Party completely broke down and that practically no one was loyal to the Duce to the last. After the proclamation put out by the King and Badoglio the upper crust of the Party scattered to the four winds."[6] This, in turn, meant that an attempt by the Nazis to resurrect a new Fascist regime in Italy, as Hitler had urged, would receive little aid from elements of the former Fascist hierarchy.

Although it threw cold water on Hitler's dream of a popularly supported Fascist revival, the memo permitted itself other flights of fancy—namely, that the Italians would stick to their word and remain faithful to the Axis. "The new Government's reiterated resolve not to acquiesce in unconditional surrender in any circumstances and not to permit Italy to be turned into a theatre for operations against her German ally is most earnestly meant and will be translated into reality."[7]

For several weeks to come, Ribbentrop would nurture the hope that the Nazis could reach an understanding with Badoglio and therefore avoid an inter-Axis clash.[8] Yet, despite its dashes of wishful thinking, the memo ended with a melodramatic caveat: "However, no one at the present time dare predict the course of future events, even for a day ahead."[9]

It was enough to give Hitler a migraine.

■ ■ ■

Even as the ink was drying on Ribbentrop's memo, the Italians were scrambling—in their own strangely half-hearted way—to jumpstart their surrender negotiations with the Allies, which had stalled yet again. The Italians had been toying with the idea of getting out of the war since late July, when Raffaele Guariglia, the foreign minister, had gone to the Vatican in an attempt to contact the Allies through the British and American diplomats in residence there. The next step had been taken on August 2, when Lanza D'Ajeta was sent to Lisbon to make contact with the Western Powers. Two other envoys were dispatched in early August, to Tangier and Switzerland respectively, but their efforts met dead-ends.

D'Ajeta did not fare much better. After arriving in Lisbon, he met with the British minister and attempted to explain Badoglio's predicament: Italy wished to extricate herself from the war but could not do so because of the increasing presence of German troops in Italy. Badoglio could break free of the Nazis only with the aid of military support provided by the Allies. D'Ajeta wanted to know whether they were open to the idea of negotiating a deal (though D'Ajeta himself had not been empowered to conduct such negotiations).[10] But the Allies, who were sitting in the catbird seat—or so it seemed at the time—did not believe that Italy was in a position to dictate terms. Unconditional surrender, tempered only by the West's sense of fairness, was the only deal on the table.

Undaunted, Badoglio decided that the Allies might be more receptive to a visit from one of his military men. He therefore selected General Giuseppe Castellano, a suave, quick-witted Sicilian who worked under Ambrosio, chief of *Comando Supremo,* to make another attempt at negotiating with the enemy.[11] He left by train on August 12 and did not arrive in Lisbon until four days later.[12] Castellano, who traveled incognito for reasons of security, could easily have taken a plane and reached his destination sooner, but was told not to hurry.[13] Badoglio, it seems, was still stalling for time as he and the king tried to figure out who posed the greater threat, the Nazis or the Allies.

A few days after arriving in Portugal, Castellano met with General Eisenhower's representatives, General Walter Bedell Smith, Ike's chief of staff, and Brigadier Kenneth W. D. Strong of the British army, who had traveled to Lisbon in a disguise that consisted of a "motley collection of garments."*[14] The peace talks took place in a cloak-and-dagger atmosphere. "Lisbon was said to be full of German spies," explained Strong, who was Eisenhower's intelligence chief, "so the fewer people who knew of our presence the better."[15]

General Castellano, it turned out, was not especially anxious to surrender Italy to the Allies.[16] Like D'Ajeta before him, he did not even possess the official authority to do so.[17] As Eisenhower's men could not help but notice, he seemed much more interested in trying to learn the details of the top-secret Allied invasion plans for mainland Italy.[18] This was information they had no intention of sharing

---

*Bedell Smith went on to become director of the CIA in 1950.

with their new would-be ally.* "What Castellano really wanted," Strong believed, "was to get the maximum amount of information before the Italians made up their minds on which side of the fence they would come down."[19]

As the Allies suspected, this seemingly strange and somewhat suspicious behavior on Castellano's part was best understood in light of the anxiety pervading Rome. Before making any deals with the West, the king and Badoglio wanted assurances that the Allies would storm the peninsula in overwhelming strength and chase the Germans right up to the Alps. As later became evident, Rome's less-than-dynamic duo had no intention of fighting the Nazis themselves, though hardier souls among their countrymen did not cower at the possibility.

Even so, Badoglio was not discouraged by the unproductive nature of the Lisbon talks. How could he be? Castellano had failed to send a single progress report back to Rome during the two weeks he was gone![20] Inexplicably, he had neglected to bring a radio along with him for use during his mission.[21] The Italian intelligence services possessed several secure communications links in the Portuguese capital, but no one had bothered to inform Castellano of this.[22]

Badoglio eventually became so frustrated by the lack of news from Lisbon that he dispatched yet another envoy, General Giacomo Zanussi, on the heels of the first. Zanussi, who was on the staff of the Italian army, left for Lisbon by plane and arrived on August 26.[23] He brought with him a British POW as a sign of good faith, but the sight of this unexpected pair merely served to create more confusion in the minds of the Allies.[24]

"The purpose of this latest visitor was far from clear," Churchill wrote of Zanussi.[25] Fearing that the Italian might be an imposter, one of Eisenhower's men even considered having Zanussi shot as a

---

*The subject of Mussolini also emerged during the talks. Over drinks, Bedell Smith asked Castellano about the Duce's whereabouts. The Italian evaded the question, but said that Hitler, too, was very much interested in this sort of information.

Nazi spy.[26] He was spared, but the peace talks remained primarily in the hands of Castellano.*

■ ■ ■

In the middle of the month, Badoglio found himself engaged in a delicate balancing act. At the same time that General Castellano was traveling to Lisbon to meet with the Allies, Badoglio was sending other of his envoys to an Axis war council at Bologna to discuss plans for defending the peninsula against the expected Allied invasion.

Hitler welcomed another Axis military conference because he believed it might prove helpful in revealing Italian intentions. Though he had received hints of Badoglio's peace offensive—he knew about Grandi's trip to Lisbon and had remarked as recently as August 11 that "everything so far indicates treason" where the Italians were concerned—he still had no definitive proof that Badoglio was planning to double-cross him.[27] So while Hitler continued to build up the German army in northern Italy, he sent two of his most trusted lieutenants to the Bologna conference on August 15 in an effort to further "clarify" how the Italians really felt about the Axis.**[28]

Erwin Rommel, commander of Army Group B in Italy, and General Alfred Jodl led the German delegation. The Italians sent General Mario Roatta, the Italian army chief of staff, and a few of his colleagues. The meeting took place just outside Bologna at a comfortable villa that had recently belonged to Fascist bigwig Luigi Federzoni but

---

*To further complicate matters, Castellano had some additional competition in the person of Dino Grandi, who was also included in the small army of Italian go-betweens who journeyed westward during August. Grandi, who had spearheaded the revolt against Mussolini in the Grand Council of Fascism on the eve of the coup, July 24–25, arrived in Portugal shortly after Castellano. Though he played no role in the negotiations, German agents followed his every move.

**When he discussed the Italian situation during a conference on August 11, Hitler remarked: "[E]verything so far indicates treason. Clarification of the situation now becomes imperative. Rommel shall negotiate." *Fuehrer Conferences,* 117.

was confiscated after July 25.[29] As the subject matter of the talks was intended to be strictly military, the Axis diplomats from both camps were told to stay at home.[30]

"From the outset," recalled Kesselring, who was also in attendance, "a palpable tension brooded over the proceedings."[31] But this was putting it mildly. Rommel had been warned, probably by Hitler, to fear for his life. "The preliminaries to the conference did not augur well," observed Manfred Rommel, the Desert Fox's son, "for my father was informed that the Italians intended to use the occasion either to get rid of him by mixing poison with his food or to have him seized by Italian troops."[32] As a result of these fears, the Germans took extensive measures for their own security.

Once the plane carrying Rommel and Jodl had touched down in Italy, the two men were escorted to the Federzoni villa by a motorized battalion of the Waffen SS, an unusual move. Upon arrival, these soldiers set up a cordon around the building, seemingly oblivious to the presence of a security detachment provided by the Italians. "Outside the open door of the conference room," according to General Warlimont, "SS men goose-stepped up and down past the Italian ceremonial guard, over whom they towered head and shoulders."[33]

Things generally went downhill from there. Though ostensibly the Axis partners had come to Bologna to discuss the best way to manage the war effort in Italy, the meeting quickly degenerated into accusations and counteraccusations. Each side spent much of the time questioning the motives of the other as well as the position of certain army divisions on the peninsula.

One issue on the table was the Italian decision to bring back to the homeland some of its divisions stationed in foreign lands. Back on August 11, the Italians had informed the Nazis that they were pulling the Fourth Army out of France and several divisions from the Balkans. It was this announcement that had triggered the August 15 meeting in the first place.[34] At Bologna, Jodl gave his sanction to the troop transfers but then, in a peak of audacity, asked Roatta whether he planned to use these additional forces against the Allies or the Germans!

"Jodl took the floor," Warlimont later wrote, "and, abandoning all pretence at courtesy, coupled the German agreement to the withdrawal of Italian troops from southern France with the question 'whether these were for use against the English in southern Italy or against the Germans on the Brenner.'"[35] Roatta claimed to be offended by the question and refused to answer.[36]

As at Tarvisio, the Axis conference on August 6, progress was almost nonexistent when it came to other important matters.[37] The meeting was so tense that even lunch became a bone of contention. Fearful of a poisoning attempt, Hitler had expressly forbidden Rommel and Jodl from breaking bread with the Italians.[38] The two Germans eventually relented and sat down for a meal at the Hotel Baglioni in the center of Bologna.[39] Just for good measure, the Nazis posted guards around the hotel and instructed a German officer to act as a personal bodyguard and sit at the table with a loaded pistol. This was apparently not enough to put Jodl's mind completely at ease. Worried that his hosts might attempt to slip him a "Mickey Finn," Jodl refused to drink his coffee.*[40]

■ ■ ■

The following day, Roatta made a report to the king and Badoglio in which he stressed the distrustful atmosphere of the Bologna conference.[41] He was particularly struck by the fact that the Nazis had surrounded Federzoni's villa with soldiers of the SS.[42] Badoglio cautioned everyone present that it was crucial to handle their allies with kid gloves for the time being.[43] Provocations on their part, he said, might cause the Germans to descend on Rome and arrest them all.[44]

The Nazis were no happier. Jodl had captured the mood in a short message he cabled to Germany in the early afternoon of August

---

*A "Mickey Finn," better known as a "Mickey," was slang for a drink laced with knockout drops.

15.[45] "Italian intentions are no clearer than before," he reported, and added, "[O]ur reasons for suspicion are still as valid as ever."[46]

A few days later, on August 19, Admiral Doenitz summarized Hitler's view: "Situation Italy: The Fuehrer's attitude remains generally unchanged. The conference of Rommel and Jodl with Roatta . . . took place in an atmosphere completely void of cordiality. *There is still no evidence of Italian treason, only certain indications lend themselves to such an interpretation.* Therefore we are carrying on as before and pouring Rommel's Army Group into Italy according to plan and without Italian interference. The safety of our forces and our supply lines is ruthlessly assured but without giving the Italians an excuse for an open break."*[47]

The bickering at Bologna merely reinforced Hitler's belief that Badoglio was dead set on betrayal. And it was this conviction, in turn, that helped to shape his strategy for defending Italy in case of an Allied invasion. This strategy was based on the notion that he could not hold on to all of Italy without the active support of the Italian military, which he now expected to join the enemy camp.[48]

"Without the Italian Army we cannot defend the entire peninsula," Hitler had said during a military conference back on July 17. "In that case we would have to withdraw to a relatively short line."[49] Under the circumstances, his primary goal was to defend the northern enclave, where much of Italy's agriculture and 80 percent of its industry were located.[50] If necessary, Hitler was prepared to retreat all the way back to the area around Florence, well over a hundred miles north of Rome.

■ ■ ■

Hitler's plans for defending Italy inevitably gave rise to a personal drama between Rommel and Kesselring. Rommel was in charge of Army Group B, the collective name given to the numerous German

---

*My italics.

divisions that were pouring into northern Italy through the Alpine passes during August. (By mid-month, half of Army Group B had made its way into Italy.)[51]

According to Hitler's thinking, once the Allies attacked the mainland and the Italians "showed their true colors," as he liked to say, Kesselring's divisions would withdraw from the south and re-group in the Rome area.[52] If all went as planned, they would then be incorporated into Army Group B, at which point Rommel would assume control of all German forces in Italy, and Kesselring would be out of a job.[53] Indeed, rumor had it that the latter was being considered for an assignment in Norway.[54]

Needlessly to say, none of this sat well with Kesselring. He liked Italy and he liked the Italians—or so he claimed—and he still held out hope that they would remain loyal to the Axis. Ever the optimist, Kesselring believed that it was better to contest every inch of Italian territory rather than hand over southern Italy, or more, to the enemy without so much as a fight.

During the summer of 1943, a rivalry developed between Kesselring and Rommel for Hitler's ear, Rommel advocating the eventual evacuation of southern and central Italy.[55] In reality, it was not much of a competition: Hitler always seemed to side with Rommel over the Italophile Kesselring, whom Hitler believed had spent too much time in the Mediterranean sun.

"I was written down as an 'Italophile' and consequently suitable for employment in Italy only for as long as my presence there could help maintain friendly relations with the royal house," Kesselring recalled after the war. "For when the time should come to grasp the nettle and talk a different language the man had been chosen, namely Rommel, whose Army Group was already standing to in my rear."[56] In contrast to Kesselring, Rommel had a reputation for being hostile to the Italians, with whom he had quarreled during the Axis retreats in North Africa.[57]

Now, in mid-August—which is around the time he transferred his Army Group B headquarters from Munich to Lake Garda in northern Italy—Rommel was one half of Hitler's temporary dual-command structure for Italy. "His area of command was for the moment limited to northern Italy," General Warlimont observed, "with the result that we now had in Italy two German senior headquarters, one behind the other, while alongside them and loosely connected to them, was the whole Italian command organization."[58]

As shall be seen later, this rivalry between Rommel and Kesselring came to a head a few weeks later when the latter made a bid for total control of German forces in Italy—with surprising results.

■ ■ ■

The Nazis' military considerations were becoming more important than ever during the second half of the month, when the Allies began to set their sights on the Italian mainland. On August 17, after thirty-eight days of fighting, Sicily fell to the Western Powers.[59] Over the course of a week prior to that date, the Nazis managed to transfer some 40,000 German troops to southern Italy via the Straits of Messina, an impressive feat under the circumstances.[60] These soldiers, who brought their vehicles and equipment with them, would live to fight another day—and the Allies would soon pay a high price for letting them escape.[61] Incredibly, no one bothered to ask Hitler's permission for this minor Dunkirk. He was so equivocal on the subject of Sicily that Kesselring and Jodl went ahead and made the decision for him.[62]

But mainland Italy was no sanctuary for the Axis. Despite ongoing talks with the Italians, Churchill decreed that "the war should be carried forward against Italy in every way that the Americans [would] allow."[63] During August and early September, the Allies frequently bombed Italian cities.[64] Large areas of Milan, Naples, Turin, and Genoa suffered severe damage as a result.[65] Rome was targeted for the second time on August 13—it had already been hit on July 19, the day of the Axis conference at Feltre—inspiring the Badoglio regime unilaterally to declare Rome an Open City the following day.[66] According to General Student, the frequent bombings of Italy seemed to undermine the idea that the Italians were forging a separate peace.[67]

Elsewhere, the Allies continued to step up the pressure. On the eastern front, where Hitler's forces had been weakened so that Italy could be fortified with additional German troops, the Russians continued to reclaim lost territory, capturing Kharkov on August 23 and Taganrog one week later.[68] August 23 was an important date for another reason. On that day, the Americans unleashed a massive bombing raid against Berlin, igniting fires that could be seen hundreds of miles away.[69] Unable to protect the Reich capital, the Nazis ultimately evacuated one million civilians from the city.[70]

With the relentless stream of bad news on the war front, Hitler was growing increasingly concerned about a possible July 25 in Germany. To counter this, on August 24, Heinrich Himmler, the SS chief (and all-around bad guy), was made Minister of the Interior, replacing the elderly Wilhelm Frick.

■ ■ ■

Badoglio had rebels on his mind as well. By the fourth week of August, anxiety in Rome had reached fever pitch. The Italians had heard nothing from Castellano since he left for Lisbon, and there were fears that the Allies might not be receptive to their desire to switch sides in the war.[71] Badoglio worried constantly about the Nazis as well as the Fascists of the Mussolini era, who he feared might join forces to overthrow his government.[72] He therefore began to clamp down on subversive activities, be they real or imagined.

It was at this time that Badoglio exposed, or manufactured, the so-called Cavallero plot, which he portrayed as a secret conspiracy involving former Fascists who were planning to topple the Italian regime in connivance with the Nazis.*[73] Ugo Cavallero, the supposed ringleader, was arrested along with other Fascist personalities—and

---

*Knowledge of this supposed plot may have been among the reasons for transferring Mussolini from Maddalena to the mainland in late August.

alleged plotters—some of whom had been locked up immediately after July 25 and subsequently released.[74]

Though Badoglio claimed he was acting in the best interests of
the nation, some Italians cried foul. They charged that the Head of
the Government was using trumped-up allegations to carry out a
preemptive strike against the remnants of the old regime, settle accounts with personal enemies, and eliminate potential rivals for
power.[75] In any event, Badoglio summoned the courage to send a
missive to the Nazis in which he complained about German involvement. Ribbentrop responded immediately, asking Badoglio to
explain himself and to identify individuals who were thought to be
involved. This, in turn, elicited a quick apology from Raffaele Guariglia, Ribbentrop's opposite number in Rome. Badoglio then reportedly received a tongue lashing from the king, who was angered to
learn that his *Capo del Governo* was provoking the Nazis with vague
accusations.[76]

Count Galeazzo Ciano, the Duce's son-in-law and onetime foreign minister, was almost snagged in Badoglio's net. Galeazzo was
married to Edda but he had voted *against* the Duce in the meeting
of the Grand Council. After the events of July 25, he had resigned
from his post at the Vatican and maintained a low profile.

There had been calls for his arrest after the coup, but Badoglio
refrained from taking action until the Cavallero plot had surfaced,
after which he apparently ordered that Ciano be arrested and sent
to Ponza, the same penal island on which Mussolini had been interned in early August. Though Ciano seems to have been innocent
of collusion with the alleged conspirators, he was under investigation for having illegally enriched himself during the Fascist glory
days.[77] In any event, he did not hang around long enough to plead
his case.

On the morning of August 27, Ciano, his wife, and their three
children were willingly spirited out of Rome and flown to Germany
by the Nazis in an operation conducted by Herbert Kappler, the
police attaché at the German embassy in Rome.[78] "No one could

understand," Edda later wrote, "why Galeazzo Ciano had thrown himself to the wolves in taking refuge with Hitler and his cohorts, whom he had been openly criticizing for many months. The truth is that we had decided together to flee Rome and take refuge in Spain because we felt the vise closing on us ever more tightly."[79]

The Cianos believed—naïvely, as it turned out—that after a brief layover in Germany the Nazis would facilitate their journey to Spain.[80] But this stopover "was transformed from hour to hour and day to day," Edda recalled, "first into a visit as 'guests' of the Führer, then . . . into a visit as 'virtual prisoners.'"[81] Galeazzo never counted on being kidnapped, according to Edda. "On the contrary, he fell—and I along with him—into a deadly trap."*[82]

But bagging Ciano, whom the Nazis viewed as a Fascist turncoat, was apparently not Hitler's biggest priority. According to Wilhelm Hoettl, an SS intelligence officer who helped plan the Cianos' escape, the Fuehrer was more concerned with the preservation of the Duce's genes.[83] "Hitler's orders," he recalled, "were emphatic that 'whatever happened, Mussolini's blood in the veins of his grandchildren must at all costs be preserved for the future.' His sole real interest was in these grandchildren whom he regarded as the only important members of the [Ciano] family."[84]

---

*The British historian F. W. Deakin has described Galeazzo's flight as a "kidnapping by consent." Deakin, 519.

Benito Mussolini. CREDIT: NATIONAL ARCHIVES.

Sunnier days: Hitler and Mussolini in Munich in the spring of 1940.
CREDIT: NATIONAL ARCHIVES.

From left to right: Mussolini (with hand on chin), Marshal Wilhelm Keitel, Hitler, and Luftwaffe chief Hermann Goering ponder the maps. CREDIT: NATIONAL ARCHIVES.

The Axis foreign ministers, Galeazzo Ciano (left) and Joachim von Ribbentrop, in 1940 Ciano was married to Mussolini's daughter, Edda. CREDIT: NATIONAL ARCHIVES.

An informal shot of Marshal Pietro Badoglio dated October 1, 1943, just a few weeks after the rescue of Mussolini.
CREDIT: NATIONAL ARCHIVES.

General Kurt Student, chief of Germany's airborne forces, watches a paratrooper drill in the fall of 1943. Student was annoyed by the fact that Skorzeny received the lion's share of the credit for rescuing Mussolini. CREDIT: NATIONAL ARCHIVES.

This photo of Otto Skorzeny was taken just days after the rescue of Mussolini and Skorzeny's promotion to major.
CREDIT: NATIONAL ARCHIVES.

"Smiling Albert" Kesselring, with characteristic grin, confers with Hitler and Mussolini. Kesselring's faith in Badoglio was an endless source of frustration to Hitler. CREDIT: NATIONAL ARCHIVES.

The disappearance of Mussolini had presented Joseph Goebbels (left) with a major PR dilemma. But the Duce's subsequent rescue helped to boost German morale. CREDIT: NATIONAL ARCHIVES.

Admiral Karl Doenitz, chief of the German navy, dissuaded Hitler from blockading the harbor at Ventotene Island. CREDIT: NATIONAL ARCHIVES.

General Alfred Jodl in 1945. Fearful of being poisoned, Jodl had refused to drink his coffee during a meeting with the Italians at Bologna in 1943.

September 3, 1943: General Walter Bedell Smith (seated) signs the Italian armistice agreement as General Giuseppe Castellano (in black suit) looks on. Brigadier Kenneth W. D. Strong, Eisenhower's intelligence chief, is partially visible behind Castellano.

The ancient prison on Santo Stefano. Hitler considered landing paratroopers here in an effort to rescue Mussolini, though the Duce had never set foot on the island.
CREDIT: PETER BARDWELL.

An aerial photo of La Maddalena taken from an altitude of 38,000 feet. Note: The "San Stefano" shown in this picture is not the "Santo Stefano" island mentioned in this book.
CREDIT: DAN HUNT.

Maddalena town as seen from the ferry. CREDIT: DAN HUNT.

Mussolini spent the last three weeks of August at the Villa Webber on La Maddalena.
CREDIT: MR. CAMERON ARCHER, DIRECTOR OF THE TOCAL AGRICULTURAL CENTRE,
PATERSON NSW, AUSTRALIA.

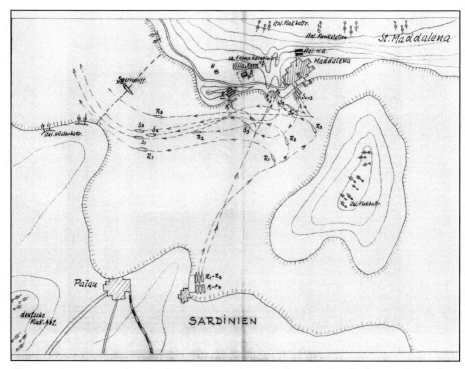

Skorzeny's postwar sketch of the proposed Maddalena raid, which was aborted at the last minute. CREDIT: NATIONAL ARCHIVES.

An Allied "identification poster" of the Heinkel 111. Note the gunner lying on his stomach in the front of the cockpit. This is where Skorzeny was positioned while taking reconnaissance photos of La Maddalena. CREDIT: NATIONAL ARCHIVES.

A World War II–era photo of the Gran Sasso region. CREDIT: NATIONAL ARCHIVES.

La Villetta in 1945. Mussolini was held at this small inn near Assergi for several days before being transferred to the nearby Hotel Imperatore. CREDIT: NATIONAL ARCHIVES.

"The highest prison in the world": A panoramic view of the Hotel Imperatore and surrounding area. The observatory in the foreground is a post–World War II addition. CREDIT: ADAPTED FROM *AFTER THE BATTLE* MAGAZINE (1978).

A closer view of the general area in which the gliders touched down. The Stork aircraft landed in and took off from the clearing on the left (opposite the hotel's right shoulder). The observatory in the foreground is a modern addition. CREDIT: ADAPTED FROM *AFTER THE BATTLE* MAGAZINE (1978).

close-up of the rear of the hotel. Skorzeny claims to have entered the radio room in e back of the building before running outside and making his way around the hotel's ft shoulder. CREDIT: *AFTER THE BATTLE* MAGAZINE (1978).

Mussolini's windows

three-quarter view of the Hotel Imperatore showing the windows of Mussolini's suite. REDIT: ADAPTED FROM *AFTER THE BATTLE* MAGAZINE (1978).

A close-up of the DFS 230 showing the single skid and two-wheel dolly. The dolly wa⟨s⟩ jettisoned after takeoff. CREDIT: NATIONAL ARCHIVES.

The DFS 230 in flight. CREDIT: NATIONAL ARCHIVES.

The Fieseler 156 Stork. This is the same type of plane that Gerlach used to fly Mussolini and Skorzeny off the mountain. CREDIT: NATIONAL ARCHIVES.

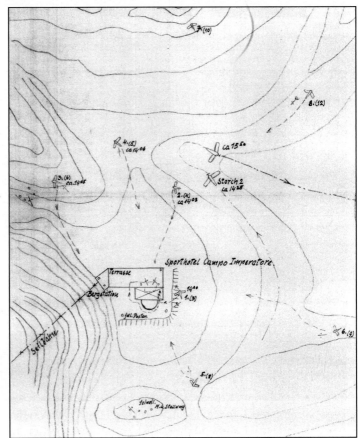

Skorzeny's postwar sketch indicating where the DFS 230 gliders landed on September 12, 1943. In this sketch, his glider is located very close to the hotel's right shoulder. The remaining DFS 230s are widely scattered. CREDIT: NATIONAL ARCHIVES.

German newsreel footage: Skorzeny (far left) and the Duce (wearing black hat) walk past the Hotel Imperatore shortly after the rescue. CREDIT: NATIONAL ARCHIVES.

German newsreel footage: Lieutenant Baron Otto von Berlepsch (left) shakes hands with Major Harold Mors on the Gran Sasso. CREDIT: NATIONAL ARCHIVES.

German newsreel footage: Mussolini gets a boost as he climbs into the Stork. The instrument panel is partially visible behind his hat. CREDIT: NATIONAL ARCHIVES.

German newsreel footage: Mussolini and Skorzeny mug for the camera after taking their positions inside the Stork. The subsequent takeoff was hair-raising. CREDIT: NATIONAL ARCHIVES.

German newsreel footage: Mussolini waves as he steps off the plane at Rastenburg on September 14, 1943, two days after being rescued. CREDIT: NATIONAL ARCHIVES.

German newsreel footage: Hitler and Mussolini shake hands near the wing of the Duce's plane on September 14, 1943. This was the first time they had seen each other since the Italian dictator's arrest. CREDIT: NATIONAL ARCHIVES.

THE HIGHEST
PRISON IN THE WORLD

Security preparations around the Gran Sasso complete.[1]
—Italian radio message intercepted by the Germans

BY THE END OF AUGUST, THE DANGEROUS AND CLANDESTINE GAME OF mutual deception that had occupied the Axis powers since July 25 was approaching a climax. On August 27, General Castellano finally returned from his covert trip to Lisbon.[2] All in all, his two-week mission had been a colossal waste of time. Rightly or wrongly, the Allies were in no mood to "negotiate," nor were they willing to divulge the details of their secret invasion plans to the Italians, whose suspicious behavior during the so-called negotiations had raised a few eyebrows.

When all was said and done, Eisenhower's men in Lisbon had merely repeated the demand for unconditional surrender and handed Castellano a brief set of nonnegotiable armistice terms, the so-called Short Terms, which the Italian general was not even authorized to sign. This abbreviated version of the armistice, intended as a temporary measure, was put forward as a way for the two sides to reach rapid agreement. Eisenhower, whose invasion of the Italian mainland was scheduled for the first part of September, dearly wanted to reach some sort of understanding with the Italians before launching his attack; in this way, the Allied troops would face only one enemy instead of two.[3]

But agreement was anything but rapid. In fact, the Italians were despondent. Their strategy of trying to bargain with the Allies for more favorable terms had backfired. After four weeks of effort and half a dozen or so different diplomatic contacts, they were still faced with a choice between unconditional surrender on the one hand and Hitler and the dreaded Nazis on the other. This was the same choice they had faced on July 25. The only change in the meantime was that Italy was now crawling with German soldiers, making an Italian surrender a much riskier proposition than it would have been in the days immediately after the coup when the Nazis had only three divisions on mainland Italy.

What was the king of Italy to do? Fearful that the Anglo-Americans could not protect Italy from Nazi wrath, a majority of the king's men recommended *rejecting* the armistice during a war council on August 28.[4] But Victor Emmanuel continued to vacillate.

At the end of the month, General Castellano flew to Allied-controlled Sicily to haggle over the Short Terms with General Bedell Smith and learn more about the imminent invasion.[5] "The Italians," remembered Churchill, "wanted to be quite sure that these landings would be strong enough to guarantee the security of the King and Government in Rome. It was clear that the Italian Government were particularly anxious that we should make a landing north of Rome to protect them against the German divisions near the city."[6]

If they were not prepared to land that far north, Castellano said, at the very least the Allies must insert an airborne division near the capital to scare the Nazis out of central Italy. Eager to reach an agreement, the Allies agreed to Castellano's request on the condition that the Italians secured the airfields near Rome and took other reasonable measures to support the operation—known as Giant Two—which was fairly complex and not without its risks. Castellano agreed.

■ ■ ■

Though Hitler knew nothing of the armistice debates going on in Rome, he was prepared for any eventuality. By the end of August, the Nazis had more or less completed their military preparations in northern Italy and finalized their planning for Operation Axis, which involved occupying the peninsula and neutralizing the Italian armed forces.[7] On August 23, Hitler personally warned Kesselring to be prepared for the worst, telling him that he had "infallible proof of Italy's treachery," though he did not explain the nature of that proof. "He begged me to stop being the dupe of the Italians," Kesselring recalled, "and to prepare myself for serious developments."[8] Though he was not fully persuaded, Kesselring took the advice to heart.

Regardless of his suspicions, Hitler had no desire to force an open break with the Italians.[9] A preemptive strike on the part of the Nazis might seal the fate of Mussolini before the Germans had a chance to find and free him. Aggression against an ostensible ally might also alienate the Axis satellite states such as Hungary and Rumania, whose loyalty the Germans already considered suspect.

It is even possible that Hitler believed he could avoid a major clash with the Italians. Though he never wavered in his belief that Badoglio was planning to betray him, he apparently clung to the hope that he could somehow keep the Italians in the Axis camp— either by bullying them into submission or by changing the rules of the game altogether by liberating the Duce and reinserting him into Italian politics.[10] Ribbentrop, for one, still believed that the Nazis might be able to do business with the Badoglio regime, even at this late date.[11]

"So the Axis powers remained unhappy bedfellows," remembered General Walter Warlimont, referring to the latter part of August, "in an alliance which had lost all form and meaning; one side was dependent upon the Allies who were slow to move; the other continued in its determination not to be the one to take the first step leading to the final break."[12] Accordingly, when Hitler got wind of the Italian peace overtures in Lisbon—and he did, of course, know about them, at least in general terms—he ordered his diplomats into action instead of his army divisions.

He decided to send an envoy to Rome to further probe Badoglio's state of mind and play for more time.[13] This move was all well
and good with Italy's leaders, who were also keen to maintain the
status quo until such time as the Allies swooped into Rome and rescued them from the Nazis. But Hitler had no intention of sending
the hapless Mackensen, the former ambassador to Italy; in fact, on
August 31, Hitler officially cleaned house at the German embassy in
Rome by firing Mackensen and the military attaché General Enno
von Rintelen, whose rosy views on Italy had frustrated the German
dictator to no end.[14]

Instead, Hitler selected Dr. Rudolf Rahn, the intelligent, bushy-
browed chargé d'affaires at the embassy.[15] Technically speaking, he
was not named as the new ambassador: Hitler's failure to make the
appointment official was probably an intentional maneuver designed to increase Badoglio's anxiety about the future.[16]

After receiving a briefing from Hitler, Rahn flew to Rome on August 30 and met with Guariglia, the Italian foreign minister.[17] He took
a carrot-and-stick approach, telling Guariglia that Hitler did not
much care whether Italy was Fascist or non-Fascist or who headed
the government. "The Fuehrer was a realist," Guariglia recalled, para-
phrasing Rahn, "and only one thing counted for him: to win the war.
If the Badoglio government intended to continue the war . . . the
Fuehrer would have the same confidence in us, and Italo-German co-
operation would be more effective than before."[18] But Rahn also told
his Italian counterpart that the Germans were aware of negotiations
in Spain or Portugal and warned that they would not hesitate to use
force if Italy attempted to forge a separate peace with the Allies.[19]

A few days later, on September 3, Rahn met with Badoglio.[20]
The latter apparently put on an Oscar-worthy performance, empha-
sizing Italy's loyalty to the Axis and pleading with Rahn to restrain
the Nazis from taking "provocative action." Badoglio then said: "I
am Marshal Badoglio—the Marshal Badoglio. I belong to the three
oldest Marshals in Europe—Mackensen, Pétain and myself. . . . The
distrust of the German government towards me is incomprehensible. I have given my word and stand by it. Please trust me."[21]

The timing of this meeting was ironic. At the same moment that Badoglio was imploring Rahn to believe in him, General Castellano was in a Sicilian olive grove signing the Short Terms on behalf of the Italian government.*[22] After weeks of debate and vacillation, Italy had officially hoisted the white flag, and done it on the sly. The armistice remained a closely guarded secret. Victor Emmanuel had no intention of broadcasting the fact of Italy's *volte-face* until the Allies had chased the Nazis out of Rome.

If everything went according to schedule, the event would come to pass in a matter of days. However, as shall be seen later, things did not go quite as the Italians had planned.

Though the Italians had inked a deal with the Allies, the king and Badoglio were in no hurry to hand over Mussolini.[23] Victor Emmanuel may very well have discouraged such a move, fearing that the Germans would get wind of it and launch an immediate strike on Rome. The Italians, in fact, had considered surrendering the Duce to the Allies right after the coup as a sign of good faith; but the king vetoed this idea because he believed the news would leak out and so betray the fact that Italy was seeking a separate peace.[24]

As was seen earlier, on August 28 Mussolini had been transferred from Maddalena Island to the Abruzzi region of central Italy, east of Rome. He was installed in a room on the second floor of a small rustic inn called La Villetta, located near the village of Assergi on the lower reaches of the Gran Sasso d'Italia, the tallest mountain ridge in the Apennines. He spent a few uneventful days at the inn under the care of his two main guardians of the moment, Police Inspector Giuseppe Gueli and Lieutenant Alberto Faiola.[25] As isolated

---

*In the evening of the same day, Castellano was handed the so-called Long Terms of the armistice, which explained the political, economic, and financial dimensions of the surrender. By signing the Short Terms, the Italians had automatically agreed to accept the Long Terms, sight unseen. These terms would be modified in Italy's favor depending on how actively the Italians assisted the Allies in the fight against the Germans during the remainder of the war.

as he was, the Duce could sense that the European Axis powers were headed for a clash, and the thought seemed to depress him. Gueli and Faiola were so concerned about his state of mind at La Villetta that when the dictator had finished his meals they quickly retrieved the knives and forks lest he use them to harm himself.[26]

At the beginning of September, Mussolini was led to a nearby cable car station and transferred skyward to what was to be his last prison, the Hotel Campo Imperatore, also known as the Albergo-Rifugio, on the majestic Gran Sasso.[27] After a ten-minute ride in the cable car, which spanned the 3,000 feet between Assergi and the hotel, the Duce got a first look at his awe-inspiring surroundings.[28] The Campo Imperatore, which was a ski resort during the winter season, was situated on a small plateau almost 7,000 feet above sea level.[29] Not far from this spot was Gran Sasso's Mount Corno, at 9,500 feet the highest peak in the Apennines.*[30]

Though large, the hotel was not much to look at; but to Mussolini it possessed a special distinction. It was "the highest prison in the world," he remarked to one of his guards, not without a touch of pride, perhaps.[31] Highest prison or not, the Duce was certainly its sole prisoner, all the guests having been evacuated while he sojourned at La Villetta.[32] The only inhabitants of the Campo Imperatore now consisted of Mussolini, two hundred or so policemen and carabinieri, and members of the hotel staff.[33]

For the Duce, who was lodged in a comfortable second-floor suite (No. 201), the succeeding days were ones of enforced leisure.[34] He passed the time listening to the radio—one of his new privileges—and playing card games such as *Scopone* with his captors, Gueli and Faiola.[35] He was also allowed to take walks near the hotel.[36] Occasionally, he caught sight of a shepherd tending his flock on one of the neighboring plateaus. "Sometimes the owners of

---

*By way of comparison, the highest peak in the American Rocky Mountains, Mount Elbert in Colorado, is roughly 14,500 feet.

the herds appeared on horseback and then vanished along the ridge of the mountain," he wrote, "standing out against the skyline like figures from another age."[37]

For the most part, Mussolini had few complaints about life on the Gran Sasso, where he enjoyed improved accommodations and expanded freedoms. The Hotel Imperatore, after all, was certainly a far cry from the fishy décor at the House of the Ras on Ponza.

Yet, at the same time, the dictator could not help but wonder whether he was being accorded the special treatment reserved for men facing the gallows.[38] As it happened, there was some truth in this presentiment: Badoglio had given orders to the effect that the Nazis "must not take him alive."[39]

Hitler, of course, was determined to do just that. At the end of August, he made this clear in emotional fashion to Edda Ciano, who had recently arrived in Germany for a stopover of indefinite duration. Edda and her husband, Galeazzo Ciano, had been lured into Hitler's clutches—or so she later claimed—with tantalizing promises of false passports, a getaway plane, and other goodies that have special appeal to couples on the lam.* In any event, when Edda showed up at the Wolf's Lair on August 31, the sight of the Duce's favorite daughter was enough to make Hitler's eyes well up with tears.[40]

"Never fear," a weepy Hitler told her when she inquired about her father. "He will be liberated. We still don't know where he is being kept prisoner, but we will know very soon. And then, I promise you, I will do everything in my power to rescue him. You can be sure that I will bring him to you safe and sound."[41]

Hitler was right about one thing: The Nazis had no clue where Mussolini was at that moment. Hitler probably did not know that the near miss on Maddalena Island in late August had led to frayed

---

*The Nazis had no evil designs on Edda, of course. It was her husband Galeazzo whom Hitler and his cronies detested.

nerves at Frascati, where an underlying tension between Skorzeny and General Student's paratroopers was beginning to bubble over.

"All was not the best in General Student's staff," Skorzeny later complained, referring to what he perceived as a noticeable lack of enthusiasm for Operation Oak. "Radl and I were astonished to learn that there were even defeatists in the general staff of an elite corps. Right after our arrival in Frascati a major asked us ironically whether we knew that the war was lost. And after the Santa Maddalena fiasco we noticed more often that they made not the least effort to really help us. They seemed to think we were crazy people who had our eye on some insane goal."[42] As fanatical SS men, he and his deputy, Radl, had little sympathy for what they perceived as doubting Thomases in the ranks of the war-weary Luftwaffe veterans.

Skorzeny did not hesitate to bring his concerns to the attention of Student, who made an attempt to handle the situation diplomatically. "The people of whom you speak," he told Skorzeny, "and who I know better than you, jumped at Narvik, Eben Emael, at Rotterdam and Crete. I am sure that they will continue to do their duty."[43] At which point Radl, "who wasn't one to hold back" according to Skorzeny, chimed in: "Allow me to state, Herr General, that an officer cannot give his best in a war that he already considers to be lost. That is a sentiment that we don't and will never understand."[44] If nothing else, the two gung ho commandos were proving why Hitler put so much faith in Himmler's ultra-loyal legions.

■ ■ ■

Exchanges such as these probably served to remind Student that he had entered a strange new realm during the summer of 1943—one that entailed a close working relationship with the SS. Instead of fighting the Allies on the front lines—or behind them—as he was accustomed to doing, Student was faced with the prospect of rescuing a fallen dictator and possibly kidnapping the government of an ostensible ally. These assignments were an unusual development in the long career of this seasoned fifty-three-year-old Luftwaffe officer.

A native of Prussia, Student had commanded a fighter squadron during World War I before going on to become the primary architect of Germany's airborne forces, pioneering what was then a brand-new form of warfare. He was considered a patriot but was not reputed to have the same unquestioning faith in the Nazi leadership so typical of Skorzeny and his brethren in the SS.

On a superficial level, Student was not a particularly forceful personality, especially after being shot in the head by a sniper during Hitler's triumphant offensive against the West in 1940. "From the point of view of outward appearance," remembered General Heinz Trettner, one of Student's most trusted subordinates, "it is impossible to say that General Student was ever an imposing figure, like a Kesselring or a von Richthofen. His high voice and—after his head wound in Holland—his hesitant manner of speech were a disadvantage to him in discussion with more accomplished speakers and his modest bearing could give the impression of mediocrity."[45]

But Student's qualities as a commander—he was known for his boldness, creative imagination, and tenacity—were reflected in the daring operations undertaken by his paratroopers, comprised of carefully screened volunteers, who quickly earned a reputation as being among the best troops of the war. "It was Student who put airborne forces on the world's military map," wrote General Sir John Hackett, a onetime British paratrooper who fought against Student's soldiers. "It is he who must be recognized as chiefly responsible for the outstanding performance of German airborne troops in the Second World War."[46]

They saw action just about everywhere. During Hitler's glory days they helped to defeat Norway and Denmark, played a crucial role in the invasion of France, and chased the British out of Crete. Later, the paratroopers were employed as hard-fighting elite ground troops during increasingly grim, defensive battles in Africa, Russia, Sicily, Italy, France, Holland, and ultimately Germany.[47] Student and his paratroopers would always be remembered for their legendary raid on the "impregnable" Belgian fort of Eben Emael. As shall be seen later, this feat would be in the forefront of Student's

mind when the Germans began planning their final attempt to rescue Mussolini.

■ ■ ■

But the dictator had to be found first. Though the friction between
Skorzeny and the paratroopers was destined to outlast the war, General Student and the SS continued to work together to locate the
Duce after the Maddalena "fiasco." According to Radl, there were
plenty of rumors in the air.

One "trustworthy" source placed Mussolini in a Roman hospital
awaiting an operation; but Herbert Kappler, the police attaché at the
embassy, discovered that this information was false.[48] Eugen Dollmann also lent his assistance, dispelling a rumor suggesting that the
Duce was being held in the Villa Savoia, which was the king's personal residence and the same place where Mussolini was arrested
on July 25.[49] There were also vague hints that Badoglio had hidden
his prisoner somewhere near Lake Trasimene in the Perugia region,
north of Rome.[50]

Then Kappler, who was participating in Operation Oak against
his better judgment, stepped forward with the crucial breakthrough. His agents, who were monitoring Italian communications,
had intercepted a terse and puzzling message on the wireless: "Security preparations around the Gran Sasso complete."[51] Gueli, one
of the Duce's captors, had apparently sent this message to his superiors.* It was this lead—along with some supporting intelligence—
that ultimately allowed the Nazis to zero in on the mile-high ski
resort known as the Hotel Imperatore.

At first, Student did not attach much value to Kappler's discovery.[52] In fact, at this stage the general was not even convinced that
Mussolini was on the mainland.[53] But events soon changed his

---

*According to some reports, the Germans were aware that Gueli was one of the
men responsible for Mussolini's security. See Foley, 50.

mind. On September 4 or 5, Student and Skorzeny paid a visit to the Italian seaplane base at Vigna di Valle on Lake Bracciano to check up on a squadron of Luftwaffe aircraft.[54] German seaplanes had been dispatched to the base in preparation for the Maddalena rescue operation.[55]

While Student was there, he heard an unexpectedly interesting story from the squadron captain.[56] A few days earlier at dawn, the officer told Student, there was an air raid. Everyone took cover and waited for the inevitable explosions, but none came.* The only thing that dropped out of the sky, as it were, was a Red Cross seaplane, which then made a landing on the lake. If that were not odd enough, he said, shortly after the appearance of the plane, an ambulance was seen leaving the base along with several other cars. There was a rumor floating around Vigna di Valle suggesting that the passenger of the ambulance was Il Duce.

Student could scarcely believe his ears: Mussolini had been transferred right under his nose! What he learned at Lake Bracciano was welcome news, of course, because it seemed to confirm that the Duce was on the mainland after all and that Kappler's intercept was probably more important than he had initially believed.[57] But Student could not help feeling that a golden opportunity had slipped through his fingers.

If it were not for the secrecy surrounding Operation Oak, the German pilots at Bracciano, who knew nothing of the plot to free Mussolini, might have nabbed the dictator themselves or called for reinforcements: The deed would then have been done.[58] Student had been "racking his brains" for weeks in the effort to find the Duce, he thought to himself, and every time he got close to his quarry, the Italians slipped him away in the nick of time.[59] "Apparently, very strict secrecy can sometimes have its disadvantages,"

---

*According to Student, the Italians used an air raid siren several times during the summer of 1943 while transferring Mussolini from one place to another. The aim, of course, was to clear the area of potential witnesses.

Student later wrote. "In this case it was the reason why a unique chance was missed."[60]

According to Radl, Kappler's Gran Sasso lead was also supported by a seemingly unrelated incident that came to their attention around this time: a car crash involving two Italian officers.[61] A red flag apparently went up when the Germans learned the identity of the victims, at least one of whom was known to be guarding Mussolini.* When they attempted to get more details about the crash, they discovered that the Italians in question had been driving from Rome to L'Aquila, or vice versa—in retrospect, Radl could not remember which. L'Aquila, of course, was the regional capital of the Abruzzi. It was only about fifteen miles or so from the lower cable car station of the Hotel Imperatore.

The ski resort now became the main focus of the search. In Student's mind it was the only logical place on the Gran Sasso in which the Italians could possibly hide Mussolini. "The hotel was secluded," he later wrote, "it was the only lodging far and wide in a jagged, romantic mountain landscape."[62] But the hotel's isolated location—it was only accessible via cable car—made it difficult for the Nazis to investigate.

Skorzeny obtained some information from a German living in Italy who had spent some time at the resort before the war. A travel agency brochure also provided a few details, including a photo of the hotel.[63] But as the first week of September drew to a close, the Nazis were acutely aware that time was not working in their favor. "The feeling that the enormous tension [between the Axis powers] would break one way or the other one of these days was universal," Student remembered.[64]

---

*Saverio Polito, Mussolini's senior jailer at Maddalena, had been injured in a car accident around August 20. However, it is not clear whether this is the crash to which Radl is referring. Polito was actually driving from Perugia to Rome at the time, so it seems unlikely that knowledge of this accident would have provided the Germans with any clues regarding the Gran Sasso. See Patricelli, 43.

At first, Student and Skorzeny could not think of a way to study the hotel without alarming the Duce's captors and triggering another transfer of their prisoner. Then they hit upon an idea involving a German medical officer on Student's staff named Leo Krutoff.* The doctor, who spoke fluent Italian and was apparently something of a charmer, was instructed to make a pilgrimage to the Gran Sasso to determine whether the Campo Imperatore could be used as a convalescent home for ailing German soldiers.[65] Krutoff, who knew nothing of the real reasons behind this fishing expedition, was told to observe the layout of the building and make a note of other important details. He left by car for the hotel, which was located about seventy-five miles from Rome, on the morning of September 8.[66] According to Radl, the Nazis had already sent at least one agent to do some snooping around the Gran Sasso before Krutoff received his mission.[67]

On that same day, Skorzeny decided to conduct some aerial reconnaissance of the site in a special Heinkel 111 equipped with automatic cameras. Radl and Captain Gerhard Langguth, Student's intelligence officer, also took part. To keep their real objective secret from the pilot, Skorzeny told him that they were intending to photograph a few ports in the Adriatic Sea (which borders Italy in the east). The pilot was instructed to fly to the target via Rimini, Ancona, and Pescara, and then make a return trip along the same route. This flight path would take them over the Abruzzi region and the Gran Sasso.

Soon after takeoff, they experimented with the cameras, which were located in the belly of the Heinkel, only to discover that they were frosted over and did not function. Fortunately, they had brought along a portable camera as a backup, but using it to take pictures of the ground below was no easy matter. Taking another postwar swipe at the paratroopers, Skorzeny and Radl later claimed that Langguth

---

*It is not clear which of them came up with the idea. After the war, Student and Skorzeny each claimed it as his own.

was singularly unhelpful in this regard. "Scarcely had we boarded the aircraft," Skorzeny recalled, "when he told us that the automatic cameras weren't working and that there was no time to repair them. Radl and I looked at each other in amazement. Langguth casually showed us how to use a heavy hand-held camera, on which the film also had to be advanced by means of a hand crank. He had no intention of doing it himself."[68]

Using the camera required some improvised gymnastics. To get a clear shot at a suitable angle, the Germans had to dangle outside the plane through an open hatch as they soared over the hotel, or so the story goes. Skorzeny went first, sticking his upper body through the opening and holding the camera with both hands.* Radl held his legs to prevent him from falling out. At this point, the Heinkel was flying at about 230 miles per hour and its altitude was 16,400 feet.[69] The temperature of the air outside the plane, according to Skorzeny, was about 18 degrees Fahrenheit.[70]

"I could never have believed that the air was so cold, the wind so biting," remembered Skorzeny. "I passed my chest through the opening while Radl held my legs. . . . Gray and brown rocks, immense bare cliffs, a few névés, and then we passed over our objective, the hotel, a massive building even when viewed from this height. I took the first photo, then, holding the fairly heavy camera in my left hand, I turned the crank which advances the roll of film. Only at this precise juncture did I realize that in these last few instants my hands had grown numb."[71] During the return trip, Radl switched places with Skorzeny and took several more photos.

The two SS men were anxious to hear what Dr. Krutoff had managed to find out. But when they returned to Rome, a few surprises awaited them. By the end of day, in fact, Adolf Hitler's mission to find and free Mussolini had suddenly come to a screeching halt—seemingly for good.

---

*Student claimed that Langguth took the reconnaissance photos and that Skorzeny was merely an "especially interested passenger" on this flight. Student, 417.

THE DOUBLE CROSS

The Fuehrer anticipated Italian treason as something absolutely certain. He was really the only one who firmly counted on it. And yet, when it actually happened, it upset him pretty badly.[1]

—Goebbels' Diary, September 10, 1943

IN THE EARLY AFTERNOON OF SEPTEMBER 8, SKORZENY AND RADL were winging their way back towards Pratica di Mare airfield near Rome. As they glanced in the direction of Frascati, they were shocked to see large black clouds of smoke billowing up on the horizon. Sometime around noon, the small town of more than 10,000 people had been severely damaged during an Allied air attack, which delivered almost four hundred tons of plummeting explosives.[2] Thousands of Frascati's residents, most of them elderly or women and children, lay dead or injured among the smoldering ruins.[3]

The target of the raid was Kesselring's GHQ, where 150 German soldiers had been killed.[4] Kesselring himself was uninjured.[5] "The first bombs fell close to my glass veranda just as I was leaving my office," he remembered. "The enemy attack caused less damage to the military staffs than to the town and its inhabitants."[6] Though the headquarters complex suffered only minor damage, Skorzeny's quarters at Frascati had been gutted.[7]

But as Skorzeny soon discovered, the air raid was merely the prelude to more important events. In the early evening he was driving through Rome on the way to meet Radl. "My car moved forward slowly," he recalled, "for there was an unwonted bustle in all the streets. People thronged around loud speakers and, as I drove into the Via Veneto, I had to move at a snail's pace. Noisy acclamations hailed a piece of news bellowed by the loud speakers . . . women embraced one another, groups of people engaged in passionate debate. More and more puzzled, I finally stopped to question a passer-by who informed me of a fresh catastrophe: Italy had laid down her arms."[8] When Skorzeny had taken to the air that morning, the Italians had been allies. They were his enemies, it seemed, by the time the sun had set.

Or were they? That was the question that had plagued Hitler's anxious lieutenants for several hours on September 8. Though Allied radio started broadcasting the news of Italy's surrender in the late afternoon, the Italians continued to deny the existence of the armistice to the Germans, many of whom learned of it only through foreign radio reports. Rudolf Rahn, who was acting as Hitler's diplomatic envoy to Rome during this time, was particularly perturbed. He first heard about the Italian surrender at 5:45 P.M. on the American radio.[9] The U.S. media, as it turned out, had broken the story prior to Eisenhower's official announcement, which aired a short time later at around 6:30 P.M.[10]

"This is General Dwight D. Eisenhower, Commander-in-Chief of the Allied Forces," Ike's voice crackled over the radio. "The Italian Government has surrendered its armed forces unconditionally. As Allied Commander-in-Chief, I have granted a military armistice. . . . All Italians who now act to help eject the German aggressor from Italian soil will have the assistance and support of the United Nations."[11]

It seemed incomprehensible. That very day at noon, Rahn had spoken to King Victor Emmanuel, who assured him that Italy would never surrender![12] "At the end of the conversation," Rahn recalled, "the King stressed the decision to continue the struggle, to the end, at the side of Germany, with whom Italy is bound in life and death."[13] After hearing the first radio broadcast, Rahn had hurriedly put in a call to General Roatta, the chief of the Italian army.[14] He dismissed the radio reports as nothing more than British propaganda.[15] But later that evening, Guariglia, Badoglio's foreign minister, finally came clean. "I have to tell you," Guariglia told Rahn in person a little after 7:00 P.M., "that Marshal Badoglio, in view of the desperate military situation, has been forced to ask for an armistice."[16] Rahn replied angrily, "This is treachery to a given word."[17]

But the Nazis were not the only ones surprised by the Allied radio reports. Incredibly, in a bizarre twist worthy of fiction, Eisenhower's decision to broadcast the news of the Italian armistice had also caught Badoglio off guard.

As was seen earlier, General Castellano, Badoglio's proxy, had signed the Short Terms in Sicily on September 3 amidst great secrecy. It was understood that the *public* announcement of the armistice would roughly coincide with start of Operation Avalanche, the Allied invasion of the mainland. But because of security concerns—the Allies still did not have complete faith in their would-be ally—Eisenhower declined to inform Rome about the date or location of the landings lest these details find their way into German hands. The Italians soon came to believe, mistakenly, that D-day was set for September 12, or possibly later—or so they claimed.[18]

This misunderstanding led to a major confrontation between the Allies and the Italians in the hours leading up to Avalanche. Having learned the true date of D-day on the evening of September 7–8, the Italians immediately got cold feet, protesting that they had not yet taken all the military measures needed to fight the Germans.[19] But Eisenhower was unimpressed by these arguments and refused to alter his timetable.

In the early evening of September 8, Victor Emmanuel hastily convened a special council to discuss his options.[20] During this meeting, the king's men, who included Badoglio and a score of other leading Italians, seriously considered denying the existence of the armistice, at least as a temporary measure, and so avoid the wrath of the Nazis.[21] But after much debate, they agreed to keep their commitments to the Allies: Badoglio made a radio address later that evening at 7:45 P.M. announcing Italy's capitulation.[22]

"The Italian Government," he said, "recognizing the impossibility of continuing the unequal struggle against the overwhelming power of the enemy . . . has requested an armistice from General Eisenhower, Commander-in-Chief of the Anglo-American Allied Force. This request has been granted. The Italian forces will, therefore, cease all acts of hostility against the Anglo-American forces wherever they may be met. They will, however, oppose attacks from any other quarter."[23] The last sentence was a veiled reference to the Nazis, though Badoglio avoided mentioning them by name; it was as if he thought this strange omission would somehow soften the blow in Hitler's mind.

Amazingly, for much of the day on September 8, Eisenhower was left guessing as to what the Italians would do.[24] He did not know whether they planned to welcome his forces as liberators or to take up arms against them. The latter scenario, he maintained, could have been disastrous for the Allies in light of the modest forces he had at his disposal for invading the Italian coast.*[25] Indeed, there was so much confusion on September 8 that several Italian aircraft actually attacked the Allied invasion force at sea.[26] The Italian navy also made a bid to stop the Allies, and this potential catastrophe was only prevented at the last minute—literally.[27]

■ ■ ■

Much like the coup of July 25, the Italian surrender announcement had caught the Nazis by surprise, at least in its timing.[28] But it did not take long for them to lash out at their new enemy, promising to square accounts with Badoglio and other Italians who dared to oppose them.

---

*Allied resources were being husbanded for the Normandy invasion scheduled for 1944 and were also devoted to the effort in the Pacific Theatre.

"With this," German radio announced at 11:00 P.M. on September 8, "the veil has been torn from a treacherous intrigue which for weeks had been enacted by an Italian clique, serfs to Jews and alien to their own people. . . . Led by the Reich, Europe is determined and strong enough to get equal with this treason. An exemplary punishment will be visited on the traitors: a punishment which they deserve for the betrayal of the Italian people. These traitors will not reap any profit from their crime; the German army will see to it."[29]

The Nazis also flashed the code word "Axis" to their commanders throughout Italy and beyond, including the Balkans and the West. This was the signal for German forces to begin neutralizing their former allies by disarming them and taking them prisoner by any means necessary. Operation Axis incorporated some of the measures that Hitler had proposed in the immediate aftermath of the Italian coup.

The military situation in Italy had changed radically during the previous six weeks. On July 25, the day that Mussolini was arrested, only three German divisions operated on the Italian mainland, and a few more were fighting in Sicily. By September 8, that number had ballooned to *sixteen* divisions, eight under Rommel in the north and another eight under Kesselring in the south, two of the latter's divisions being positioned near Rome. Nine of these sixteen had entered Italy in the weeks following the coup. Another four divisions had managed to escape from Sicily in mid-August along with their equipment, and these forces—battered and depleted from their recent battles against the Allies—were placed under Kesselring's command.

The sudden announcement of Italy's *volte-face* created a volatile and unpredictable situation throughout the Italian peninsula, where all hell began to break loose in the face of Avalanche. During the early hours of September 9, thousands of American and British forces (General Mark Clark's Fifth Army) began landing on the beaches of Salerno, located on the southwestern coast of Italy below Naples, where they struggled to establish a beachhead under enemy fire. A small Allied force on the southern tip of Italy (General Sir Bernard

Montgomery's Eighth Army), which had crossed over from Sicily to Calabria back on September 3, was already moving northward, albeit rather slowly, to link up with the main invasion force at Salerno. Skirmishes between German and Italian units began to break out near Rome and in other parts of the country.*

No one, perhaps, was more shocked by the Italian surrender than Kesselring, who had retained an almost unquestioning faith in his Axis ally until the bitter end. But as the commander of German forces in southern Italy, "Smiling Albert" quickly accepted the reality of the situation by hurling the German Tenth Army into action against the Allies at Salerno. (Montgomery's Eighth Army was so far south at the time that it did not pose an immediate threat.) Fortunately for the Nazis, Kesselring had anticipated a landing in the Salerno area—it was a predictable choice—and had made his preparations.[30]

For the next several days, the fighting at Salerno was intense. But though Rommel had eight divisions in the north, Kesselring received no aid whatsoever from the former's Army Group B. "This Italian duumvirate of myself and Rommel," Kesselring complained, "with Hitler's almost obsequious submissiveness to Rommel, was responsible for the rejection of my priority calls for reinforcements."[31] Rommel did not believe it was worth fighting for southern Italy, and he had no intention of sacrificing his own units for the sake of what he viewed as a lost cause.

Yet even without reinforcements, Kesselring soon found himself on the verge of a stunning victory. At one pivotal moment on September 13, the Nazis came within a hair's breadth of driving to the sea through an open gap in the Allied forces and threatening their flanks, a potential knockout blow that may very well have led to disaster and even defeat for General Clark's invasion force.

---

*On September 9, the Allies also landed a small force (the British First Airborne Division) at Taranto, on Italy's heel. This landing was conducted in the absence of enemy resistance.

"The situation deteriorated to such an extent," remembered Kenneth Strong, Eisenhower's intelligence chief, "that at one point plans for the evacuation [by sea] of at least part of the beachhead were being actively canvassed."[32] *Evacuation.* The very idea was unthinkable. But after making a supreme effort, the Allies finally managed to save the day thanks largely to naval gunfire, air power, and desperate and heroic fighting on the part of the troops;[33] indeed, the situation became so desperate at one point that the Americans threw cooks and typists into the fray.[34]

"After the war Eisenhower said he thought of all his battles, Salerno was the one where the Allies came nearest to a tactical defeat," wrote Strong.[35] Mark Clark also admitted that Salerno was almost a disaster.[36]

After the climactic battle on September 13, the situation began to stabilize as reinforcements arrived to buttress Clark's position and Kesselring realized that he could not push the Allies into the sea. Somewhat after the fact, Monty's Eighth Army arrived on the scene to take part in what everyone hoped would be a speedy drive to the Eternal City.

■ ■ ■

For Badoglio and other Italians in high places, that is precisely where the real crisis was taking place. In the aftermath of the surrender, the five Italian divisions guarding Rome were facing the chilling prospect of going one-on-one with the Nazis without help from the Allies. "All Italians who now act to help eject the German aggressor from Italian soil," Eisenhower promised, "will have the assistance and support of the United Nations."[37] But because the Allies had chosen to land at Salerno, about 140 miles south of Rome, his statement did not have much practical effect.[38]

This unfortunate state of affairs had come about in part through the failure of the Italians to coordinate their military plans with the Allies, who had grudgingly agreed to make a risky airborne insertion into Rome on September 8.

The American troops were needed, the Italians said, to assist their local forces in defending Rome against German attacks. More important, it was also hoped that a landing near the capital would spook the Nazis and force them to clear out of southern Italy altogether in an effort to avoid being cut off and trapped.[39] Because Rome was a major road and rail center, whoever controlled the capital could sever the Nazi supply routes to southern Italy, where Kesselring's divisions were engaging the Allies.

But although the Italians had pleaded for the help of General Matthew Ridgway's Eighty-Second Airborne Division, they made no real effort to give Ridgway the military support he required to carry out his planned series of airdrops and landings.[40] On the Italian side, this involved seizing control of the antiaircraft guns protecting Rome, securing airfields, and providing trucks and fuel for Ridgway's men.

The Allies were so worried about whether the Italians could give meaningful support to the American paratroopers that they took the unusual step of sending General Maxwell Taylor, disguised as a downed Allied airman, on a clandestine mission to Rome on September 7 to assess the viability of the plan.[41] "He and his companion, Colonel Gardner, were picked up by an Italian frigate and smuggled into Rome in a Red Cross ambulance at great personal risk," recalled Strong.[42]

After some delays, General Giacomo Carboni, the commander of the Italian forces guarding Rome, eventually made an appearance and informed Taylor that the airborne operation could not be carried out as planned. By way of explanation, Carboni made some dubious assertions involving a lack of fuel and ammunition and German troop positions.[43] When Taylor eventually caught up with Badoglio, in the early hours of September 8, the marshal backed up Carboni.

This last-minute backpedaling erased all doubt from Taylor's mind: The airborne operation would have to be cancelled. As a result, the Romans would have to face the Nazis on their own, and they had no one to blame but their own leaders. "The air landing would, like all such operations, have been risky," reflected Strong, "but I believe it might have been carried out with relatively small losses if Badoglio had possessed more courage. The ... Italian divisions, though admittedly immobile, together with our airborne units, could conceivably have been adequate to hold Rome and perhaps to prevent the Germans from sending reinforcements to Salerno."[44]

■ ■ ■

But even this lost opportunity did not, in itself, doom the Eternal City. After all, the Italians had five divisions in the Rome area with which to repel the Nazis.[45] Kesselring, who had his hands full at Salerno, could afford to detail only two of his eight divisions to seize Rome: the Third Panzergrenadier Division and General Student's Second Parachute Division, the same paratroopers who had been rushed to Rome in the wake of the July 25 coup.[46] But it soon became evident that the local effort to protect Rome was botched from the beginning. It was the hasty flight of the decisionmakers that truly sealed the city's fate.

In the wee hours of September 9, Badoglio got wind of German attacks on the outskirts of the city. Fearing that the Nazis might capture them, he and the king, along with a motley assortment of other high-ranking Italians, fled Rome in a long convoy of vehicles and headed eastward toward the opposite coast. They eventually arrived in Pescara on the Adriatic, boarded a nearby corvette, and sailed to Brindisi, on the heel of Italy, arriving on September 10.

"If the Government remained in Rome," Badoglio later wrote in his defense, "its capture would be inevitable and the Germans would rapidly substitute a Fascist Government who would repudiate the armistice. This disaster must be avoided at all costs, for it would mean the complete ruin of Italy."[47]

Perhaps. But in his speedy flight from the capital, Badoglio did not give the Italian army specific orders regarding the German threat.[48] Without clear direction from the top, the Italian forces in and around Rome, and throughout the country, began to fall apart.

Although isolated units did fight bravely and soldiers and Roman citizens alike participated in individual acts of gut-wrenching heroism, most of the resistance ceased on September 10. On that day, Kesselring, who had threatened to raze the capital with the Luftwaffe, accepted the surrender of the Eternal City.

The precipitous flight of Badoglio and the king exposed the bankruptcy of their post-Mussolini strategy, which was based on avoiding risk and allowing the West to do all the fighting against the Germans. By dragging out the peace process for weeks and refusing to lend military support to the Allied invasion, the new Italian government had made it much easier for the Nazis to gain the upper hand in the aftermath of the surrender.*

■ ■ ■

On September 11, the day after Badoglio and company found safe harbor in Brindisi, the Italian people received a call to arms.[49] It came not from the king or his *Capo del Governo,* but from Italy's newfound friends, the Allies. In a joint statement, Churchill and Roosevelt exhorted the Italians to rise up against the hated Nazis:

"Now is the time for every Italian to strike his blow," the message urged. "The liberating armies of the Western World are coming to your rescue. We have very strong forces and are entering at many points. The German terror in Italy will not last long. They will be extirpated from your land and you, by helping in this great surge of liberation, will place yourselves once more among the true and long-proved friends of your country from whom you have been so wrongfully estranged. Take every chance you can. Strike hard and strike home."[50]

---

*In fairness, it can also be argued that the Allies made a misstep by clinging stubbornly to the unconditional surrender formula during the summer of 1943. This stance made it difficult to reach a speedy agreement with the Italians and may have undermined their incentive to provide maximum support.

Under the circumstances, the message fell flat. The Badoglio regime had already fled Rome, the Italian army was left without specific orders or firm leadership, and Allied soldiers were fighting for their very lives at that moment on the beaches of Salerno. The Nazis, on the other hand, were cementing their control over most of Italy at this time and securing the all-important communications networks, such as roads and railways, leading to the south.[51]

"Most of the northern Italian cities are in our hands," Goebbels was already reassuring himself on September 11. "Above all, contact with our troops in the south has been re-established and secured. Thus the main problems connected with our security in Italy have been solved."[52]

The Nazis were also well on their way to disarming Italian soldiers throughout the country either by negotiation or by force. Those stationed in foreign lands, such as France and the Balkans, also laid down their arms under the shadow of German bayonets. Most Italian troops—hundreds of thousands of them—were taken prisoner on Hitler's orders; Kesselring, whose forces were already stretched to the limit, allowed the soldiers in his sphere of command to return to their homes.*

There were a few bright spots for the new partnership between Italy and the Allies. The Italian navy, its reputation never having suffered the indignities leveled at Mussolini's army and air force, managed to score a victory of sorts by escaping the clutches of the Nazis. This was not through a dramatic feat of arms but rather the result of a theatrical deception on the part of the Italians. Admiral Raffaele De Courten, chief of the navy, had met with Kesselring on September 7, one day before the surrender.[53] He informed the gullible Kesselring that the Italians were preparing to take to the seas in a heroic effort to do battle with the enemy.

---

*By September 14, the Germans had disarmed fifty-six Italian divisions, and another twenty-nine were partially disarmed. They captured 700,000 Italian soldiers along with mountains of war equipment. Lamb, *War in Italy,* 21.

With tears in his eyes, De Courten informed the German commander that the navy would either destroy the Allied fleet or die trying. "Admiral de Courten explained that according to all the signs an Allied landing on the mainland was imminent," recalled General Siegfried Westphal, Kesselring's chief of staff, "and that the Italian Navy did not want to remain idle in harbour while this vital struggle was in progress. . . . Therefore the Navy's heaviest units would shortly make a surprise sortie from La Spezia to steam around the western cape of Sicily and seek an engagement with the British fleet, which would end either in victory or on the sea's bed. . . . The emotion with which de Courten made his statement, his tears and his invocation of the German blood that flowed in his veins from his mother's side, did not fail to make a deep impression."[54]

By the time the Nazis got wise to De Courten's ruse, most of the fleet had already escaped by sea, bound for the safe haven of Allied-controlled Malta. The fleet, which departed Genoa and La Spezia on the evening of September 8, did not have the luxury of air cover. The Luftwaffe managed to sink the *Roma* and damage the *Italia,* but the majority of vessels arrived in Malta on September 11 in one piece.[55] "The splendid prize of the whole fleet of what had been a victorious Power of the first rank thus fell into our hands," Churchill boasted.[56]

Angry about losing the fleet, the Nazis executed several Italian commanders at La Spezia who, having failed to get away, had scuttled their ships rather than hand them over to the Germans.[57] It was just one instance of the widespread brutality exhibited by the Nazis throughout the peninsula in the several days following Italy's surrender.

■ ■ ■

Now that the Germans had more or less stabilized the situation on the peninsula, they needed to figure out their next move: What was to be Hitler's strategy for defending Italy now that it had switched sides in the war? For Hitler and Rommel, the answer was fairly obvious. Kesselring was to evacuate southern Italy and hand over his divisions to Rommel, his rival, who was to assume command of all German forces in Italy and defend the northern enclave against the Western armies.

Just two days after the surrender, Goebbels repeated this refrain. "Naturally we shall not be able to hold southern Italy," he confided to his diary on September 10. "We must withdraw northward beyond Rome. We shall now establish ourselves in the defense line that the Fuehrer always envisaged; namely, the line of the [northern] Apennine Mountains. The Fuehrer hopes we can withdraw that far and at that point build up a first line of defense."[58]

But Kesselring, for one, was beginning to have his doubts about the wisdom of handing Italy over to the Allies as a gift, even the southern and central regions. True to form, he was inclined to view the situation in a much more favorable light. The defection of the Italian navy notwithstanding, he could barely believe his good fortune in the days after Avalanche. Despite the surrender of Italy and an Allied invasion, four-fifths of the country remained firmly in German hands.[59]

He was lucky, of course, that the Allies had not mounted an assault closer to Rome: Such a move would have instantly sent the Germans in southern Italy scurrying to the north in an effort to avoid being cut off and trapped. "An air landing on Rome and sea landing nearby, instead of at Salerno, would have automatically caused us to evacuate all the southern half of Italy," Kesselring later admitted.[60]

The choice of Salerno as the invasion point was decided primarily by the limitations of Allied air power and the desire to capture a major port—Naples—early in the campaign. The fighters based on Sicily had an effective combat radius of 180 miles, and this factor eliminated potential landing sites north of Salerno. Aircraft carriers might have changed this equation, but they were unavailable in sufficient quantity.[61] The Allies' obsession with air cover, which Kesselring had anticipated, helps to explain how the Nazis were able to predict a landing in the Salerno area.

If anyone had the right to feel vindicated by the events of September 8, that man was Adolf Hitler. It was Hitler, after all, who had predicted the Italian surrender for weeks on end, beginning on the night of July 25. He had argued about it with his subordinates. He had barked at the doubters among the Germans, he had bullied and cajoled them. And yet when the moment finally arrived, it came as a heavy blow.

Goebbels, who had joined him at the Wolf's Lair in the wake of the armistice, noted the depth of Hitler's reaction. "The Fuehrer anticipated Italian treason as something absolutely certain," Goebbels noted on September 10. "He was really the only one who firmly counted on it. And yet, when it actually happened, it upset him pretty badly. He hadn't thought it possible that this treachery would be committed in such a dishonorable manner."*[62] Upset indeed! Why, the Italian surrender was nothing less than a "gigantic example of swinishness," Hitler told Goebbels.[63]

Needless to say, Badoglio's double cross presented the Germans with a monumental PR dilemma. Italy's defection was bound to send shudders through the homeland as well as such Nazi satellite states as Hungary and Rumania, which had already been shaken by the fall of Mussolini. In light of these factors, Hitler could no longer maintain his media silence. After dodging the German people for months and ignoring the special pleading by Goebbels and Doenitz, the Fuehrer reluctantly took to the airwaves on September 10. In so doing, he tried to put a Nazi spin on the loss of Italy and minimize its impact at home and abroad.

"Freed from the heavy burden of expectation weighing on us for a long time," Hitler said in a sixteen-minute recorded speech, "I now consider that the moment has come again to address myself to the German people without having to resort to lies, either to myself or to the public. The collapse of Italy, which has now taken place, was an event that could have been anticipated for a long time." It could have been expected, Hitler explained, because there were

---

*The suspense had become almost unbearable for Hitler. On September 7, the day before the surrender announcement, he had decided to force the issue by giving Badoglio an ultimatum requiring him to explain his suspicious behavior or face the consequences. Hitler had intended to deliver this message on September 9.

"certain circles" in Italy that had been working for some time to undermine the Rome-Berlin alliance. "What these men had been aspiring to for years has now been achieved. The Italian leaders of state have gone over from the German Reich, ally of Italy, to the common enemy."[64]

Though the Duce's domestic foes had tried to undermine his Fascist regime as well as his relationship with Hitler, Germany, by way of contrast, had been a faithful friend of Italy and had repeatedly come to its aid during the war, notably in North Africa and the Balkans. Hitler had allowed Germany to make these sacrifices only because of his admiration for one man: Mussolini.

> The German Reich, and I as its Fuehrer, could only adopt this attitude because it was known that one of the most outstanding men of modern times was at the head of Italy, the greatest son of Italian soil since the collapse of the ancient empire. . . . His fall and the disgraceful insults to which he was subjected will be felt with the deepest shame by future generations of the Italian people. . . . I personally was seized with understandable sorrow at the unique historic injustice inflicted on this man, at the shameful treatment meted out to a man who for twenty years lived only for his people and who is now treated as a common criminal. I was and still am happy to describe this great and loyal man as my friend.[65]

The speech also included several warnings. One was aimed at Germans who contemplated a regime change in the Reich. "Hope of finding traitors here rests on complete ignorance of the character of the National Socialist State; a belief that they can bring about a July 25 in Germany rests on a fundamental illusion as to my personal position as well as about the attitude of my political collaborators and my field marshals, admirals and generals."[66]

The second warning was for Italy. "The measures decreed for the protection of German interests in the face of events in Italy are very hard. In so far as they affect Italy they are being applied according to plan and already with good results. The example of Yugoslavia's betrayal had given us in advance a salutary lesson and valuable experience."[67]

This was an ominous reference. As everyone knew, Hitler's Luftwaffe practically razed the capital of Yugoslavia (Belgrade) when that country's new leaders attempted to break free of the Nazis. About 17,000 civilians were killed during the Belgrade bombings alone.[68] Yugoslavia fell to the Germans within a matter of days.

13

A SIMPLE PLAN

We didn't have much time. The Allies had just invaded the Italian peninsula. Gen. Student wanted to mount the operation quickly. So I had my plan ready in a matter of hours.[1]

—Major Harold Mors on the Nazis' final
attempt to snatch Mussolini

THE SURPRISE ANNOUNCEMENT OF ITALY'S SURRENDER DID NOTHING to alter Hitler's plans to rescue Mussolini. If anything, the changed circumstances forced the Nazis to redouble their efforts. "Each day, indeed each hour of delay," Skorzeny recalled, "increased the danger of the Duce's being transferred to still another place of confinement. Then there was that other eventuality which we dreaded most: Suppose the prisoner were handed over to the Allies who had doubtless requested this."[2] Just for good measure, Himmler sent a telegram to Rome on September 9 reminding the would-be rescuers that the liberation of Mussolini was still a top priority, armistice or no armistice.

These were the days of violence and confusion in the Eternal City. At first, Student and his Second Parachute Division—which, along with the Third Panzergrenadier Division, was facing five Italian divisions in Rome—were too busy trying to subdue their former allies to contemplate a rescue of the Duce. "All considerations and preparations concerning the liberation of Mussolini were temporarily pushed into the background," Student remembered.[3]

On the day of Himmler's telegram, for instance, the paratroopers had carried out an operation of a different nature: a bold airborne assault on Italian army headquarters at Monterotondo, outside Rome. "I made an attempt to seize the Italian General Headquarters by dropping on it from the air," Student recalled. "This was only a partial success. While thirty generals and a hundred and fifty other officers were captured in one part of the headquarters, another part held out."[4] By Student's own admission, the Italians had put up a fierce resistance.[5]

But by September 10, the day on which Rome fell and the local situation began to stabilize, the Mussolini task force was already turning its attention back to the Gran Sasso, where they believed the dictator was being held.[6] The testimony of Leo Krutoff, Student's Italian-speaking medical officer, had helped confirm the location. Back on the morning of September 8, before the Axis powers came to blows, he had made an attempt to visit the Campo Imperatore to find out whether the Italians would allow German soldiers to recuperate there.

Krutoff, who knew nothing of Operation Oak, never made it to the hotel. In fact, as he later informed Student and Skorzeny, he ran into an Italian roadblock before reaching the lower cable car station near Assergi, the small village on the lower reaches of the mountain. He did manage to speak to a few locals from whom he learned that the carabinieri had taken over the hotel recently and stationed a couple of hundred men there. As Student later wrote: "Doubts were hardly possible any more."*[7]

■ ■ ■

On the evening of September 10, Student made up his mind to spring Mussolini from his lofty prison on the Gran Sasso a few days

---

*There are reports that Skorzeny and his men also tortured two Italian carabinieri officers to confirm that Mussolini was being held on the Gran Sasso. See Infield, 37; and McRaven, 198.

hence.[8] But how was he to accomplish this tricky feat? It would no doubt be a "very risky business," he thought.[9] The Campo Imperatore, after all, was situated on a stark plateau at an elevation of almost 7,000 feet. It was accessible only by way of the small cable car that traveled the 3,000 feet between the hotel and Assergi. (In 1943, there was no useable road connecting Assergi with the hotel as there is today, just a narrow mule track.)[10]

The most straightforward option involved sending an assault team up the slope of the mountain, but this plan was rejected for several reasons. A large number of soldiers would be required to surround the plateau to prevent the Italians from escaping with their prisoner at the last moment. Heavy German casualties could be expected. As Skorzeny later pointed out, it would be difficult for a large ground attack to achieve the all-important element of surprise. "Our trump ace should be total surprise," he wrote, "for, beyond all strategic considerations, we feared the carabinieri might have received orders to kill their prisoner rather than let him escape."[11]

A skydiving commando was also considered. But though Student's men were experts at paratrooper operations, there was no enthusiasm at Frascati for applying these methods to the Gran Sasso. For one thing, the troops might descend too rapidly in the thin atmosphere. Assuming they *did* land safely, the unpredictable wind gusts surrounding the plateau would probably scatter the soldiers over a wide area, making it difficult for them to organize themselves quickly for a concentrated attack against the hotel.

The only method that seemed at all feasible was a potentially hazardous glider landing. Using conventional aircraft was out of the question because there was not a proper airstrip on the Gran Sasso. But it was thought that a dozen or so troop-carrying gliders, which were able to land on almost any surface, might be able to swoop down onto the plateau more or less intact. The sheer implausibility of the idea was likely to provide just the sort of psychological shock necessary for a lightning assault.

"Our only solution, therefore," according to Skorzeny, "lay in the landing of several gliders. But was there any ground, close to the hotel, that would permit such a landing?"[12] Skorzeny believed that there was. During his reconnaissance mission over the Gran Sasso, he had noticed what appeared to be a small meadow adjacent to the building. With a little luck, he thought, it might be possible to land the gliders there.

The aerial photos were not much help. Skorzeny's plans to have them enlarged were foiled by the Allied bombing of Frascati, which destroyed the main photography facility. He eventually managed to have the pictures developed, but the prints were only four inches square and resembled a bad batch of vacation snapshots.[13] Yet, with a little squinting, one could discern the outlines of the meadow that Skorzeny had spied while dangling outside the Heinkel. After examining the photos, Student made a decision. "By looking at them it was clear that the undertaking, if at all possible, could only be executed using small gliders that were put to the test when taking Fort Eben Emael."[14]

This, of course, was a reference to the dramatic paratrooper mission targeting the Belgian stronghold of Eben Emael at the beginning of the war. By 1943, the operation was already the stuff of legend, having earned the highest admiration of military men around the world. It was General Student and his soldiers who had planned it and carried it out.

The general concept for the raid reportedly originated with Hitler, who in the fall of 1939 was brooding over his future plans to invade France.[15] These called for a fast-moving offensive through Holland and Belgium coupled with a surprise thrust through the Ardennes forest. But Eben Emael, a famous fort located on the Albert Canal, threatened to wreak havoc with his invasion. For the Germans to make speedy progress through Belgium, it was necessary for them to capture the three main bridges over the canal before the enemy had a chance to destroy them. The guns of Eben Emael, nestled snugly in the confines of this large and seemingly impregnable fortress, could quickly destroy the bridges in the event of a German attack.

Hitler reckoned that a conventional assault against the fort—which was situated on a 150-foot ridge and designed to withstand artillery shelling and aerial bombardment—would take hours or days and would not prevent the Belgian gun crews from bringing down the bridges before his soldiers had a chance to stop them.[16] The German dictator, who was generally enthusiastic about unorthodox ideas, believed that glider aircraft might provide the solution.

Though the idea of using gliders in combat may seem somewhat odd on its face, these types of planes possess several important advantages. Gliders, for instance, can land on almost any surface and are virtually silent. They also make it possible to accomplish the swift insertion of a small number of soldiers at a *specific* target behind enemy lines. An airborne drop, by way of contrast, tends to disperse men over a wider area, and this was especially true before the advent of high-tech parachutes.

In late 1939, Hitler presented his idea to General Student, who along with his staff officers then developed a more detailed plan.[17] Gliders had never been used in combat before—Eben Emael was to be their debut—but the forward-looking Luftwaffe already had a plane at the ready.[18] During the 1930s, the air force had commissioned a company called the German Institute for Gliding Research (DFS) to develop a military glider.[19] The result was the DFS 230, basically the modified form of a glider developed in the early 1930s to transport meteorological equipment. Aside from the pilot, the plane was designed to carry a maximum of nine men and their equipment.

Early on the morning of May 10, 1940—the day of Hitler's great offensive against the West—a small squadron of DFS 230 gliders appeared in the sky over Eben Emael.[20] Dodging antiaircraft fire, they landed hard on the grassy surface of the fort.[21] Small bands of Luftwaffe combat engineers then scrambled out of the half-wrecked planes and made a mad dash for the steel cupolas and concrete casemates enclosing the main guns, which were quickly put out of commission with shaped charges, another novelty at the time.[22]

The Belgian defenders were left stunned. Though Student's sixty-nine-man assault team had been outnumbered ten to one, it achieved complete tactical surprise and managed to accomplish its main objectives, namely, destroying the guns capable of taking out the canal bridges, within twenty minutes.[23] The Germans counted six men dead, the Belgians twenty-five.[24] Eben Emael subsequently went down in history as one of the most spectacular commando operations of all time. It also helped pave the way for a stunning German *Blitzkrieg* that defeated the combined armies of France and Britain in short order.

Of course, any similarities between Eben Emael and a possible raid on the Hotel Imperatore were superficial at best. For Eben Emael, for example, Student's paratroopers had rehearsed almost every aspect of the operation for months on end.[25] The Germans had also possessed good intelligence on the fort, including a set of blueprints, and knew the location of each of the guns that they were responsible for destroying.[26] Meticulous planning and numerous rehearsals conducted under real-life conditions were important factors in the success of the mission.

The Gran Sasso raid, on the other hand, would have to be an improvised affair out of necessity. There would be no time to rehearse the operation and iron out potential problems. The landing zone was relatively small—only four or five acres—especially when viewed in light of the unpredictable wind conditions on the mountain.*[27] Yet the glider pilots would be required to land successfully on their first, and only, attempt.

Detailed intelligence was also lacking. The Germans did not possess proper schematics of the hotel.[28] And even if they had acquired them, no one could say for sure in which part of the building Mussolini would be at the moment of the landings. What was more, the hotel's defenses were also a matter of speculation. A few well-placed machine guns on the perimeter of the resort could put a quick end to the mission, though the element of surprise would help to offset this possibility. The Nazis were also counting on the likelihood that the Italians would not fight to the death over the po-

---

*According to military writer and U.S. Navy Seal William H. McRaven, the landing area on the Gran Sasso was much smaller than that on the surface of Eben Emael, which was "massive" by comparison. McRaven, 70 (in an endnote).

litical corpse of the Duce—especially at a time when the Italian armed forces were in a state of collapse.

■ ■ ■

After considering the alternatives, General Student gave his final approval for a glider assault, which he scheduled for the morning of September 12. He later claimed that he had worked out many of the mission details himself and had assigned a paratrooper battalion under the command of Major Harold Mors to carry it out.[29] Other reports, however, suggest that Mors was the primary architect of the Gran Sasso raid.*[30]

At the tender age of thirty-two, Mors was already a seasoned officer. He had led airborne troops during the German invasion of the Low Countries and the successful, but costly, assault on the island of Crete in the Mediterranean.[31] "We didn't have much time," recalled Mors, who received the assignment on September 11, just one day before the raid.[32] "The Allies had just invaded the Italian peninsula [on September 9]. Gen. Student wanted to mount the operation quickly. So I had my plan ready in a matter of hours."[33]

It was to be a two-phase operation. At the heart of it was an airborne assault involving twelve DFS 230 gliders, the same type of planes used at Eben Emael, which would attempt to make a landing on the small plateau surrounding the Hotel Imperatore. "The air operation was the crucial part of the mission," Student recalled.[34]

Each glider would be filled to capacity. Assuming that everything went smoothly, the aircraft would be able to disembark 108 combat

---

*It should be noted that Skorzeny also claimed to have played a major role in the planning of the operation. In fact, Skorzeny and Radl both accused Student and his paratroopers of being reluctant to carry out a glider assault in the first place. According to the SS men, some of Student's officers predicted that such an attack would result in 80 percent casualties. Marco Patricelli, who wrote a detailed (Italian-language) study of the Gran Sasso raid and interviewed several of the surviving paratroopers, gives the lion's share of the credit to Mors.

soldiers, not counting the twelve pilots, who were also expected to lend a hand. But the gliders would not reach the target en masse. The commandos would arrive in small groups, each glider coming down one minute behind the next. It was during the landing sequence that the Germans would be most vulnerable to Italian defensive fire.

Lieutenant Baron Otto von Berlepsch was given command of the glider assault team, most of whose members would be drawn from the First Company of Mors's battalion.[35] In addition to this group of ninety paratroopers, Skorzeny persuaded Student to include himself and about seventeen of his Friedenthal commandos.

"Skorzeny asked Gen. Student if he could go along," recalled Mors. "Since Skorzeny's efforts had helped locate Mussolini, Student felt he couldn't say no. Then Skorzeny talked Student into letting him take about 15 of his own men along on the gliders. He could be persuasive. But Von Berlepsch was furious, having to leave behind 15 paratroopers."[36]

According to Student, the paratroopers were intended to be the primary strike force. "While von Berlepsch and his paratroopers were responsible for breaking a possible resistance and making sure the entire operation on the mountain goes smoothly," Student later wrote, "Skorzeny was to function as a police organ for the personal protection of the Duce. Besides, he would personally bring Mussolini to Germany afterwards."[37]

The second part of the operation would be conducted in the valley below the mountain. In a move designed to cover Berlepsch's rear, Mors and the rest of his battalion, as well as a dozen or so of Skorzeny's men, would travel overland to Assergi—cutting telephone and telegraph lines as they went—and occupy the lower cable car station.[38] It was the job of Mors and his men to prevent reinforcements from coming to the aid of the Italians on the Gran Sasso.[39]

The two phases of the mission—the airborne assault and the ground operation—were scheduled to take place at the same time.[40] "Major Mors himself was to lead most of his battalion by land to the valley station of the funicular in Assergi in a motorized column, occupy the station . . . and get in contact with the company that would have landed on the peak and support them in case of emergency. The most important assignment of Major Mors was to cover the coup de main of the company that landed on the Gran Sasso from a possible intervention by the Italians from Assergi. To make this possible, the arrival of the battalion at the valley station and the landing of the company on the mountain had to be simultaneous."[41]

■ ■ ■

The mission may have looked logical enough on paper, but no one knew how it would play out in real life. Even in a best-case scenario, the Germans who managed to land safely on the Gran Sasso would be outnumbered two to one by the two hundred or so Italians that Skorzeny believed were guarding Mussolini.[42] These odds would only grow worse if some of the gliders crashed into the mountain or went drastically off course.

The biggest wildcard, according to Student, a onetime glider pilot himself, was the "unknown and totally unpredictable wind currents of the high Abruzzi. Not even a small sport glider had ever flown over it."[43] To his mind, it was far from clear how a group of heavily loaded DFS 230s would fare under such conditions, though he believed it was a "challenge" worthy of the Luftwaffe pilots.[44]

The element of surprise was key. Student and Skorzeny both reckoned that it would take several minutes for the Italians to comprehend what was happening. This brief time interval was a window of opportunity for the aggressors. A new type of automatic rifle built especially for the paratroopers, the FG–42, would also help to even the odds should there be a firefight.[45]

Even as the Germans put the finishing touches to their plan, Skorzeny continued to worry about their chances of success. "We knew that they were pretty slim," he recalled. "First, no one could possibly guarantee that Mussolini was still in the hotel or that he would remain there until daybreak [on the day of the raid]. Second, it was not at all certain that we could overcome the Italian detachment quickly enough to prevent the Duce's execution."[46] The second concern was particularly troubling.

Then Radl, Skorzeny's deputy, had a brainstorm, or "brainwave," as they used to say at the time. "Suddenly Radl had an idea of genius: we should take a higher Italian officer with us!" Skorzeny remembered. "His mere presence would probably serve to create certain confusion in the minds of the carabinieri, a sort of hesitation which would prevent them from resisting immediately or from assassinating the Duce. This would help us to strike before they found time to collect themselves."[47]

It sounded like a good idea to Student, who approved it "immediately."[48] The Nazis eventually settled on an Italian carabinieri general named Fernando Soleti. Despite the collapse of the Axis, Soleti was contacted on September 11 and asked to rendezvous with the Germans early the next morning, the day of the raid.*[49] He was not told the real reason for the appointment.[50]

Two days after the Italian surrender, while the Nazis and the Allies were still fighting it out on the beaches of Salerno, Goebbels found himself pondering the fate of Mussolini. "The question still remains as to where the Duce is," Goebbels confided to his diary on September 10. "Nobody knows the answer. . . . We fear that he has already been handed over to the English and is on a British man-of-war."[51]

As it turned out, this was a wildly pessimistic assumption. Mussolini was not even close to being in Allied custody at that moment, though he probably should have been. The West, after all, had demanded that he eventually be turned over, and the Italians had assured Eisenhower that the dictator would be kept in a secure location until then.[52]

---

*According to Radl, Soleti confirmed to Herbert Kappler that Mussolini was on the Gran Sasso, at least as of September 8.

Eisenhower, for one, held some strong views on the Duce's future, according to Captain Harry Butcher, his naval aide. "Ike would like to be directed to try Mussolini himself," Butcher noted in his diary on September 6, 1943, "that onetime famous gentlemen being committed by the agreement to be delivered to the Allies. If Ike had a directive to try the dictator, he said this morning, he certainly would find him guilty and would take great pleasure in seeing him hanged. However, we concluded that any trial of Mussolini would be conducted on a 'high level'—with jurists from at least several of the United Nations."[53]

But the Italian duumvirate of the king and Badoglio did nothing to bring these grand plans to fruition. In fact, in their haste to flee Rome on September 9, the two men made no effort to take the Duce with them to Brindisi or to have him transferred to some other Allied safe haven, which would have prevented him from falling into German hands.*[54] As it happened, the royal convoy en route to Pescara had driven through the Abruzzi region not far from the Hotel Imperatore.[55]

The motives behind this failure to act remain murky. Perhaps Victor Emmanuel still felt a twinge of loyalty for his old *Capo del Governo,* whom he frankly admired (and whom he had given a promise of protection on July 25). It is also possible that the king and Badoglio—who were by no means certain that their escape to Brindisi would be successful—were worried that Hitler might hold them personally responsible if Mussolini ended up in an American brig to await execution.

Whatever the reasons, after September 8 life continued to go on more or less as usual at the Campo Imperatore, which was well

---

*According to the historian Denis Mack Smith, the Germans were not the only ones contemplating a rescue mission. During the chaotic days after the Italian surrender, there was a "not very serious plot" brewing among a group of Italian air force officers that involved rescuing Mussolini and flying him out of the country to safety. Denis Mack Smith, *Mussolini,* 300.

within the German occupation zone. Due to its elevation and isolated location, the hotel remained eerily undisturbed by the chaos
and violence that broke out all over Italy in the days following Operation Avalanche. Police Inspector Giuseppe Gueli, who was the
Duce's senior jailer on the mountain, felt it prudent to enhance his
security measures and set up a few machine guns outside the resort.[56] But in the absence of new orders, he decided merely to watch
and wait. The suspense began to intensify when word of Rome's
collapse reached the mountaintop.

When the Eternal City fell, Mussolini observed, "a strange atmosphere of uncertainty and expectation reigned on the Gran Sasso.
It was now known that the Government had fled, together with the
King. . . . The officials in charge of me seemed embarrassed, as if
faced with the performance of a particularly unwelcome task."[57]

But for the Duce, the most important revelation of this period
was of a profoundly personal nature. On the evening of September
10, while listening to Berlin radio, he heard something that caught
his attention.[58] It was not Hitler's speech of that same day, which he
apparently missed, but a brief news item about the Italian armistice
terms: "Allied General Headquarters have officially announced that
among the Armistice terms is included the handing over of Mussolini to the Allies."[59]

One of the Duce's guards quickly noted that this announcement
had been made earlier and that London had denied it. But other media outlets were also reporting on the West's determination to bring
Mussolini to justice. "According to trustworthy sources," reported
the French journalist known as "Pertinax" (Andre Geraud) in a
story carried in the New York Times on September 10, "the United
States and British Governments are determined to have Benito Mussolini put on trial at the earliest date. He is a prisoner of the Badoglio government, not having been allowed to escape, and can be
surrendered at any moment."[60]

There was truth to these reports. Though the Short Terms of the
Italian armistice, which were merely a temporary expedient, made

no mention of the Duce or his Fascist henchmen, the longer version did. Article 29 of the Long Terms stated: "Benito Mussolini, his Chief Fascist associates and all persons suspected of having committed war crimes or analogous offences whose names appear on lists to be communicated by the United Nations will forthwith be apprehended and surrendered into the hands of the United Nations."[61] (The contents of the Long Terms were officially kept secret until 1945.)[62]

When the Berlin radio report reached the Gran Sasso and Mussolini's ears on September 10, it led to one of the most dramatic (or melodramatic) incidents to take place during the Duce's confinement. Later that evening, Mussolini, vowing that he would never allow himself to be surrendered to the Allies, reportedly tried to slit his wrists with a Gillette razor blade.[63] It is not clear whether the Duce was really trying to commit suicide or was simply making a show of it.[64] But just to be on the safe side, Lieutenant Faiola removed all the razors and other sharp objects from the dictator's room.[65]

However, as he later admitted, Faiola believed that it was more likely that the Nazis would attempt to snatch Mussolini before he could be delivered to the West.[66] If this happened, Badoglio's standing orders remained in place: The Nazis were not to take Mussolini alive.[67]

14

FREEING MUSSOLINI

The plane gave a slight nosedive and there we were at the edge of the plateau. Swerving towards the left, the machine seesawed in the void. . . . I held my breath, awaiting the inevitable, horrible crash.[1]

—Skorzeny, *Skorzeny's Secret Missions*

FOR STUDENT AND SKORZENY, SEPTEMBER 12 WAS THE CULMINATION of six weeks of frantic searching. Despite the efforts of Italian Military Intelligence (SIM), they had managed to track their elusive quarry from Rome to the Pontine Islands in the Tyrrhenian Sea, from there to *Isola Maddalena* near Sardinia, and finally to the majestic heights of the Gran Sasso in central Italy. Along the way, they had received crucial assistance from Herbert Kappler and a host of others, some of whom were openly scornful of the enterprise. The Nazis had concocted no less than three schemes to "liberate" Mussolini during this period. On at least one occasion (Santo Stefano), Hitler himself had played an active role in devising the rescue operation.

Of course, much else had happened during this brief time. The fortunes of the Third Reich had visibly begun to unravel. For one thing, the Nazis had lost their strongest European ally, the Italians, and witnessed the first successful invasion of mainland Europe (though, on September 12, the success of that invasion was still in doubt). In Russia, Stalin's armies had pushed the Germans back on their heels all summer long, putting an end to Hitler's aspirations in the East. In Western Europe, the Anglo-Americans had launched mighty air attacks against Hamburg, Berlin, and other Axis targets.

"Nobody doubts any longer that this is a war to be or not to be," Goebbels solemnly confided to his diary on September 11, one day before the Gran Sasso raid. "The Eastern Front is causing the German people considerably greater worry now than in past weeks. The state of depression because of air raids has increased as a result of the most recent heavy attacks."[2] No one was more aware of this disturbing trend than Adolf Hitler. Isolated, and medicated, in the gloomy swamps of the Wolf's Lair, he may well have fantasized that the rescue of the Duce would be the first step in a new and revitalized version of the Axis—an Axis rearmed with the "miracle weapons" of German technology, such as ballistic missiles and jet airplanes.

On September 12, a Sunday, while the battle for Salerno was raging 140 miles south of Rome, the SS chief, Heinrich Himmler, sent another gratuitous telegram to the Eternal City reminding Student and Skorzeny that the Mussolini rescue operation was of the utmost importance.[3] Little did he know that the Germans' hastily conceived plan to snatch the Duce from the Hotel Imperatore seemed to be going awry even before it had begun.

On the eve of the assault, Skorzeny had been blindsided by a news bulletin that seemed to make the notion of Operation Oak irrelevant. According to the report, which he heard on Allied radio, Mussolini had already been surrendered to the West as part of the Italian armistice agreement. Supposedly, one of the Italian warships that had taken flight from the port of La Spezia had delivered him to Tunis in North Africa, where he was currently being held as a POW. Alarmed, the Germans did some mental calculations and determined that the Duce probably could not have arrived in Tunis so swiftly. They decided to ignore this revelation.

At the same time, a more troubling problem arose concerning the timing of the glider assault. According to the mission profile, the Nazis were scheduled to swoop down from the sky at 7:00 A.M., which meant that they would lift off from Pratica di Mare airport, located about twenty miles south of Rome, one hour earlier.[4] The gliders had a better chance of landing safely during the early morning hours when the air currents swirling around the mountaintop were relatively weak. The element of surprise was also involved: By attacking early in the morning, the Germans would be more likely to catch Mussolini's captors off guard and bleary-eyed.

However, on the evening of September 11, Major Mors informed Student that the operation would have to be postponed for several hours.[5] Mors wanted to be certain that he and his battalion would have enough time to reach the cable car station near Assergi at the same time the gliders began to descend on the hotel, as the plan called for.[6] Mors apparently wanted to have a margin for error just in case his progress was slowed by skirmishes with hostile Italian forces.[7] In response to Mors's request, Student reluctantly pushed Zero Hour back to 2:00 P.M., the glider takeoff set for 1:00 P.M.[8] During the early hours of September 12, Mors and his battalion left for Assergi in a motorized column, officially setting the rescue operation in motion.[9]

Student's decision was not taken lightly. It meant that the action on the mountain would now have to be carried out in broad daylight in the middle of the afternoon. "In the heat of midday," he reckoned, "all the difficulties . . . would only be more severe."[10] Even so, he was not willing to defer the rescue until the following day. "Mussolini could have been taken down from the Gran Sasso at any time and brought to one of the Adriatic ports and handed over to the Americans by sea. Therefore no time could be lost. The risks had to be taken and the flight had to be made under the especially tough conditions of midday."[11]

■ ■ ■

On the morning of the raid, General Fernando Soleti of the Italian carabinieri was also the cause of a few anxious moments. As mentioned earlier, Soleti was the key to Radl's last-minute scheme to baffle the Duce's captors and prevent them from firing on the Germans.

The Italian general had earlier agreed to a rendezvous with Radl that morning. But when the SS man arrived at the Ministry of the Interior in Rome at around 7:30 A.M., Soleti was nowhere to be found.[12]

He finally appeared at 9:00 A.M. and eventually agreed to accompany Radl to nearby Pratica di Mare.[13] There, General Student took Soleti aside and explained that the Germans were planning to rescue Mussolini later that same day.[14] Soleti's presence would be necessary during the operation, Student said, to avert a violent gun battle between former allies. The Italian gave his consent without much fuss, according to Radl, and the matter seemed to be settled.[15]

Only the gliders were still unaccounted for at this point. The twelve DFS 230s were scheduled to fly the eighty miles from Grosseto to Pratica di Mare early that morning.[16] But by 10:00 A.M. they had not yet shown up and no one seemed to know what had happened to them. Finally, about an hour later, the twelve gliders and their tug aircraft appeared in the skies over the airfield.[17] "It was high time," Student thought to himself.[18]

Though the DFS 230s were a welcome sight to the Germans, their arrival led to a rude awakening for General Soleti, who was eating breakfast with Radl in an airport building as the gliders broke free of their tugs and began to touch down.[19] Soleti could see the planes landing outside the window, but did not know what to make of them. According to Radl, General Student had not gone into great detail with the Italian about the particulars of the rescue operation.[20]

However, Soleti was curious about the machines and, assuming that Radl was a paratrooper (Skorzeny and his Friedenthalers were all disguised as paratroopers), he asked the SS man whether he had done much flying in them.

"Yes, very often, Herr General," said Radl disingenuously, trying to soften the blow in advance. "It makes an extremely comfortable impression, not only because there's no engine noise, which makes it difficult to talk, but also because one in fact feels like a bird-man; *uomouccello*!"[21]

"Really, what are these machines for?"[22]

Radl braced himself. "Simple, Herr General," he said. "Later we will take off in these gliders and land on the massif of Gran Sasso and free the Duce."[23]

Soleti smiled: He thought that Radl was making a joke.[24] Once he realized that this was not so, and that he was being asked to participate in some sort of ill-conceived airborne operation, Soleti became physically unwell and a doctor was summoned.[25] Later, he made a desperate appeal to General Student and Herbert Kappler, but to no avail.[26] He soon realized that the Germans would not take no for an answer. According to Skorzeny, he and General Student were prepared to bring Soleti by force if necessary "in order to avoid a bloodbath."[27] The Italian general was kept under guard thereafter.[28]

■ ■ ■

Shortly after the gliders landed, General Student gave a briefing for the newly arrived pilots and selected paratrooper officers of Lieutenant Baron Otto von Berlepsch's company in an office on the grounds of the airfield.[29] Also present were Berlepsch, Langguth (Student's intelligence officer), Skorzeny, and Radl; Major Mors and his battalion were already en route to Assergi.[30] Most of the men in the room were naturally surprised to learn the nature of the special mission they would be executing a few hours hence.[31] Indeed, security concerns had prevented them from being told anything about it beforehand.

"The entire liberation operation was based on the element of surprise," Student remembered telling them.[32] The shock value of the raid would be great.[33] The main job of the glider pilots was simply to put Berlepsch and his paratroopers safely on the ground—they would take care of the rest.[34] It was regrettable that the pilots would be required to make their landings in the middle of the afternoon, when the wind currents were believed to be stronger, but this could not be helped.[35]

He also cautioned them about the lack of up-to-date intelligence. There was no guarantee, he said, that Mussolini was still on the mountain.[36] On the other hand, Italian morale was believed to be low, especially in light of the collapse of the country's armed forces.[37] In addition, the Germans were bringing along an Italian general named Soleti, whose presence might serve to defuse the situation.[38]

When he had finished his briefing, General Student left Pratica di Mare and returned to his HQ at Frascati.[39] Langguth and Skorzeny then offered the men additional details with the aid of maps and drawings.[40] The first and perhaps most dangerous phase of their mission, the flyers learned, involved landing the twelve DFS 230 gliders in the relatively small clearing around the Hotel Imperatore.

As the pilots huddled around the four-inch-square reconnaissance photos, they began to sense the challenge that lay before them. The plateau was surrounded on all sides by deep chasms and higher mountain slopes: Overshooting one's mark or getting swept off course by a strong gust of wind could easily result in catastrophe. The detailed features of the landing zone were also difficult to see clearly because of the size and poor quality of the snapshots. It was particularly hard to discern the possible slope of the ground.[41]

But landing was not the only worry. Captain Langguth pointed out that the pilots might face obstacles even before reaching the target. He was particularly concerned about a mountain ridge east of Tivoli that rose to a height of 4,265 feet.[42] This was apparently the first significant ridge they would encounter during the flight, and Langguth was not certain whether the gliders and their tugs would be able to gain enough altitude by that time to clear this hurdle.[43]

But it was not a serious problem as far as Langguth was concerned. If the altitude of the glider convoy was in doubt, the lead plane, which he would be flying, could simply perform a horizontal 360-degree turn.[44] This involved banking to one side, gaining sufficient height while flying a broad loop, then returning to the original flight path. The rest of the convoy would be required to follow suit, repeating the same maneuver. (It is not clear whether Langguth mentioned this loop maneuver during the briefing.)

■ ■ ■

According to the plan, each glider would carry nine combat troops in addition to the pilot and would be towed to the Gran Sasso by an engine-powered Henschel aircraft.[45] (The tugs were probably Hs 126s; these single-engine planes were doing a lot of glider towing at this time in the war.)[46] Once the gliders had reached the mountain, the 131-foot-long cable towlines would be released and the planes would aim for their designated landing points near the hotel.[47] If everything went smoothly, the gliders would land at a rate of one per minute in a specified order, unloading a total of 120 soldiers.[48]

Lieutenant Berlepsch was in command of the assault team.*[49] The forces under him—a mixed bag of paratroopers and Frieden-thalers (SS)—were divided into twelve glider groups.[50] Though no one knew it at the time, the ostensible ordering of the first few gliders—coupled with an in-flight surprise—was destined to spark a bitter controversy that lasted for decades.

Captain Langguth, who had taken part in the September 8 recon-naissance flight and was therefore familiar with the route, was chosen to fly the leading Henschel tug.[51] Berlepsch and eight of his para-troopers were to ride in the glider attached to Langguth's plane.[52] This tug-and-glider combination comprised the first "chain." Skor-zeny and the reluctant General Soleti would fly in the DFS 230 of the second chain, accompanied by seven SS commandos from Skorzeny's Friedenthal Battalion.[53] Radl and eight more of Skorzeny's SS men were assigned to the glider of the third chain.

The rest of the gliders would be filled with Berlepsch's para-troopers. These troops would provide general support for the assault and also carry out specialized assignments. One glider squad, for in-stance, was responsible for occupying the upper cable car station (as

---

*The command of the glider assault team is another matter of dispute between Skorzeny and the paratroopers. Student and Mors later maintained that Berlepsch was designated as the commander on the mountain. According to Skorzeny, he and Berlepsch had a sort of joint command, Skorzeny assuming control of the attackers until such time as he entered the hotel, after which the command fell to Berlepsch.

opposed to the lower) and securing an underground tunnel that connected the station with the hotel.

Though the assault teams were bringing along plenty of fire-power—FG–42 paratrooper rifles, machine guns, and light mortars—they had no intention of using it if they could avoid doing so.[54] It was hoped that the frightening nature of their lightning attack would be sufficient to shock the Duce's guards into submission without the need for a bloody clash.[55]

Skorzeny, for his part, later claimed to have learned an important lesson from a British commando assault carried out against Rommel's headquarters in North Africa earlier in the war. During this misadventure, the British inadvertently set off a violent fiasco by firing their guns in the early stages of the operation, which immediately triggered return fire and created a situation that they were unable to control.

"After studying this action," Skorzeny explained, "I made up my mind to instruct the soldiers of my special unit to shoot only when it was an absolute necessity. . . . I found an effective, proven means of preventing my soldiers from firing: namely to go in first and not fire myself."[56]

■ ■ ■

By 12:30 P.M., the Germans were preparing to board the gliders and tow aircraft. But as they began to do so, they were frozen in their tracks by the shrill sound of an air raid siren. Suddenly, a group of enemy aircraft, twin-engine Mitchells, appeared in the skies above their heads and began dropping bombs on the airport.[57] This was not a clever preemptive strike on the part of the Allies, who apparently knew nothing of the rescue scheduled for that day, but rather sheer bad luck. The Germans dashed for cover in the bushes and trees on the outskirts of the airfield as the sound of explosions and AA guns filled the air.[58]

"While we scattered for shelter," Skorzeny recalled, "I thought bitterly that this spelled the end of the magnificent operation we had devised. What hellish bad luck it was to suffer such a mishap at the last moment!"[59] Once the danger had passed, they slowly emerged again to survey the compound. Miraculously, none of the gliders had been hit and the airfield had sustained only minor damage.[60] They decided to proceed as planned.

No sooner had this crisis passed than there was another eruption of a different sort near Skorzeny's DFS 230. General Soleti was at the center of it. He was apparently making one last attempt to avoid the inevitable. "I don't want any part of this!" he was shouting. "This is suicide!"[61] According to Radl and General Student, Soleti made an attempt to shoot himself before being subdued and bundled into Skorzeny's glider by a couple of SS men.[62] It should be noted that Soleti was not the only one feeling uneasy. Radl later admitted that he and another Friedenthaler were having trouble controlling their bladders while waiting to board the planes.[63]

It is not hard to understand their anxiety. In the eyes of the uninitiated, the rudimentary design of the DFS 230 did not inspire confidence. Being composed primarily of tubular steel rods surrounded by a fabric skin, the plane had a flimsy feel to it.[64] Though it had a length of thirty-seven feet and a wingspan of seventy-two feet, the aircraft weighed less than one ton when empty.[65] The DFS 230's lightweight construction made it particularly vulnerable to enemy fire.[66] To help offset the danger of being shot out of the sky, these gliders often came equipped with machine guns that could be used to keep hostile ground forces in check during, and after, combat landings.[67] But on this day, the Germans were not planning to fire these guns unless they had to.[68]

Once it was fully loaded on the afternoon of September 12, each DFS 230 was filled to capacity and therefore must have been close to its maximum weight allowance, which was a little more than 4,600 pounds.[69] There was not much wiggle room on the inside. The Germans had to straddle a long bench that ran down the center of the interior and place their equipment wherever they could find the space.[70] After takeoff, each glider was supposed to jettison its wheels (two-wheel dolly) in preparation for a landing on the single skid attached to the undercarriage.[71] For this mission, the Germans had wrapped barbed wire around the skids to create a source of friction during the landings.[72] A parachute pack beneath the rear fuselage could also be used to slow the craft.[73]

At 1:00 P.M.—right on schedule—the Henschel tugs and their gliders began lifting off from Pratica di Mare.[74] At the head of the pack was Captain Langguth, who was flying in the lead chain.[75] Skorzeny and Soleti flew in the glider of the second chain.[76] "As for the Italian general," Skorzeny later wrote, "I took him with me in the . . . glider and placed him exactly between my legs astride the narrow beam we sat on, squeezed together like sardines. We had barely enough space to park our weapons."[77]

Once Langguth was in the air, he began to guide the unwieldy convoy to the northeast in the direction of the Hotel Imperatore, seventy-five miles from Rome.[78] The normal towing speed for a DFS 230 was about 112 miles per hour, but that could be increased to 130 miles per hour if necessary.[79]

Like the other gliders, Skorzeny's DFS 230 was enveloped in the brilliant sunshine of the early afternoon. As the temperature increased inside the cabin, he noticed that several of his men were feeling the effects of airsickness. Soleti, a former cavalry officer, was faring no better.[80] "A stifling heat filled our transport glider," Skorzeny recalled. "The Italian general was turning white about the gills; a while later, his complexion was as gray-green as his uniform."[81] One of the SS commandos in Radl's glider, which was in the chain behind Skorzeny's, had vomited inside the aircraft, filling the cabin with a sickening smell.[82]

Not long after taking off, the head of the convoy began to approach the 4,265-foot mountain ridge east of Tivoli. This was the potential trouble spot that had worried Langguth. Even now, he was not sure whether all the glider chains would be able to overfly this obstacle, so he made a fateful decision: He decided to swing the entire convoy around in a circle to gain sufficient altitude and ensure the safety of the troops.[83] He therefore banked his Henschel to one side and began to fly a broad, horizontal loop, dragging Berlepsch and his glider with him.[84]

There was only one problem. When Langguth glanced outside his window, he was horrified to discover that none of the other glider chains were following suit.[85] Instead, the decapitated column continued flying straight over the ridge, unscathed, and onward to the target. "The order of the unit was now changed," General Student noted in retrospect. "The chain with Skorzeny was now first."[86]

According to Skorzeny, the cause of this misunderstanding was a huge bank of clouds in the area over Tivoli, which had obscured Langguth's sudden change of plans.[87] When Skorzeny's chain emerged from the mist, its pilots could find no sign of Langguth, who seemed to have vanished into thin air. There being no radio contact between the various chains compounded the mix-up.[88] Cut off from the rest of the assault squadron, Langguth was unable to warn the other pilots that he and Berlepsch had taken a detour. (Student later claimed that the pilots of Skorzeny's chain simply failed to understand the significance of Langguth's course change.)[89]

In any event, the convoy was now flying blind—and without its commander. When the pilot of Skorzeny's glider, a young lieutenant named Elimar Meyer, shot a glance in the direction of the cabin and asked what they should do, Skorzeny shouted, "We're taking over the lead!"[90]

He could not get a clear view of the ground through the small plastic windows, which were dirty and scratched, so he took out a knife and cut several slits in the canvas fuselage.[91] "I decided that the primitive structure of these gliders possessed certain advantages," he remembered.[92] Using various landmarks and geographical features, he was able to keep the convoy on track by giving instructions to Meyer, who then relayed the necessary information to the pilot of the glider's Henschel tug.[93]

A little less than one hour into the flight, Skorzeny looked down and spotted the small town of L'Aquila, the provincial capital of the Abruzzi region.[94] This was an indicator that the target was not far off. Soon afterward, he could make out a small dust storm surrounding the trucks of Major Mors's column.[95] They had already passed Assergi and were making their way along the winding road that led to the cable car station.[96] The timing was nearly perfect: The two phases of the operation would be carried out simultaneously as planned.[97]

Skorzeny could now see the Hotel Imperatore beneath his DFS 230, which was flying at an altitude of approximately 9,843 feet.[98] No longer in need of the tug plane, Meyer released the tow cable and allowed the glider to descend slowly toward the 7,000-foot-high plateau. He flew the plane in wide circles as Skorzeny surveyed the ground below. The latter soon spied a small clearing that had been designated as one of the landing zones.

This was the so-called "meadow" that Skorzeny had seen during his September 8 reconnaissance flight. He had never seen it up close before, and the sight was enough to sicken him. "I felt we were in for it now," Skorzeny recalled, "because the 'gently sloping meadow' was, in point of fact, a steep, indeed precipitous abyss. Triangular in shape, it was much like the platform for a ski jump."[99] It was also strewn with rocks and boulders—features that had not shown up well on the aerial snapshots.[100]

Pilot Meyer turned to look at Skorzeny, as if asking him what he should do. For a moment or two Skorzeny did not have an answer. He had to make a split-second decision: Should he abort the mission entirely, or roll the dice and pray that the Luftwaffe pilots could find a way to put the planes on the ground without killing the whole lot of them?

"Steep approach!" Skorzeny finally shouted, telling the pilot to land as close as possible to the hotel.[101] In that moment he had committed himself and the other gliders flying behind him. He knew that they would follow his lead and descend through the thin air into an uncertain fate. Radl was watching from his own glider as Skorzeny's began to dive. "The blood freezes in my veins," he remembered. "I'm thinking he's going to crash."[102]

Skorzeny's glider came down in a hurry. "The whirring of the wind increased and rose to a howl as we approached the ground," he recalled. "I saw Lieutenant Meier [sic] loose the parachute brake. There was a violent jolt, a sound of something cracking and shattering. Instinctively I closed my eyes. Then I felt that we had touched earth and, after a final spasm, the glider stood its ground, stock still."[103]

Miraculously, the damaged glider, tilting to one side on its skid, had come to rest about fifty feet from the corner of the hotel (the rear corner on the hotel's right shoulder).[104] It had run over numerous rocks and debris, but these obstacles had served to prevent the craft from overshooting its target.

■ ■ ■

Sitting by a window in the Campo Imperatore, Benito Mussolini was idling away another uneventful afternoon on the mountain when Skorzeny's DFS 230 suddenly fell to earth. "It was exactly 2:00 P.M.," he later remembered, "and I was sitting by the open window with my arms folded when a glider landed a hundred yards from the building. . . . The alarm was sounded. . . . In the meantime, Lieutenant Faiola burst into my room and threatened me: 'Shut the window and don't move.'"[105]

Though a bit shaken up, the SS commandos immediately began to pour out of the open hatch of the glider, the door of which had been conveniently torn off its hinges during landing.[106] Skorzeny followed close behind them with gun in hand.[107] Soleti was also swept up in the current. When he exited the glider, he began shouting in Italian, "Don't shoot, don't shoot!"*[108]

As Skorzeny dashed toward the back of the hotel, he encountered a dazed-looking Italian guard who stood motionless, apparently paralyzed by the spectacle. Skorzeny simply shouted *"Mani in Alto!"* (Hands up!) and rushed toward the first door he saw.[109] He burst into a room and found a lone soldier working the dials of a radio transmitter. Skorzeny kicked the chair out from under him,

---

*The manager of the Hotel Imperatore, who was there at the time, claimed that Soleti had a gun pressed against his ribs.

knocking the man to the floor. He put the radio out of commission by smashing it with the butt of his submachine gun, conscious that any firing on his part was likely to spark a battle.

The hotel had now been breached—or so it seemed. Once inside the radio room, Skorzeny looked for an entrance into the rest of the building, but found none. The room was a dead-end. He hurried back outside and began scanning the rear of the building, which was shaped like a semicircle, but he could see no other doors. The pre-operation intelligence was apparently so lacking that he had no way of knowing where all the entrances were located.

Skorzeny ran all the way around the left shoulder of the building and had to scamper over a wall to reach the ground in front of the hotel. The main entrance was now in view, though it was still some distance away. He looked up and saw a face at a window.[110] It was the Duce.

Mussolini was looking down on the Germans from his suite. "At the head of this group was Skorzeny," he remembered. "The Carabinieri had already got their guns at the ready when I noticed an Italian officer among Skorzeny's group whom, on approaching nearer, I recognised as General Soleti, of the Metropolitan Police Corps."[111] He began shouting, "Can't you see? There is an Italian general there. Don't fire! Everything is all right."[112]

Skorzeny could hardly believe it. The man that he had been chasing for weeks was alive and tantalizingly close to being in his grasp. All the same, he believed that Mussolini would be safer out of the line of fire. "Duce, get away from the window!" Skorzeny shouted.[113]

Meanwhile, Radl, whose glider had landed about three hundred feet in front of the hotel, was beginning to run toward the main entrance with his squad.[114] He could see Skorzeny and several of his men moving along the front of the building.[115] General Soleti was with them.[116] One of Radl's commandos had broken an ankle on the uneven ground and was doing his best to crawl behind the others.

When Skorzeny reached the main entrance, he found himself face-to-face with two Italian machine-gun emplacements. He and several of his Friedenthal men knocked the guns aside and bullied the crew out of the way. Shouts of *"Mani in Alto!"* permeated the air as Skorzeny made a beeline for the front door. Italian carabinieri were running this way and that in a state of near panic. "I pushed against the carabinieri who were bunched up in front of the entrance and fought my way against the stream in a not too gentle fashion. I had seen the Duce on the second floor to the right."[117] He bounded up a nearby staircase and burst through a door.

"The occupant of the room was Benito Mussolini," Skorzeny remembered, "flanked by two Italian officers whom I lined up against the wall."[118] Only three or four minutes had elapsed since Skorzeny had come crashing down from the sky.[119] Another Friedenthaler from Skorzeny's glider, a Lieutenant Schwerdt, followed Skorzeny into the room and quickly led the officers into the hallway. Two more Germans suddenly appeared at the window, having climbed up the lightning rod on the exterior of the building.[120] So far, not a shot had been fired.[121]

Skorzeny looked out the window and saw Radl and his team in front of the hotel. "Everything in order here!" Skorzeny yelled to Radl. "Secure below!"[122]

■ ■ ■

While all this was going on, more DFS 230s were dropping out of the sky from almost every direction and skidding to a halt in the small field around the Campo Imperatore. Several of the gliders literally appeared out of nowhere from the center of low-lying clouds—surely a frightening sight—before making their landings and disgorging small squads of German paratroopers.[123] Some of these soldiers began to take up positions around the outside of the building. Others stormed the upper cable car station and the underground passage between the station and the hotel. Lieutenant Berlepsch was among the new arrivals (apparently his glider chain had swung round and rejoined the convoy).[124]

Most of the gliders managed to land safely, but one of them was not so fortunate.* "Next, suddenly," Skorzeny remembered, "I saw Glider 8, caught in a gust; to my horror it took off from its plane while the plane was still circling, and plummeted like a stone to crash into bits on a heap of rubble."[125] Radl, who by this time had joined Skorzeny in Mussolini's suite, looked out the window and saw survivors crawling on the ground near the downed glider.

Skorzeny then heard the sound of shots being fired in the distance.**[126] Worried that the Italians were beginning to recover from their paralysis, he stepped into the hallway on the second floor and demanded to speak to someone in charge. "The carabinieri now had to be disarmed as quickly as possible."[127] Within minutes, the Italians formally surrendered the Hotel Imperatore, putting an official end to the raid.

With two of his men guarding the door, Skorzeny took advantage of the brief respite to say a few words to Mussolini.

"Duce," he said dramatically, "the Führer has sent me to set you free."[128]

Mussolini, who was never one to overlook an historic moment, replied by saying, "I knew my friend Adolf Hitler would not abandon me."[129]

Overall, the Gran Sasso raid had been carried off in spectacular fashion.*** Casualties had been minimal. The ten paratroopers in the glider that had crashed were taken to the hotel and treated by German and Italian medics.[130] Their injuries were not life-threatening.[131]

----

*The number of gliders that actually landed on the plateau is uncertain. According to Skorzeny, only eight did so. The others, he claimed, had either failed to leave Pratica or had dropped out while in flight.

**At some point during the raid, a nervous paratrooper apparently fired off a few rounds. These may have been the shots that Skorzeny heard.

***It should be noted that eyewitness accounts of the raid vary in some respects. For a slightly different version of events, see the hotel manager's account in Iurato and Antonelli, "With Mussolini at the Campo Imperatore," 250–253.

"We had undoubtedly been extremely lucky," Skorzeny recollected.[132] At the cable car station in the valley, skirmishes between German and Italian troops had resulted in several minor casualties among the latter.*[133] But both ends of the cable car were now in German hands and they were operable.

The dramatic glider landings and the presence of General Soleti had no doubt come as a great surprise to the Italians and may very well have helped to undermine any thoughts of resistance. But there was another factor at work of which the Germans had no knowledge. Earlier that afternoon at about 1:30 P.M.—just half an hour before the arrival of the first glider—a mysterious telegram was sent from German-occupied Rome to Police Inspector Giuseppe Gueli, Mussolini's chief jailer on the mountain: "Recommend to Inspector General Gueli maximum prudence."[134] It was signed by Carmine Senise, Badoglio's chief of police.[135]

It was a puzzling and cryptic message, and its meaning has never been fully explained. It is possible that Badoglio and other Italians in high places, fearing German reprisals of one sort or another, were reluctant to interfere with Hitler's plans to rescue the Duce. In any event, the telegram's air of caution provided Gueli with the "out" he was looking for. Shortly after Skorzeny's glider landed, Gueli reportedly gave the order not to open fire on the Germans.[136] He later explained to Lieutenant Faiola, another of Mussolini's captors, that the Senise telegram gave them the authority to surrender the Duce to the Nazis.[137]

The speedy submission of the Italians did nothing to detract from the performance of the Luftwaffe glider pilots. "All but one of the gliders landed smoothly," Student later wrote.

> Considering the extremely difficult terrain it was quite a special accomplishment. The pilots released the tug ropes at an altitude

---

*According to the Italian writer Marco Patricelli, two of the Italians injured in the valley died of their wounds. See Patricelli, 90–91.

of 3,000m [9,843 feet]. While they were gliding, the sight of the hotel was sometimes obscured by cumulus clouds. Only as they were almost right above the destination were they able to realize that one of the two places to land, determined with the help of the aerial pictures, was a steep slope. The pilots who were supposed to land there tore their gliders around and landed on a tiny surface close by. One of the gliders was forced to land on a spot where no smooth landing was possible and crashed. And still, the pilot was able to land in a way that all the passengers, though more or less wounded, stayed alive.[138]

■ ■ ■

By mid-afternoon, Skorzeny and the paratroopers on the Gran Sasso were congratulating themselves on the success of their mission, which was practically finished. All that remained was to transport Mussolini back to Pratica di Mare airfield and put him on a plane bound for Germany. But in this seemingly minor detail arose one of the most hair-raising moments in the story of Operation Oak.

For reasons that are not entirely clear, the Germans rejected the most obvious option—namely, to send the Duce down to the valley via the cable car and then onward to Rome under the protection of Major Mors's battalion. Skorzeny later claimed that traveling overland with Mussolini would have been too risky, presumably because of the possibility that Italian troops in the area might stage some sort of ambush.[139] It is also conceivable, though unlikely, that the Germans were fearful of interference on the part of angry civilians who were hostile to the Duce.[140]

Before the raid, General Student had decided that Mussolini was to be flown back to Pratica di Mare in a Fieseler 156 *Storch* (Stork) aircraft.[141] The Stork was a lightweight (one-ton), slow-moving two-seater that could take off and land in tight spaces. Its long, stalk-like landing gear featured heavy-duty shock absorbers that allowed the plane to hit the ground fairly hard during touchdown. The Stork was also known to have some unusual properties. Under the right wind conditions, this gravity-defying aircraft could almost hover in mid-air like a helicopter.[142] According to Student's plan, a second Stork would be used to transport Skorzeny, who would then rendezvous with the Duce at Pratica and escort him to Germany.[143]

Captain Heinrich Gerlach, General Student's personal pilot, was given the job of chauffeuring Mussolini. (Gerlach was the pilot who flew Student and Skorzeny from the Wolf's Lair to Rome on the morning of July 27, two days after the Italian coup.) On the day of the raid, while Skorzeny was bounding into the Campo Imperatore and the gliders were diving through the clouds, Gerlach was flying circles over the mountaintop. Once the Duce had been freed and the hotel secured—the Germans hung sheets out of the windows to signal their success—Gerlach was faced with a decision: He could attempt to land his Stork on the plateau near the hotel as the gliders had done, or he could land in the valley below. A skilled pilot, Gerlach chose the former option "in spite of the obvious difficulties" (as Student put it).[144]

To everyone's amazement, the thirty-year-old Gerlach landed the Stork almost perfectly, making use of a headwind and bringing the plane down on an incline to help decelerate the craft.[145] But this feat was overshadowed shortly thereafter when Skorzeny dropped an unexpected bombshell. He told the flyer that he, Skorzeny, had decided to accompany Gerlach and Mussolini during their journey to Rome. Skorzeny's Stork had landed in the valley near the lower cable car station, but had damaged its undercarriage in the process.[146]

Gerlach was flabbergasted by the request. The mountainous terrain and the thin air would make the takeoff tricky enough without the added burden of Skorzeny's stocky, six-foot-four-inch frame. The stunned pilot flat-out refused to do it.

Skorzeny later tried to justify his seemingly absurd demand. "Suppose the take-off resulted in a catastrophe," Skorzeny reasoned, "my supreme consolation could only be to blow out my brains. How could I ever face Hitler to announce that my mission had succeeded but that Mussolini had died shortly after being freed? And as there remained no other possibility of conveying the Duce securely to

Rome, I preferred to share the dangers of this flight, though my presence in the plane could not but increase them."*[147]

Needless to say, this was a somewhat paradoxical position. But Skorzeny could be persuasive when he needed to be, and eventually Gerlach acquiesced, adding angrily that if anything went wrong during takeoff it was not his responsibility. "In spite of huge doubts," Student later wrote, "Gerlach finally let himself be talked round and agreed. Then Gerlach and Skorzeny together convinced Mussolini."[148]

The Duce, himself a pilot, showed no enthusiasm for the Stork flight—with or without Skorzeny—but ultimately consented to it.[149] All he asked was that he be allowed to return to Rocca delle Caminate, his country estate in the Romagna.[150] As was seen earlier, he had made the same request to Badoglio shortly after being arrested. But again Mussolini was to be denied. Skorzeny had orders to take the ex-dictator straight to Germany after a brief layover at Pratica, where the two men would change planes. Skorzeny sweetened the pill by informing him that his wife and their two teenage children were already en route to Munich. They had been "liberated" from Rocca delle Caminate that same afternoon by Skorzeny's SS commandos.

■ ■ ■

When the Duce exited the Hotel Imperatore, he was introduced to Major Mors, who had arrived in the cable car. Technically, Mors was in charge of the entire rescue operation.[151] "He was unshaven and looked ill," Mors remembered. "He said he was glad that it was the Germans who rescued him and not the English. He told us not to shoot anybody."[152] The Germans eventually let most of the Italian soldiers go free.

Mussolini then found himself staring into the lens of a whirring movie camera. The propaganda-savvy Germans had brought along

*In contrast to General Student's account, Skorzeny claimed that the Germans had discussed three possible plans for bringing Mussolini back to Rome. According to Skorzeny, flying the Duce off the mountain was the third, and least desirable, option.

a cameraman, by way of the cable car, to document for posterity the triumphant scene on the Gran Sasso.[153] In the newsreel footage released afterward, the Duce could be seen standing in front of the hotel wearing a dark overcoat, which was too big for him, and black felt hat, flanked by a dense crowd of smiling German soldiers.[154] Mussolini himself looked tired and wore a faint smile.

He then walked across the windy plateau and stepped into the Stork. As he strode toward the plane, the German soldiers, as well as some of the Italian carabinieri, raised their arms in the Fascist salute and chanted "Duce!"[155] Mussolini took his place in the second seat, right behind the cockpit. Skorzeny wedged himself into the luggage space behind the Duce. It was a tight squeeze.

At 3:00 P.M. or so they were ready to depart.[156] It was to be an aircraft-carrier-style takeoff: The improvised "runway" was just a downward slope about two hundred yards long, and at the end of it was a deep chasm.[157] Gerlach applied full power to the single 240-horsepower engine of the Stork, but the machine did not budge.[158] On the pilot's instructions, some German soldiers were holding on to it so that Gerlach could build the rpms.[159] Finally, at his signal, the men let go of the Stork and it sprang down the hill to the cheers of the soldiers. The aircraft was jostled roughly as it rolled over half-buried stones that could not be removed.[160]

About two-thirds of the way down the slope, a narrow ditch ran directly across the Stork's path. At the last moment, Gerlach yanked back on the stick and the plane rose a few inches, tipping slightly to the left before slamming back onto the ground. "The left wheel of the landing gear struck the soil violently once again," wrote Skorzeny, whose two hands were gripping the steel frame. "The plane gave a slight nosedive and there we were at the edge of the plateau. Swerving towards the left, the machine seesawed in the void. I closed my eyes. All my efforts had been in vain! I held my breath, awaiting the inevitable, horrible crash."[161]

"There was still some shouting," Mussolini remembered of the final moments of takeoff, "some waving of arms; and then came the silence of the upper air."[162] Radl, who was standing guard over the Duce's luggage, watched anxiously as the Stork rolled down the slope, hopped over the ditch, and then disappeared beyond the edge of the plateau: "My knees fail. Completely," he remembered. "My legs are gone. I feel myself falling."[163]

Radl collapsed onto the luggage. An eerie silence then swept through the crowd as they listened for the sound of the Stork.[164] "Everything is in vain," Radl thought to himself. "They crashed."[165]

The Stork did, in fact, plummet straight into the abyss. But instead of trying to pull the nose up, Gerlach, demonstrating nerves of steel, consciously put the plane in a terrifying nosedive in order to achieve the airspeed necessary to gain control of the craft. Within a few seconds he was able to level the plane out. "As I opened my eyes," Skorzeny recalled, "Gerlach got the plane under control and slowly raised it to a horizontal position."[166] Radl and the other onlookers were elated when they suddenly saw the Stork reappear on the far side of the chasm. Student later called the takeoff a "masterpiece" of piloting.[167]

Once he had regained control, Gerlach descended into the valley and set a southwesterly course for Rome, skimming the treetops to avoid detection by enemy aircraft.[168] The passengers of the Stork could finally emit a collective sigh of relief. (Due to the strain on the craft, the engine was not functioning properly, but Gerlach kept that piece of information to himself.)[169] Without thinking, Skorzeny placed a hand on Mussolini's shoulder.[170] "Now, indeed," Skorzeny later wrote, "we could consider his rescue accomplished."[171]

■ ■ ■

It nearly was. After flying for about an hour, Gerlach made a neat two-point landing at Pratica di Mare, the left wheel having been damaged during takeoff.[172] "Then the plane stopped," Skorzeny wrote. "Everything had worked wonderfully well; we had had much luck from the beginning to the end of our adventure."[173] Student later grumbled, "It had almost turned into a catastrophe because Skorzeny insisted on flying in the same plane with them."[174]

Skorzeny and the Duce promptly boarded a Heinkel 111 and set off for Austria. Stormy weather near Vienna caused the pilot some difficulties in locating the city, but he finally managed to touch down at Aspern airport at about 11:00 P.M.[175] The two men then proceeded to the Hotel Imperial, where they had arranged to spend the night; the next day, they planned to fly on to Munich, where Mussolini would be reunited with his wife.[176]

Soon after they arrived at the hotel, the switchboard began to light up with calls. All the major players in the Third Reich, it seemed, were anxious to offer Skorzeny their congratulations and to verify that the news was true. Close to midnight, a local SS colonel appeared out of nowhere, produced a handsome-looking medal, and hung it around Skorzeny's neck.[177] It was the Knight's Cross. It belonged to the colonel, but an elated Hitler had ordered him to present it to Skorzeny as a symbolic gesture.

Hitler himself then came on the line. "Today, you have carried out a mission that will go down in history," he told Skorzeny from the Wolf's Lair. "You have given me back my old friend Mussolini. I have given you the Knight's Cross and promoted you to Sturmbann-führer [major]."[178] It was the first time that this prestigious decoration had been earned and awarded on the same day.[179] Himmler, Goering, and Marshal Wilhelm Keitel (chief of OKW), also spoke to Skorzeny that evening.[180]

As for the Duce, he thanked Hitler briefly by telephone, but said that he was exhausted and went directly to bed.[181] "He informed the Führer that he was tired and sick," Goebbels noted, "and would first of all like to have a long sleep."[182] While Mussolini slumbered, Skorzeny reportedly walked off with the dictator's diary and personal papers.*[183] These were eventually copied, translated into German, and presented to Hitler.[184]

No one bothered to ask the newly liberated Duce for his permission.

---

*Among these were the *Pontine and Sardinian Musings,* extracts of which appear earlier in this book.

EPILOGUE

■

THE AFTERMATH

THE RESCUE OF MUSSOLINI—WHICH WAS NATURALLY VIEWED AS A jailbreak by the Allies and the Badoglio regime—became an instant and enduring classic in the annals of special operations and surprised a war-weary world, most of which had no inkling as to the depths of Machiavellian intrigue that were animating the European Axis powers during the summer of 1943. Even today, despite its being one of the most dramatic stories of World War II, the dissolution of the Rome-Berlin alliance remains one of the lesser-known chapters of the war, at least in the popular mind.

One day after the Gran Sasso operation, the Nazis broadcast the news of the Duce's rescue in a matter-of-fact statement that highlighted the role played by Skorzeny and the SS. "Members of the armed SS Guards and Secret Security Service," read the announcement as reported by the *New York Times,* "aided by members of parachute troops, today carried out an undertaking for liberation of the Duce. The coup de main was a success. Mussolini is at liberty and his delivery to the Anglo-American Allies, which was agreed [sic] by the Badoglio government, has been frustrated."[1]

Though Hitler deeply regretted the Italian surrender, he could console himself with having saved the Duce's skin and given a sorely needed boost to German morale.[2] More important, he had reinforced Italy with enough German troops during August to defend the peninsula for some time to come. "Taken with the German success in occupying the greater part of Italy and holding the Allies well south of Rome," wrote Hitler's biographer Alan Bullock, "the restoration of Mussolini could be presented as a triumphant ending to the crisis which had threatened in the summer [of 1943] to leave the southern frontiers of the Reich directly exposed to Allied attack."[3]

Nazi-controlled Paris radio predicted ominously, though overoptimistically, that the Duce's liberation would pave the way for a resurgence of Fascism in Italy: "Mussolini is now free to take Italy in hand again and lead her along the road from which Badoglio tried to make her swerve, free to take vengeance for insults that have soiled the Italian flag, free at last to take a stand again with his army on the European side. Italy has again found her leader."[4] Japan, Hitler's Axis ally in the Far East, offered its hearty congratulations. "The whole Japanese nation," its information bureau informed the world, "was overwhelmed with joy" at the news of the Duce's rescue.[5]

The story was naturally viewed with more cynicism by the Allied press, which was quick to point out that the Nazis had little else to crow about. "The serio-comic thriller—'The Rescue and Liberation of Benito Mussolini'—was told, retold and heavily embroidered today by the German radio," read an article in the *New York Times* on September 14, "which turned with apparent delight to this new subject after weeks of labored explanations of Nazi defeats in Tunisia, Russia, Sicily, and Italy."[6]

The same article noted dryly that the Germans had made friendship a central theme in their propaganda: "A feature of Berlin's story earlier in the day was that the kidnapping of Mussolini from his Italian guards was made possible through the personal friendship and Fascist brotherhood of Adolf Hitler, who, in his speech Friday [September 10], waxed heavily sentimental over the former dictator of Italy. The German propagandists said it was understood that 'Hitler himself prepared the plan for freeing his friend' and gave the orders for carrying it out."[7]

There is no evidence that Hitler helped to develop the Gran Sasso operation, but he certainly lit a fire under the would-be rescuers and followed the ups and downs of Operation Oak with intense interest.

The article continued: "One of the first acts of Mussolini, they said, was to telephone Hitler. They added that it was 'difficult to express in words the feelings which animated Hitler and Il Duce during this historic conversation.'"[8]

It fell to Winston Churchill to explain how the big fish had gotten away. "We had every reason to believe that Mussolini was being kept under a strong guard at a secure place," he told the House of Commons on September 21, "and certainly it was very much to the interests of the Badoglio Government to see that he did not escape. Mussolini has himself been reported to have declared that he believed that he was being delivered to the Allies. This was certainly the intention, and is what would have taken place but for circumstances entirely beyond our control."[9]

Churchill, who never underestimated the importance of propaganda and had employed it to great effect during the darker years of the war, was also inclined to tip his hat: "But the stroke was one of great daring, and conducted with a heavy force. It certainly shows there are many possibilities of this kind open in modern war. . . . The Carabinieri guards had orders to shoot Mussolini if there was any attempt to rescue him, but they failed in their duty, having regard to the considerable German force which descended upon them from the air, and would undoubtedly have held them responsible for his health and safety. So much for that."[10]

■ ■ ■

The Nazis hailed Skorzeny as the star of Operation Oak, a role that suited the cocky Austrian to a tee. With Hitler's blessing, he took to the German airwaves shortly after the rescue operation and announced to the world that he was the man who had liberated Mussolini. The newly promoted major was also draped with prestigious medals and decorations. He received the Knight's Cross from Hitler and the Air Force Medal in Gold from Goering.[11] The Duce presented him with the Order of the Hundred Musketeers.[12] (Radl, Skorzeny's deputy, was promoted to captain.)[13]

"The Gran Sasso raid naturally transformed this unknown Captain [Skorzeny] into the hero of the hour," recalled Wilhelm Hoettl, an SS intelligence officer who had helped plan the Cianos' escape in August. "But he has to thank Dr. Goebbels for the fact that his fame has spread so far and survived so long. For propaganda purposes Goebbels was greatly in need of some German success and Skorzeny was to provide a mighty dramatic one."[14]

Goebbels himself was ecstatic. "The liberation of the Duce is the great sensation at home and abroad," he wrote in his diary a few days after the raid. "Even upon the enemy the effect of the melodramatic deliverance is enormous . . . the entire German people . . . are profoundly happy."[15] He added: "There has hardly been a military event during the entire war that has so deeply stirred the emotions and evoked such human interest. We are able to celebrate a first-class moral victory."[16]

But not everyone was in the mood to rejoice. As Skorzeny was enjoying his new celebrity status, General Student and Major Harold Mors were stewing. They believed that Skorzeny and his SS commandos were hogging all the credit for what they maintained was essentially a Luftwaffe operation—one that was planned and executed by German airborne forces. As they saw it, the simple fact that Skorzeny and Radl had landed on the Gran Sasso before any of the paratroopers—contrary to the prepared plan—had allowed the SS to grab the Duce as well as the glory.

Though just about everyone who played a role in Operation Oak received honors of one sort or another—including Herbert Kappler, Mors, Gerlach, Meyer (Skorzeny's glider pilot), and many of the Luftwaffe officers and pilots who participated in the rescue—it was Skorzeny who received the lion's share of the credit.* Accord-

---

*Mors was awarded the German Cross in Gold. Gerlach and Meyer each received a Knight's Cross. Kappler was promoted to Lieutenant Colonel and given the Iron Cross. Priebke, Kappler's deputy, was bumped up to captain and also received the Iron Cross.

ing to Student, Mussolini never even bothered to thank him or the paratroopers for their role in the operation.[17]

"It sounded more or less as if Skorzeny and his SS-commando performed this sensational mission by themselves," remembered Student, who received the Oak Leaves to his Knight's Cross about two weeks after the rescue (he had already earned a Knight's Cross earlier in the war).[18] When Mors attempted to lodge an official complaint, Hitler turned a deaf ear. He preferred to shine the spotlight on Skorzeny and the fanatically loyal SS, the one organization in which Hitler still believed he could trust.[19] However, this did not stop Student and his paratroopers from returning to the Gran Sasso with a camera crew to restage the rescue on film from their point of view.[20]

In a slightly comical footnote to history, the American novelist John Steinbeck also made a brief appearance in the Mussolini rescue saga. As the Allies were struggling to establish a foothold at Salerno in the wake of the Italian surrender, Steinbeck was snooping around on the island of Ventotene, where he believed he had come close to bagging Il Duce. "Accompanying a British American tank force that recently took Ventotene island off Naples (on Sept. 9)," reported the *New York Times* on September 13, "Mr. Steinbeck said he missed Mussolini there by less than twelve hours."[21]

As was seen earlier, the Duce was never imprisoned on Ventotene, though the island had captivated Hitler during the first half of August. (Steinbeck's investigations also determined, correctly this time, that Mussolini had been imprisoned on Ponza as well.)

Two days after his liberation, Mussolini was reunited with Hitler—who, during their ten-year relationship, had played the roles of protégé, mentor, and savior in turn—at the Wolf's Lair in East Prussia.* The triumphant reunion of the two dictators was captured by German

---

*Mussolini flew to the Wolf's Lair from Munich, where he had been reunited with his wife and family after the rescue.

newsreel footage, which was broadcast throughout the Third Reich and beyond. In jerky black-and-white images, Hitler could be seen greeting the Duce enthusiastically as the latter stepped off a Junkers 52 at an airport near Rastenburg. Mussolini, who was wearing a dark-colored suit and a fedora, resembled a tired businessman after a lengthy flight. The two men shook hands for a long time and exchanged what appeared to be warm words. Hitler reportedly had tears in his eyes.[22]

The mood behind the scenes was less convivial. Hitler had expected the Duce to be brimming with diabolical energy, but instead he seemed depressed and unresponsive. To begin with, the German dictator exhorted his friend to exact swift revenge on Galeazzo Ciano and the other traitors of July 25 who had voted against Mussolini in the Grand Council of Fascism. A handful of these men had fallen into German hands, and Hitler was determined to make an example out of them.

Ciano, who was still married to the Duce's daughter Edda, had fled to Germany in late August in the naïve hope that the Nazis would facilitate the next leg of his journey to Spain. But Hitler despised Mussolini's son-in-law, as did most of the Nazi hierarchy, and Ciano's ill-advised plans to publish a tell-all book helped to seal his fate. "Ciano intends to write his memoirs," Goebbels noted in his diary. "The Fuehrer rightly suspects that such memoirs can only be written in a manner derogatory to us, for otherwise he could not dispose of them in the international market. There is therefore no thought of authorizing Ciano to leave the Reich; he will remain in our custody."[23]

But when Hitler demanded that Ciano and the others pay with their heads, the Duce hesitated.[24] Weary and physically unwell, he was no longer the blustering dictator of former days, and he had no enthusiasm for enacting an Italian version of Hitler's infamous Night of the Long Knives. The notion of signing Ciano's death warrant was particularly troubling to Mussolini, but Hitler remained unmoved by arguments concerning family ties.

In the outlaw world of the Nazis, Mussolini's lack of bloodlust was interpreted as a sign of weakness. "The Duce has not drawn the moral conclusions from Italy's catastrophe that the Fuehrer had expected of him," Goebbels wrote in his diary. "He was naturally overjoyed to see the Fuehrer and to be fully at liberty again. But the Fuehrer expected that the first thing the Duce would do would be to wreak full vengeance on his betrayers. But he gave no such indication, and thereby showed his real limitations. He is not a revolutionary like the Fuehrer or Stalin. He is so bound to his own Italian people that he lacks the broad qualities of a worldwide revolutionary and insurrectionist."[25] As for Goebbels, he believed that Ciano should be executed and Edda "whipped."[26]

Hitler got another knock on the head when the Duce expressed a desire to retire from public life and return to Rocca delle Caminate, his country estate in the Romagna, to avoid an outbreak of civil war in Italy.[27] But Hitler quickly vetoed this option, telling his friend that such a development would reflect badly on Germany and undermine the legitimacy of the new Fascist state that Hitler was planning to establish in German-occupied Italy.[28] Mussolini eventually acquiesced to Hitler's wishes, perhaps in the hope that he could protect his countrymen from Nazi brutality.

Ultimately, both men were disappointed by their reunion at the Wolf's Lair in September, and by their newest incarnation of the Axis. Mussolini's attitude gave Hitler little hope that he could expect much from the resurrection of the Italian dictator. "We may consider him absolutely disillusioned concerning the Duce's personality," wrote Goebbels about his boss, though he added that there was "no actual quarrel."[29] Goebbels, it should be said, was jealous of Mussolini's bond with Hitler and took a certain degree of pleasure in watching the Duce's stock fall in Hitler's eyes.[30] In the final analysis, Mussolini was "nothing but an Italian," Goebbels huffed, "and can't get away from that heritage."[31]

Hitler's disappointment ran deep. "Belief in Fascist Italy as a pillar of the Nietzschean paradise had been part of his psychological structure," according to the Axis expert Elizabeth Wiskemann. "He was now forced to admit that a major pretence of his life had been nonsense, that Italy had been no better in this war than in the last, and that Mussolini was excessively Italian. His Mentor, his twin-Superman for twenty-one years, was a perfectly ordinary man."[32]

There was something ironic about this revelation. Though the rescue of the Duce had given the German public something to feel good about, that same event seems to have disillusioned Hitler in private.

■ ■ ■

As for Mussolini, his regrets were already etched on his face. "The resurrected dictator looked old, tired and wan," recalled the SS man Eugen Dollmann, who saw the Duce on September 27, "and only his eyes retained their old Palazzo Venezia fire. . . . I congratulated him on his release from the Gran Sasso and reassumption [sic] of power, but he dismissed my remarks with a gesture of resignation and the light in his eyes grew dim."[33] Rachele Mussolini later wrote that "after July, 1943, Benito Mussolini, my husband, thought that his star had completely faded; from that time he spoke of himself solely as 'Mussolini defunto,' or the late Mussolini. He greatly feared German intentions for the future of Italy and was conscious that as head of the Italian Social Republic he was merely protecting the Italians from German revenge."[34]

The Italian Social Republic was the name of the Duce's new neo-Fascist regime, which came into being that September. Because nobody knew exactly when Rome might fall to the Allies, Mussolini's government was established on the western shore of Lake Garda near Salò in northern Italy—Lake Garda being almost equidistant between Milan and Venice.[35] It was also believed that the Duce's presence in Rome might prove to be too politically explosive in light of the anti-Fascist feeling in the city. Historians later dubbed the new regime the Salò Republic, but by any name it was a puppet kingdom created under the aegis of the Nazis. Though Mussolini was its nominal leader, Hitler and the Germans pulled most of the strings. During the remainder of his life, the Duce never again saw the Eternal City.[36]

Under pressure from Hitler, Mussolini convened a kangaroo court in January 1944 at Verona to dispense summary justice to Ciano and five other Fascists who had cast their votes against the Italian dictator during the Grand Council meeting several months earlier.[37] (Altogether, nineteen men had voted against Mussolini on the evening of July 24–25, but most of them, including Dino Grandi, had escaped the grasp of the Nazis. At Verona, thirteen of them were sentenced to death in absentia.)

Ciano's wanderings came to an end at Fort Procolo, a few miles outside Verona in northern Italy, where he and four other defendants were shot by a firing squad (the sixth was given a long prison sentence). As a sign of contempt, the men were shot in the back, but Ciano managed to turn around at the last moment to face his executioners.[38] Edda, who had begged her father to spare her husband's life, was crushed by Galeazzo's death and nearly had a nervous breakdown.*

■ ■ ■

During his second incarnation as dictator, Mussolini found a home at the Villa Feltrinelli in the small town of Gargnano on Lake Garda.[39] He was "virtually a prisoner" of the Germans, according to the Italian historian Paolo Monelli.[40] Hitler's SS troops guarded the villa day and night and followed the Duce almost everywhere he went. They were ostensibly there to protect his person, but they also spied on him and even monitored his telephone calls. (Mussolini liked to refer to General Karl Wolff, commander of the SS in Italy, as his jailer.)[41] Further

---

*Edda's attempts to save her husband's life and smuggle his diaries out of Italy read like fiction but are outside the scope of this book. At the heart of the story is a female Nazi spy who became a de facto double agent after falling for Ciano's charms during his brief prison term.

complicating matters, the Villa Feltrinelli was noisy and crowded. The house was practically overflowing with the Duce's sizable family, which included his wife, children, daughters-in-law (who fought with each other), and several grandchildren.

Mussolini found domestic life suffocating and began to spend more and more of his time at his nearby office, the Villa delle Orsoline. He also devoted an increasing amount of time to his philosophical ruminations and left the business of state largely to his various Fascist ministers. To some of those around him, the Duce seemed to be out of touch with the real world. "He lives by dreams, in dreams, and through dreams," observed Fernando Mezzasoma, a young Fascist who grew close to Mussolini during the Salò Republic years. "He has not the least contact with reality, he lives and functions in a world which he constructs for himself, a completely fantastic world; he lives outside time."[42]

The Duce's mistress, Claretta Petacci, and her family were installed on a nearby estate. However, under pressure from his wife, Mussolini did not visit Claretta as often as he might have wished. He found other ways to occupy his time, such as badmouthing the Nazis behind their backs, playing Beethoven or Verdi on his violin (in his less-than-graceful, machismo style), reading Plato and Goethe, and complaining about his insomnia and other health problems.

"He was an old man," wrote the historian Martin Clark, "defeated in life, wasted by sickness, abandoned by his daughter, surrounded by a squabbling family, bullied by the Germans, without friends and without hope. Still, he deserved his fate. He was an arrogant bully, and he had miscalculated."[43]

His gloom could only have deepened as he watched a bitter civil war flare up behind the German lines. "Mussolini's bid for a Fascist revival plunged Italy into the horrors of civil war," Churchill later wrote. "In the weeks following the September Armistice, officers and men of the Italian Army stationed in German-occupied Northern Italy and patriots from the towns and countryside began to form partisan units and to operate against the Germans and against their compatriots who still adhered to the Duce."[44]

The 80,000 or so Partisans (more than half of whom had joined the Communist-controlled Garibaldi brigades) did everything they could to make life harder for Mussolini and the Nazis.[45] They employed the standard tricks of the trade: assassinations, sabotage, and surprise attacks.[46] The Germans responded by launching vicious attacks of their own against Partisans and civilians alike, sometimes setting entire villages aflame.*

■ ■ ■

The last Axis summit took place at the Wolf's Lair on July 20, 1944, just hours after an assassin's bomb had nearly killed Hitler.** The two dictators spent part of the time rehashing the usual issues, according to Eugen Dollmann, who was present for the bizarre tea party. "The only new feature," he observed, "was that there had at last been a putsch against Hitler in his own Reich, and that the Italians need no longer suffer taunts about 25 July and 8 September in silence."[47]

The scene became more interesting when an argument erupted among some of Hitler's top lieutenants—Goering, Doenitz, and Ribbentrop—who began to squabble over the Third Reich's military failures and point fingers at one another.[48] Mussolini listened silently as all this was going on, crumbling a piece of cake with his fingers and creating tiny sculptures with the remains.[49]

Hitler also remained mum, apparently pondering his close call with death. Then he proclaimed: "Never have I felt more strongly

---

*There were also thousands of former Allied POWs roaming around German-occupied Italy, many of whom were aided by ordinary Italians at great personal risk.

**Admiral Canaris, head of the Abwehr, was implicated in the plot to kill Hitler and was subsequently thrown into a concentration camp. He was executed on Hitler's orders in 1945. After the fall of Canaris, the victorious Schellenberg absorbed German Military Intelligence into the SS, ending the Nazi intelligence wars once and for all.

that providence is at my side—indeed, the miracle of a few hours ago has convinced me more than ever that I am destined for even greater things and shall lead the German people to the greatest victory in its history."[50]

Though a ghost of his former self by that time, the Duce mustered a nostalgic response. "I must say you are right, Führer," he said. "Our position is bad, one might almost say desperate, but what has happened here today gives me new courage. After the miracle that has occurred here in this room today it is inconceivable that our cause should meet with misfortune."[51]

When the meeting had ended and the two men said their goodbyes at the train station, Hitler looked Mussolini in the eye for what seemed like an eternity and reaffirmed his friendship.[52] "I know that I can count on you," Hitler told him, "and I beg you to believe me when I say that I look on you as my best and possibly only friend I have in the world."[53] When the Duce's back was turned, Hitler reportedly drew aside Rudolf Rahn, the German ambassador to Fascist Italy, and told him to keep an eye on Mussolini—but it is not clear whether this cryptic aside was made in a spirit of distrust or affection.[54]

"One pale and ageing man [Hitler] . . . extended his left hand to another pale and ageing man," remembered Dollmann. "The two incongruous friends gazed deep into each other's eyes once more, as in the days of their glory, but the light in those eyes was extinguished, almost as though they guessed that this was their last meeting."[55]

■ ■ ■

They met their ends the following year. By the spring of 1945, Mussolini's kingdom in northern Italy was beginning to shrink rapidly under the pressure of the Allied advance and the increasing activity of Italian irregulars. Hitler sent his last message to the Duce on April 24, informing him that "the struggle for existence or non-existence has reached its climax."[56] Shortly afterward, Mussolini and Claretta

Petacci were captured by Partisans at a roadblock outside the village of Dongo (in the region of Lake Como).[57] He was disguised as a German soldier at the time, wearing an army overcoat, helmet, and dark sunglasses.[58] On April 28, the Duce of Fascism and his lover were shot dead by the side of a road near the hamlet of Mezzegra on the western shores of Como.[59]

The executions were conducted without fanfare or the semblance of a trial. The corpses were transported to Milan, where they were abused by the crowd and hung by their heels from a rafter in the Piazzale Loreto along with the dead bodies of several other captured Fascists.[60] The setting for this spectacle was strangely fitting: Milan was the city in which Mussolini had proclaimed the Axis almost ten years earlier.*

As the Duce dangled from a rope in Milan, Hitler was living in an underground bunker in Berlin. He had left the Wolf's Lair for good in November 1944;[61] in January 1945, he ordered that it be destroyed, but German engineers did not have enough explosives to finish the job.**[62] Half mad, his body nearly paralyzed from nervous tension and crazy drug cocktails, Hitler was still clinging to his center of power when he was informed of Mussolini's demise.

"Hitler had heard of Mussolini's shameful death," remembered Traudl Junge, one of Hitler's secretaries. "I think someone had even shown him the photos of the naked bodies hanging head downwards in the main square of Milan. 'I will not fall into the enemy's hands either dead or alive. When I'm dead, my body is to be burned so that no one can ever find it,' Hitler decreed."***[63]

---

*An autopsy conducted in 1945 failed to shed much light on Mussolini's mysterious health problems; it did, however, reveal a small scar indicative of an ulcer.

**The remains of the Wolf's Lair are now a tourist attraction in Poland.

***In his *Last Days of Hitler*, the historian Hugh Trevor-Roper maintains that Hitler could not have seen the photos of Mussolini's corpse and may have been unaware of the gruesome details.

On April 30, Hitler and Eva Braun, who had taken marriage vows the previous day, took their own lives. Goebbels, who had stayed by Hitler's side until the bitter end, also chose death rather than face the tender mercies of the Russians, who were already fighting in the streets of Berlin. (Admiral Doenitz inherited the leadership of the Third Reich, albeit briefly.)

■ ■ ■

During the Saló years, Mussolini expressed the gratitude he felt at being rescued from the Gran Sasso. "The Greek philosopher, Thales," wrote the Duce, making one of his beloved scholarly references, "thanked the gods for creating him a man and not a beast, a male and not a female, a Greek and not a barbarian. I thank the gods for having spared me the farce of a vociferous trial in Madison Square, New York—to which I should infinitely prefer a regular hanging in the Tower of London."[64]

In what may have been a moment of greater honesty, Mussolini also admitted privately in the months before his death that he and Hitler had succumbed to their own illusions like a pair of madmen.[65]

After the Gran Sasso raid, Skorzeny enjoyed a special status in the eyes of Hitler and was often entrusted with special missions that the German dictator considered especially important. "Throughout his military career," wrote William H. McRaven, a U.S. Navy Seal, "Skorzeny used tactical deception and acts of extreme bravado to throw the enemy off guard and gain an advantage."[66] Though not all his efforts were successful, he managed to score several more coups before war's end that increased his notoriety.

One of Skorzeny's most well-known exploits during World War II took place during the Battle of the Bulge, which was sparked by a surprise German offensive that Hitler launched in the West in December 1944. The primary attack force consisted of conventional army units. But, in one of his final brainstorms, Hitler instructed Skorzeny to send

a group of commandos behind enemy lines dressed as American soldiers (Operation Greif). After receiving months of training, dozens
of these bogus GIs were set loose in Allied territory, where they
proceeded to commit acts of sabotage by misdirecting road traffic,
snipping telephone lines, and generally creating havoc. Although
Skorzeny's commandos did little actual damage, their presence
caused a mass panic that was out of all proportion to their numbers.

During this period, Allied soldiers had difficulty distinguishing
friend from foe and had to subject one another to endless cross-
examinations. In the furor, authentic GIs were swept up and arrested on the suspicion of being Nazi spies. The privileges of rank
offered little protection. An American general by the name of Bruce
Clark was arrested by overzealous MPs and detained for five hours.

As a result of Operation Greif, "a half-million GI's played cat and
mouse with each other each time they met on the road," recalled General Omar Bradley, a three-star general who was repeatedly stopped
at Allied roadblocks and given the third-degree. "Three times I was
ordered to prove my identity by cautious GI's. The first time by iden-
tifying Springfield as the capital of Illinois (my questioner held out
for Chicago); the second time by locating the guard between the center and tackle on a line of scrimmage; the third time by naming the
then current spouse of a blonde named Betty Grable."[67]

If that were not enough, the idea soon took hold in the Allied
psyche that Skorzeny was planning to seize Eisenhower himself. As a
result of these concerns, the Supreme Commander of Allied Forces
was practically put under house arrest by his own security men.

"Security officers," recalled Kay Summersby, Eisenhower's secretary, "immediately turned headquarters compound [at Versailles]
into a virtual fortress. Barbed wire appeared. Several tanks moved
in. The normal guard was doubled, trebled, quadrupled. The pass
system became a strict matter of life and death, instead of the old
formality. The sound of a car exhaust was enough to halt work in
every office, to start a flurry of telephone calls to our office, to in-
quire if the Boss were alright."[68]

Hitler's offensive ultimately failed. But by the end of the war, Skorzeny had become something of a legend. When he finally surrendered in May 1945, the Allied press reports betrayed a grudging fascination with the boastful Austrian. "A rather handsome man," wrote a *New York Times* reporter, "despite a scar stretching from his left ear to his chin, he smilingly disclaimed credit for heading a mission to murder members of the Allied High Command last winter . . . and declared that if any German soldiers operated behind the American lines in American uniform it was something that somebody else, not he, had cooked up."[69]

But there was one subject about which Skorzeny could not keep silent. "After he had tried impatiently to convince his questioners that he was just an ordinary soldier whom gossip had maligned, Skorzeny settled down to telling a story he was obviously proud and eager to relate. It was the narrative of how he and a handful of picked men had snatched Mussolini from the fate that finally overtook him in northern Italy."[70]

Although Skorzeny's roguish charm has captivated certain writers and historians in the succeeding years, it has disgusted others, who consider him little more than a resourceful terrorist.

In 1947, it was the opinion of an American military tribunal that mattered most. Skorzeny was charged with various offenses related to Operation Greif, including the murder of captured American soldiers. During his trial, the judges heard dramatic testimony from Wing Commander Forrest Yeo-Thomas, a legendary British agent who had worked closely with the French Resistance. Yeo-Thomas, known during the war as the White Rabbit, explained to the court that he had ordered his own operatives to carry out special missions disguised in German uniform. As a result of this and other testimony, Skorzeny was eventually acquitted of all charges, but was not immediately released.

He subsequently spent months languishing in a detention camp at Darmstadt in Germany awaiting the de-nazification process. Several Allied countries, such as Czechoslovakia and Belgium, expressed an interest in having Skorzeny extradited to face additional charges. When he appealed for help to Yeo-Thomas, the British hero gave a concise reply: "Escape."[71] Shortly afterwards, Skorzeny did just that. In July 1948, three former SS officers dressed as American military police drove to Skorzeny's internment camp at Darmstadt, presented some official-looking papers, and whisked their celebrity prisoner to freedom (or so the story goes).*

The remainder of Skorzeny's life, much of which was spent in South America and Spain, was shrouded in mystery. It was also the subject of fantastic rumors and wild speculation, some of which may well be true. During his postwar years, some writers claim, Skorzeny lent his sinister services to the CIA, went to work for Juan and Evita Peron in Argentina (it is even said that Skorzeny and Evita had a romantic affair), and played a key role in founding the so-called Odessa network, a covert organization that aimed to smuggle former SS men and other Nazis out of Germany and help them evade justice.

Truth often being stranger than fiction, it was revealed in 1989 that Skorzeny had also worked as a temporary agent of the Mossad, Israel's version of the CIA, during the early 1960s.[72] According to press reports, Skorzeny helped the Mossad to foil an Egyptian plan to use former Nazi scientists to develop a missile program.[73]

He died of cancer in 1975 in Madrid.

In the decades after World War II, the name of Otto Skorzeny became synonymous with the rescue of Mussolini, and that was the way he liked it. His fame was apparently an endless source of irritation to Student and the German paratroopers, whose grievances with Skorzeny outlasted the cold war. According to author Charles Whiting, who interviewed General Student in the 1970s, the former paratrooper chief was still griping about Skorzeny thirty years after the Duce was snatched from the Gran Sasso. Student died in 1978.

---

*Some writers have alleged that the CIA aided Skorzeny in his escape with the view that he might prove useful to them in the future.

Before his death in 2001, Major Mors also continued to champion the Luftwaffe cause. "Yes, it was the paratroops who planned and carried out the operation," Mors explained in an interview published in the *Los Angeles Times* in 1987. "But for more than 40 years, Skorzeny has gotten all the credit. His version is something of a fairy tale. . . . The point is, Skorzeny and his SS commandos went along as passengers; Von Berlepsch commanded the assault team."[74]

Mors said that his own critical role in the mission had been obscured because he remained in the valley. "I chose to stay with the two companies in the valley, because if anything went wrong with the glider force, I would still be in position to supervise the operation and decide what to do. Later, some people didn't understand this, but my job was to command the whole operation, not just one aspect."[75]

Another paratrooper officer, Arnold von Roon, who had been a major on General Student's staff during the war, later contended that politics had clouded the issue. "Once Hitler decided that it was Skorzeny and the SS commandos who led the operation," Roon said, "it was difficult to do anything about it. Gen. Student didn't want to get into a row with Goering over who got the credit. So he never protested. He thought history would provide the truth."[76]

Both Mors and Roon concede that Skorzeny was an imposing figure and quite a character. "He was huge, robust, intelligent, but not intellectual," Roon recalled. "He was quite a charmer, too, and could be very persuasive. It is simply that he did not plan or lead the Mussolini operation."[77]

While not denying the role played by German airborne troops, some military historians continue to emphasize the Skorzeny factor. "Clearly Mors played a significant role in both the planning and execution of the mission," McRaven argued in a 1995 book devoted to the subject of special operations. "But it was Skorzeny who conducted the aerial reconnaissance, it was Skorzeny who was the first to land at Gran Sasso, it was Skorzeny who controlled General Soleti, and it was Skorzeny who first reached Mussolini. Whether

Skorzeny was a straphanger or the mastermind of the operation is inconsequential. Ultimately, success resulted from Skorzeny's actions at Gran Sasso and not from Mors's."[78]

It is fair to say that the competing claims of Skorzeny and the German paratroopers have added yet another chapter to the complicated story of Operation Oak.

Once the summer of 1943 had faded into history, the curtain opened on a much larger drama: the battle for Italy. "From September 1943 until the end of April 1945," wrote the historian Richard Lamb, "Italy suffered the disaster of being occupied by two conquering armies at war with each other, and the peninsula became a battleground."[79] In some ways, the six short weeks following the Italian coup of July 25 had determined the course of this long and brutal struggle. By failing to obstruct the German infiltration of Italy and declining to lend support to the Allied invasion (in the Rome area or elsewhere), the king and Badoglio had helped set the stage for the grim consequences that followed.

However, these consequences were not readily apparent in the wake of September 8. After their victory at Salerno, the Allies began to cast a covetous eye at the rest of the peninsula. Much like Hitler and Rommel, they believed that the Nazis would be forced to turn tail in the face of the Allied invasion, evacuate the region south of Rome, and make a stand in the north somewhere near Florence, more than one hundred miles from the Eternal City. Most of the country would therefore fall into Allied hands with little, if any, fighting. The capture of Rome would be the icing on the cake; but then again, considering its psychological value as a former Axis capital, perhaps Rome was the whole cake. Needless to say, most Italians preferred this upbeat scenario as well because it would spare much of the nation from the horrors of war.

"At first Hitler had intended to keep hold only of North Italy after Italy's retirement from the war," remembered General Westphal, Kesselring's chief of staff. "Rommel was to absorb Kesselring's forces into his army group in the [northern] Apennines and to make his stand in these mountains. Kesselring, who according to rumour was too soft with the Italians, was then to be transferred with his staff to some other war theatre—possibly Norway."[80]

But Kesselring, who viewed the Allies as cautious and predictable from a military standpoint, managed to turn this situation on its head. He was so successful in foiling the enemy's advance in the weeks after September 8 that Hitler gave Rommel his walking papers in November and named Kesselring the commander of all German forces in Italy. Kesselring, whose gullibility had so often made Hitler wince during the months of crisis, had finally beaten out his rival once and for all.*

■ ■ ■

Kesselring's efforts at redemption created endless difficulties for the Allies. One glance at their timetable told the story. The Anglo-Americans had planned to liberate the nearby port of Naples by Day Three.[81] It ultimately took them three weeks to get there (Naples fell on October 1), General Clark's Fifth Army suffering 12,000 casualties (killed, wounded, or missing) in the process.[82] Many in the Allied camp clung to the hope that Rome could be captured later that fall, perhaps by the end of October 1943.[83] Tragically, for the Allies and Italians alike, this prediction was about eight months off target.

The 140-mile distance from Salerno to Rome may have looked somewhat modest on a map, but the view from the ground was depressingly different.[84] The American and British soldiers whose job it was to slug their way up the boot of Italy were faced with moun-

---

*In the fall of 1943, Hitler instructed Rommel to apply his formidable talents to the task of defending the Western frontiers of the Reich. Rommel, who so often had expressed his admiration for Hitler during the Italian crisis, was later implicated in the attempted assassination of the German dictator in July 1944 and forced to commit suicide.

tains, rivers, and accurate German artillery. Kesselring forced them to fight for every inch of territory. Exploiting the lay of the land, he established a series of natural defensive lines on the rivers that run from the Apennines into the sea. The Germans held on to each line for as long as possible before falling back to yet another position—which they had thoroughly prepared beforehand—scorching the earth as they went. Kesselring's tactics took on a monotonous regularity, but they were enormously effective.*

"The mountainous terrain of central Italy was Kesselring's greatest ally," according to the military historian Carlo D'Este. "Not only were the mountains themselves formidable obstacles, but the many rivers, the freezing winter weather, the wind, mud, and rain, and the limited road net made any advance against a well-prepared defender a potential nightmare."[85]

The Gustav Line, which brushed by the town of Cassino, about eighty miles south of Rome, was one of Kesselring's toughest barriers.[86] By January 1944, the Allies had ground to a halt before it. When brute force failed to shatter the stalemate, the Allies attempted to outmaneuver the Nazis in late January by landing additional troops at Anzio, which was situated north of the dreaded Gustav Line. If everything went according to plan, the Germans would be trapped between two Allied armies—one in front of them at Cassino and another in their rear at Anzio.

But things did not go as planned. Having taken the Germans by surprise, the Allied soldiers who landed at Anzio were easily able to establish a bridgehead. However, by the time they were ready to break out into other parts of the country, Kesselring had effectively bottled them up on the beaches. (Otto von Berlepsch, the ostensible commander of the glider assault force at Gran Sasso, took part in the fighting at Anzio and was killed in action there.)[87]

---

*Student's paratroopers made up part of Kesselring's forces. The rescue of Mussolini proved to be their last notable airborne success. For the remainder of the war, they were employed as high-quality ground troops.

The Allies—who were now stalled on two fronts—remained stuck at Cassino and Anzio for several months, unable to penetrate the suffocating German defense. The static nature of the fighting, and the heavy casualties that resulted, conjured up memories of brutal World War I trench warfare.

■ ■ ■

This deadlock was finally broken in the spring after a mighty effort on the part of the Allies. American soldiers from Clark's Fifth Army entered Rome on June 4, 1944—nine months after the Salerno landings.

The city had not fared well under the German occupation. "Rome was an 'open city' whose walls shook under the waves of German military movements and the thunder of Allied bombs," wrote the historian Robert Katz, referring to the occupation. "Swollen to nearly twice its usual size by refugees from the countryside, Rome was a city of spies, double agents, informers, torturers, escaped war prisoners, hunted Jews, and hungry people."[88]

During this period, approximately 2,000 Jews from the city were shipped to concentration camps in the Third Reich (though most Roman Jews managed to avoid capture).* Understandably perhaps, many other Romans felt let down by their own leaders as well as by the Allies, whose promises of speedy liberation had never materialized. While the Allies were bogged down at Anzio, one bitter Roman scribbled an ironic piece of graffiti on a city wall: "Americans, hold on!" it read, mocking the promises of Allied propaganda. "We'll be there soon to liberate you!"[89]

But the Romans reserved their true anger for the Nazis. Throughout the occupation, the Germans were harried by the activity of vari-

---

*Thanks to the efforts of the Italian people, about 80 percent of the Jews living in Italy escaped the clutches of the Nazis during the German occupation, though 8,000 died at their hands. During the Salò years, Mussolini also managed to save a number of Jewish lives.

ous groups belonging to the Roman resistance. After one violent attack in March 1944, in which thirty-three German SS men were killed while marching along the Via Rasella, Hitler reacted with fury and ordered the immediate execution of hundreds of Romans. Herbert Kappler, who had been transformed from a mere attaché into the much-feared head of the Gestapo in Rome, carried out Hitler's command (aided by his subordinate, Erich Priebke). Ultimately, 335 men were rounded up and shot dead in the Ardeatine Caves just outside Rome.*[90]

Though this massacre remained the most infamous example of German brutality in the Italian mind, the Nazis carried out other atrocities in other cities and villages throughout occupied Italy. Kesselring, who had so often been criticized for being too "soft" when it came to the Italians, swung to the opposite pole in the years following the Italian surrender and advised his commanders to apply draconian measures in the fight against the Partisans.

His new attitude was reflected in orders such as those issued in August 1944: "Every act of violence must be followed immediately by appropriate counter-measures," part of the order read. "If there are a large number of [Partisan] bands in a district, then in every single case a certain percentage of the male population of the place must be arrested, and, in cases of violence, shot. If German soldiers are fired at in villages, the village must be burnt. The criminals or else the leaders must be publicly hanged."[91]

■ ■ ■

Shortly after liberating Rome, the Allied drive began to lose momentum. The culprit was Allied grand strategy, which involved the

---

*After the war, Kappler was convicted of war crimes and spent several decades in Italian prisons. Priebke fled to South America, where he lived as a free man for fifty years. In the mid–1990s, he was unmasked and extradited to Italy, where the octogenarian was sentenced to fifteen years of house arrest.

Normandy invasion in June 1944 and an additional landing in southern France in August. To carry out the latter, dubbed Operation Dragoon, several divisions were removed from the Italian theater.

By August 1944, the Germans had established the Gothic Line (in the mountains north of Florence), which their adversaries found to be another formidable barrier.[92] Incredibly, this was the defensive line to which the Nazis had planned to retreat during the summer of 1943, before Kesselring had convinced Hitler to fight tooth and nail for Italy. Come winter, the Allies had run out of steam a few miles short of the Po Valley, which remained in German hands for several more months. The Allies finally made a breakthrough in the spring of 1945, but some parts of northern Italy remained under German control almost until the end of the war.*

The German army in Italy laid down its arms on May 2, 1945— nearly two years after Victor Emmanuel and Badoglio had toppled Mussolini in the hopes of putting a speedy end to the war.** When all was said and done, according to Carlo D'Este, the war in Italy was "the longest and bloodiest campaign fought by the Anglo-American Alliance in all of World War II."[93]

---

*In March 1945, Hitler gave Kesselring command of the German armies in the Western theater. After the war, he was convicted of war crimes in connection with German anti-Partisan activities in Italy. He served a brief prison term and was released in 1952.

**In June 1944, the Badoglio regime was replaced with a broad-based coalition government. In 1946, the Italians voted to get rid of the monarchy altogether and establish a republic. In 1948, the Italians banned the king and all his male descendents from ever again setting foot in Italy. This ban was lifted in 2002.

THE STORY OF OPERATION OAK

■

To some degree, the story of Operation Oak has always been colored by myth and legend. Indeed, the distinguished Oxford historian Sir William Deakin once referred to it as "both intricate and confused, and also obscured by the personal vanity of certain of the direct participants."[1] The postwar friction between Skorzeny and Radl on the one hand and Student and the German paratroopers on the other can make separating fact from fiction particularly challenging. Each side tends to emphasize its own role while downplaying the contributions made by the other.

In piecing together this tale, I have relied heavily on firsthand accounts, including those by Skorzeny, Student, and Radl. However, the reader should keep in mind that these accounts do not always agree. A typical, but not terribly important, example of this involves the September 8 reconnaissance flight over the Gran Sasso. Skorzeny and Radl claim that they took the aerial photos, and they provide numerous details to buttress their position, but Student gives the credit to Langguth.

So that I could tell a smoothly flowing story, I declined to interrupt the narrative with a detailed discussion of competing claims. Where the facts are less than clear—and opposing points of view cannot be reconciled—this approach inevitably involves a certain measure of subjectivity. Nevertheless, I have pointed out some of the starker disagreements between Skorzeny and the paratroopers in footnotes and endnotes.

My depiction of the Gran Sasso raid deserves a few words of explanation. In describing this event, I have frankly given more weight to the accounts of General Student and the paratroopers. This seems fitting considering that the raid was a Luftwaffe enterprise for which Student had the ultimate responsibility.

However, in the interest of fairness, it should be noted that Skorzeny and Radl paint a different picture. According to the SS men, Skorzeny played a major role in the planning of the operation and was designated as the commander of the glider assault squads. Although the latter claim seems somewhat implausible—after all, Skorzeny had no training as a paratrooper—it is always possible that Skorzeny and his deputy played a larger role behind the scenes than the paratroopers would have the world believe. The exact truth of the matter is difficult to untangle.

For readers who are interested in more detail, several points of dispute between Skorzeny and the paratroopers are listed briefly below:

- *Mission planning.* The paratroopers take full credit for conceiving and planning the Gran Sasso raid. They flatly deny Skorzeny's claim that he was the primary architect of the operation.

- *Command.* Student and Mors both agree that Berlepsch was the commander of the glider assault teams on September 12. Skorzeny, on the other hand, claims that he was in charge (but that Berlepsch was designated to assume command once Skorzeny had entered the hotel).

- *Glider sequence.* According to Student, Berlepsch flew in the first glider. While en route to the Gran Sasso, Berlepsch's chain flew a broad loop to gain more altitude. This "detour" inadvertently allowed Skorzeny to take over the lead. In his memoirs, Skorzeny claims that Berlepsch was assigned to the fifth glider. The SS man said that he and Soleti flew in Glider No. 3, which assumed the lead when the two gliders ahead of him (neither of which contained Berlepsch) mysteriously dropped out of the convoy.

- *Escape plan.* In Skorzeny's version, flying Mussolini off the mountain was a last-resort measure that became necessary only when other, more preferable options proved unworkable. However, Student does not corroborate this.

- *Bombing of Pratica di Mare.* All parties agree that Allied bombers flew over the airfield on September 12 just before the departure of the gliders. Skorzeny claims that the bombing caused some minor damage to the airport, but Student denies that *any* bombs were dropped during this raid.

Notes

■

Prologue

1. Close to 9:00 A.M.: Benito Mussolini, *Memoirs*, 78. Brilliant sunshine: Ibid. Palazzo Venezia was in the center of Rome: Denis Mack Smith, *Mussolini*, 167.

2. Hibbert, 212.

3. Stuffed hand grenades into their briefcases: Monelli, 212; and Davis, *Who Defends Rome*, 99.

4. A ten-hour meeting: Denis Mack Smith, *Modern Italy*, 414.

5. Benito Mussolini, *Memoirs*, 64.

6. Hoettl, 235 (from Mussolini's *Pontine and Sardinian Musings*).

7. Benito Mussolini, *Memoirs*, 78.

8. Surrounded himself with yes-men: Denis Mack Smith, *Mussolini*, 279; Denis Mack Smith, *Modern Italy*, 391; and Brendon, 559.

9. Corvaja, 314.

10. Ibid., 320.

11. "Mussolini is always right": Hibbert, 208; and Dombrowski, 3. Note: Dombrowski wrote that this slogan could be seen in every Italian city.

12. Mussolini was greeted by the crowd: Benito Mussolini, *Memoirs*, 80; Monelli, 215; Davis, *Who Defends Rome*, 134; and Hibbert, 219. Note: Dollmann, *Interpreter*, 229, claimed that Galbiati informed him that Mussolini had received a favorable reception that afternoon.

13. Benito Mussolini, *Memoirs*, 80.

14. Instructed Galbiati to empty his wallet and distribute money to the victims: Davis, *Who Defends Rome*, 134; and Hibbert, 219.

15. Did not generally carry cash: Hibbert, 219.

16. Pride in his reception: Katz, *Battle for Rome,* 19, noted that Mussolini bragged about it to his wife on July 25.

17. Steamy summer in Rome that year: Hibbert, 246; and Plehwe, 39.

18. Hoettl, 236 (from Mussolini's *Pontine and Sardinian Musings*).

19. Bearing soup: Rachele Mussolini, 249; and Hibbert, 219.

20. Hoettl, 236 (from Mussolini's *Pontine and Sardinian Musings*).

21. Rachele begged Mussolini to cancel his meeting with the king: Rachele Mussolini, 249; and Hibbert, 219.

22. He told Rachele that he had nothing to fear from the king: Rachele Mussolini, 251.

23. He told Rachele that the king was a friend: Davis, *Who Defends Rome,* 138; and Katz, *Battle for Rome,* 19.

24. *Gran Consiglio:* Denis Mack Smith, *Modern Italy,* 414.

25. Alfa Romeo: Davis, *Who Defends Rome,* 139. Iron gates: Hibbert, 223. The Villa Savoia was on the outskirts of Rome: Badoglio, 41 (in a footnote).

26. Dark-blue suit and a black felt hat: Hibbert, 219–220. Note: Rachele Mussolini, 251, also said that Mussolini was wearing a blue suit and a hat.

27. Behind the king's shrubbery: Katz, *Battle for Rome,* 21.

28. No trace of foreboding: Benito Mussolini, *Memoirs,* 80.

29. Five feet tall: Davis, *Who Defends Rome,* 38.

30. Exchange about the hot weather: Hibbert, 224.

31. Discussed the vote and minimized its importance: Hibbert, 224; and Monelli, 218.

32. Benito Mussolini, *My Rise and Fall,* page 71 of the section titled "Fall of Mussolini."

33. Monelli, 218.

34. Benito Mussolini, *My Rise and Fall,* page 71 of the section titled "Fall of Mussolini."

35. Ibid.

36. Badoglio, 42. Note: Badoglio took this quote directly from the king, and it is consistent with other accounts; see, for instance, Monelli, 218. Mussolini sat down: Davis, *Who Defends Rome,* 141.

37. Davis, *Who Defends Rome,* 141. Admiration for Mussolini: Ibid., 40.

38. Benito Mussolini, *My Rise and Fall,* page 72 of the section titled "Fall of Mussolini."

39. Twenty minutes: Monelli, 217; and Davis, *Who Defends Rome,* 141.

40. At 5:20 P.M.: Monelli, 218.

41. Benito Mussolini, *My Rise and Fall,* page 72 of the section titled "Fall of Mussolini."

Chapter 1

1. Skorzeny, *Secret Missions*, 43.
2. Three lieutenant colonels and two majors: Ibid., 40.
3. Looped-wool carpet: Ibid.
4. Foley, 41.
5. Resigned from office for reasons of poor health: Wiskemann, 305; Gilbert, 55 (in a footnote); and Dombrowski, 39.
6. Lounge of the Hotel Eden: Skorzeny, *Secret Missions*, 35.
7. Ibid.
8. Ibid.
9. Ibid., 36.
10. Thousands of tons of bombs on Republican forces and Spanish civilians: Green, *Warplanes*, 406–407.
11. Discussed the strange goings-on in Italy: Note: Radl, 20–24, claimed that he did not meet Skorzeny at Tempelhof but that another of Skorzeny's men brought him his uniform.
12. About 320 miles and was nearing Masuria: Skorzeny, *Secret Missions*, 38.
13. Fir and pine trees: Corvaja, 231.
14. Skorzeny, *Secret Missions*, 39.
15. Ibid.
16. Stuttgart landscaping company . . . installed artificial trees and moss: Hoffmann, *Hitler's Personal Security*, 224–225.
17. Skorzeny, *Secret Missions*, 40.
18. Ibid.
19. Ibid., 41.
20. Ibid.
21. Blue-gray eyes: Trevor-Roper, *Last Days*, 116.
22. Skorzeny, *Secret Missions*, 42.
23. Ibid., 43.
24. Ibid.
25. 200,000 German-speaking ex-Austrians: Wiskemann, 23.
26. Skorzeny, *Secret Missions*, 43.
27. Ibid.
28. Ibid.
29. Hitler grew more animated as he spoke: Ibid.
30. Ibid., 43–44.
31. Ibid., 44.
32. Ibid.

33. Ibid., 45.

34. Guensche appeared again and told him that Student was waiting: Skorzeny, *My Commando Operations*, 231.

35. Sniper's bullet in 1940: Barnett, *Hitler's Generals*, 470.

36. Skorzeny, *My Commando Operations*, 232.

37. Skorzeny, *Secret Missions*, 46.

38. Ibid., 46–47.

39. Skorzeny, *My Commando Operations*, 232–233.

40. Skorzeny, *Secret Missions*, 47.

Chapter 2

1. Gilbert, 57.

2. Contempt for the bourgeois and upper classes: Bullock, *Hitler,* 220.

3. Warlimont, 326–327 (from a May 20, 1943, Hitler conference).

4. They had been caught napping: Note: After the war, Wilhelm Hoettl and Walter Schellenberg, both of whom worked in SS intelligence, claimed that the SS had tried to warn Hitler about the deteriorating situation in Italy. However, Hitler preferred to put his faith in the rosy reports issued by Mackensen, who was inclined to tell the Fuehrer what the latter wanted to hear. See Hoettl, 221–225; and Schellenberg, 385–386.

5. Dollmann, *Interpreter,* 229.

6. With Mussolini's blessing: Denis Mack Smith, *Mussolini*, 290.

7. Westphal, 167.

8. Allowed thousands of merchant vessels to cross: Buderi, *Invention,* 168.

9. Doenitz, 341.

10. Endless sorties into Germany during the first half of the year: Liddell Hart, *Second World War,* 600.

11. Sanctioned the use of carpet-bombing: Rhodes, *Atomic Bomb,* 471.

12. Nothing less than "unconditional surrender": Garland and Smyth, 11.

13. Hitler noticed trembling in his left arm and leg: Bullock, *Hitler,* 419. Note: Irving, *Secret Diaries of Hitler's Doctor,* 52, indicates that this trembling occurred early in 1943.

14. Tremors grew worse despite treatment: Bullock, *Hitler,* 419. Crossed his right hand over his left, and pushed his foot against stationary objects: Ibid., 420.

15. A slight limp: Ibid., 420; and Irving, *Secret Diaries of Hitler's Doctor,* 52.

16. Hitler was a hypochondriac: Irving, *Secret Diaries of Hitler's Doctor,* 10. Large amounts of drugs: Bullock, *Hitler,* 420. Various drugs, vitamins, glucose injections, hormones: Irving, *Secret Diaries of Hitler's Doctor,* 60–72.

17. Morell became indispensable: Bullock, *Hitler,* 420–421.

18. Contributed to Hitler's deterioration: Ibid. Used Hitler as a guinea pig: Irving, *Secret Diaries of Hitler's Doctor,* 61.

19. Seventy-seven different medications: Irving, *Secret Diaries of Hitler's Doctor,* 60.

20. Corvaja, 299.

21. Liddell Hart, *Rommel Papers,* 428.

22. In mid-July: Shirer, 1000.

23. Warlimont, 334.

24. Corvaja, 147.

25. "Arrogant islanders": Trevor-Roper, *Testament,* 42 (Hitler said this in 1945).

26. Second largest city: Rhodes, *Atomic Bomb,* 471.

27. Aim was to destroy the city: Ibid.

28. Coin the term *Feuersturm:* Ibid., 473.

29. Temperatures of 1,400 degrees Fahrenheit, killing tens of thousands and destroying eight square miles: Ibid., 474.

30. Roasted alive: Ibid. Trapped in melting asphalt: Buderi, *Invention,* 191.

31. Gilbert, 39–40.

32. Ibid., 40.

33. Ibid., 40–41.

34. Ibid., 41.

35. Ibid.

36. Ibid., 42.

37. Ibid.

38. Hewel, Ribbentrop's man: Trevor-Roper, *Last Days,* 190 (in a footnote).

39. Gilbert, 43.

40. Ibid., 44.

41. Ibid., 47.

42. Badoglio had issued a cover story: Plehwe, 42–43, 65.

43. Purely a domestic matter: Ibid., 42.

44. Italy would continue to fight: Ibid.

45. Hitler did not reply: Ibid., 65.

46. Gilbert, 48.

47. Ibid.

48. Ibid.

49. Ibid. About thirty-five miles north of Rome near Lake Bolsena: Garland and Smyth, 283.

50. Squeezed into the northeastern corner: Stokesbury, *Short History of World War II,* 294.

51. Gilbert, 49.

52. Ibid.

53. Ibid.

54. Ibid.

55. Ibid., 50–51.

56. Ibid., 51–52.

57. Ibid., 52.

58. Junge, 114.

59. Thirteenth meeting: Denis Mack Smith, *Modern Italy,* 413; and Hibbert, 196.

60. Wear down the enemy, conserve German forces, and delay an assault on the Third Reich: Alfieri, 229.

61. Ibid. (from a memo dated July 12).

62. Ibid.

63. Trevor-Roper, *Bormann Letters,* 14 (the letter is dated July 23).

64. Hitler's 60,000 Germans versus invasion force of 500,000 men: See Liddell Hart, *Second World War,* 440, 445.

65. Garland and Smyth, 242.

66. Ibid.

67. Whip up the martial spirit: Shirer, 996; Bullock, *Hitler,* 412; Plehwe, 28; and Warlimont, 339.

Chapter 3

1. Alfieri, 93.

2. First made contact in the early 1920s: Denis Mack Smith, *Mussolini,* 172.

3. Hitler, 681.

4. Italian trains to run on time: Monelli, 101.

5. Doled out cash and offered assistance: Denis Mack Smith, *Mussolini,* 172–173.

6. Flattered by Hitler's admiration: Ibid., 173.

7. Asking for a signed photograph: Hibbert, 95; and Monelli, 128.

8. Monelli, 129.

9. A bronze bust of Mussolini; the Munich headquarters: Denis Mack Smith, *Mussolini,* 173. In his office: Toland, *Hitler,* 247.

10. Disarmed and politically isolated: Shirer, 209.

11. Austria was a security buffer: Denis Mack Smith, *Mussolini,* 218.

12. Believed he could overrule *Anschluss:* Ibid., 183.

13. Ibid., 183 (from *Documents Diplomatiques Français*).

14. War and race: Ibid., 185; and Starhemberg, 147–148.

15. Dombrowski, 7.

16. Compared Hitler to a broken record: Denis Mack Smith, *Mussolini*, 185.

17. Rachele Mussolini, 144.

18. Ibid., 145.

19. Starhemberg, 166.

20. Ibid., 167.

21. Ibid.

22. Hitler's aggressive swagger: Note: Wiskemann, 44, indicates that relations between Hitler and Mussolini were very bad during the first half of 1935.

23. Keeping Hitler in check was important: Note: According to Denis Mack Smith, *Mussolini*, 193, Mussolini needed a measure of security on Italy's northern border before launching the Ethiopian war.

24. Starhemberg, 212.

25. More popular than ever among the Italians: Denis Mack Smith, *Modern Italy*, 386. New Italian empire: Ibid., 392; and Monelli, 139–140, 143.

26. She was then twenty-four (1936): Monelli, 153.

27. Shortly after the Ethiopian war: Ibid., 152.

28. Photograph under her pillow: Ibid., 154.

29. Ciano was thirty-three: Denis Mack Smith, *Mussolini*, 206.

30. Ciano was cunning: Ciano, *Diary*, xi-xii.

31. Alfieri, 201.

32. Believed that the Western powers were on the decline: Denis Mack Smith, *Mussolini*, 206.

33. Favored an alliance with the Nazis: Ibid.

34. Muggeridge, 56.

35. The Nazis could dominate Eastern Europe and Mussolini could expand his empire: Denis Mack Smith, *Mussolini*, 208.

36. Ciano thought he could manipulate Hitler: Ibid.

37. *United States and Italy*, 2.

38. "Eight million bayonets": Denis Mack Smith, *Mussolini*, 214.

39. Could raise 1.5 million soldiers: Denis Mack Smith, *Modern Italy*, 403.

40. Warplanes and artillery were out of date: Ibid., 400. Armed with 1890s-style rifles: Ibid.; and Brendon, 568.

41. Blue-gray-colored uniform: Brendon, 565.

42. Maifeld: Shirer, 301. The Maifeld was near the Olympic Stadium: Brendon, 565. Coached on how to cheer: Ibid.

43. *New York Times*, September 29, 1937.

44. Ibid.

45. Made a profound impression: Denis Mack Smith, *Mussolini,* 215; and Brendon, 565.

46. Denis Mack Smith, *Modern Italy,* 393.

47. Dollmann, *Interpreter,* 107.

48. Shirer, 343.

49. Hibbert, 112.

50. Nazi salute was modeled on the Roman salute: Wiskemann, 26; Denis Mack Smith, *Modern Italy,* 389; and Monelli, 128.

51. Racial laws were decreed in the summer and fall of 1938: Brendon, 570. Affected the 40,000 to 70,000 Jews living in Italy: Denis Mack Smith, *Mussolini,* 221.

52. Jews were maligned in the press: Denis Mack Smith, *Mussolini,* 221.

53. Jews were to be expelled from Italian schools, purged from the military, forbidden to marry gentiles, and excluded from owning land or certain types of businesses: Brendon, 570.

54. Racial laws were not well received: Denis Mack Smith, *Mussolini,* 222; Wiskemann, 113; and Brendon, 570.

55. Many Italian Jews were Fascists and looked fondly on Mussolini: Brendon, 553; and Lamb, *War in Italy,* 35.

56. Starhemberg, 92 (Mussolini made this remark in 1932).

57. Ibid. (Mussolini made this remark in 1932).

58. Ibid., 24 (Mussolini made this remark in 1930).

59. Hibbert, 98–99.

60. World war was inevitable within three or four years: Shirer, 436.

61. Wring a few concessions by playing the peace card: Denis Mack Smith, *Mussolini,* 224.

62. Ciano, *Diary,* 146 (from an entry dated October 23, 1938).

63. Referred to Hitler as untrustworthy and considered aligning himself with the Western powers: Denis Mack Smith, *Mussolini,* 228.

64. Jealous: Ibid., 230.

65. Bumbling and meaningless adventure: Ibid., 230–231.

66. Was aware in the spring of 1939 (i.e., April and May) that Hitler was planning to invade Poland: Ibid., 232; and Shirer, 482.

67. Assured the Italians in May that Germany did not want war for four years: Wiskemann, 143; and Shirer, 482.

68. The king disapproved, but Mussolini brushed off his reservations: Monelli, 174.

69. Mussolini dubbed it the Pact of Steel: Denis Mack Smith, *Mussolini,* 231.

70. *Patto di Sangue:* Wiskemann, 145.

71. *Documents on German Foreign Policy,* vol. 6, 562.

72. Ibid., 618–619.

73. Hitler's father was a civil servant: Shirer, 6. Mussolini's was a black-smith: A.J.P. Taylor, *War Lords,* 17.

74. Made deals with big business: Wiskemann, 342.

75. Neither knew much about economics: Denis Mack Smith, *Mussolini,* 69.

76. Monelli, 119.

77. Mussolini made it known he wanted men killed: Denis Mack Smith, *Mussolini,* 115; Denis Mack Smith, *Modern Italy,* 387; and Monelli, 172.

78. Both praised *The Crowd:* Denis Mack Smith, *Mussolini,* 127.

79. Five feet six inches: Hibbert, 88; and Monelli, 122.

80. Duodenal ulcer first surfaced in 1925: Wiskemann, 9.

81. Good for most of his life and began to fail in 1943: Bullock, *Hitler,* 420.

82. Kesselring, 180.

83. Worked tirelessly: Denis Mack Smith, *Mussolini,* 111; and Monelli, 123. At the expense of his personal comfort: Hibbert, 52.

84. Man of culture and learning, and had a tendency to exaggerate his erudition: Denis Mack Smith, *Mussolini,* 131–132.

85. Mussolini insisted on writing a thesis paper: Monelli, 103.

86. Irving, *Hitler's War,* xxxi.

87. Ribbentrop, 28, 30–31.

88. Wiskemann, 342.

89. Hibbert, 11.

90. Alfieri, 92.

91. Never had real friends and considered this fact a virtue: Dennis Mack Smith, *Mussolini,* 4, 299.

92. Ibid., 11.

93. Imitation of the Duce's gestures: Ibid., 216. Used rouge: Hibbert, 115; and Dollmann, *Interpreter,* 109.

94. Had little regard for the Italians: Denis Mack Smith, *Mussolini,* 240.

95. *Kampfzeit:* Trevor-Roper, *Hitler's Table Talk,* xiv.

96. Ibid., 10 (this remark was made on the evening of July 21–22, 1941).

97. Ibid., 266 (this remark was made on January 31, 1942).

98. Ibid., 135 (this remark was made on November 20, 1941).

99. Mussolini was a former Socialist: Hibbert, 37.

100. Denis Mack Smith, *Mussolini,* 240.

101. A.J.P. Taylor, *War Lords,* 24.

102. Trevor-Roper, *Hitler's Table Talk,* 10 (this remark was made on the evening of July 21–22, 1941).

103. Ibid., 3 (this remark was made on July 5, 1941).

104. Rachele Mussolini, 152.

105. Alfieri, 93.

106. His alliance with Italy was a burden: Bullock, *Hitler,* 460.

107. *Fuehrer Conferences,* 67 (this remark was made on May 14 at the Wolf's Lair).

108. Deakin, 799–800 (from *Testament of Adolf Hitler*).

109. Trevor-Roper, *Testament,* 85.

110. Too many guitar players, not enough warriors: Ciano, *Diary,* 72–73.

111. Dollmann, *Interpreter,* 315.

112. Ciano, *Diary,* 332 (from an entry dated March 18, 1940).

113. Rachele Mussolini, 153.

114. Ciano, *Diary,* 333 (from an entry dated March 19, 1940).

115. Denis Mack Smith, *Mussolini,* 260.

116. Ciano, *Diary,* 590 (from an entry dated December 23, 1943).

117. Bullock, *Hitler,* 368.

118. Gilbert, 33 (from a May 20, 1943, Hitler conference).

119. Ciano, *Diary,* 258 (from an entry dated August 13, 1939).

120. Ibid., 330 (from an entry dated March 12, 1940).

121. Made his subordinates run to his desk: Denis Mack Smith, *Mussolini,* 202. Distance to his desk was twenty yards: Ibid., 125.

122. Monelli, 211.

123. Schmidt, 65.

Chapter 4

1. Goebbels, 407.

2. Near the Gulf of Genoa: Liddell Hart, *Rommel Papers,* 432 (Rommel mentions this point in a diary entry dated July 26).

3. Warlimont, 362 (from a July 26, 1943, Hitler conference).

4. Liddell Hart, *Rommel Papers,* 432.

5. Trevor-Roper, *Bormann Letters,* 16. (The letter is dated July 26.)

6. Within a week unless the Nazis seized Rome: Goebbels, 408, 416.

7. Goebbels, 405–406.

8. Semmler, 95.

9. By the time Hitler's advisors arrived: Bullock, *Hitler,* 414. Note: Bullock wrote that Hitler had these plans at the ready at least in theory by July 26.

10. Operation Oak was the mission to find and rescue Mussolini; Operation Student called for the armed takeover of the Italian capital: Shirer, 1000; and Martienssen, 184.

11. Operation Black was the military occupation of the Italian peninsula: Shirer, 1000; and Martienssen, 184.

12. Operation Axis was the capture or destruction of the Italian fleet: Shirer, 1000; and Martienssen, 184.

13. Goebbels, 416.

14. Goering and Ribbentrop adopted Hitler's point of view: *Fuehrer Conferences,* 104.

15. Ibid.,103–104.

16. Ibid., 104.

17. Ibid.

18. Nicknamed "Smiling Albert": Barnett, *Hitler's Generals,* 276. Kesselring had a reputation for being an Italophile: Plehwe, 86.

19. *Fuehrer Conferences,* 104.

20. Gilbert, 31 (from a May 20, 1943, Hitler conference).

21. Trevor-Roper, *Bormann Letters,* 14.

22. Goebbels, 411.

23. Shirer, 343.

24. Dissolved the Fascist Party on July 27: Delzell, 238.

25. Deakin, 495 (from a Mackensen telegram dated July 26).

26. Alfieri fled to Switzerland: Dombrowski, 112.

27. Deakin, 495 (from a Mackensen telegram dated July 27).

28. Goebbels, 417–418.

29. Deakin, 498 (from a Mackensen telegram dated July 29).

30. Ibid. (from a Mackensen telegram dated July 29).

31. Deliver Hitler's birthday present to the Duce: Plehwe, 66.

32. The gift would be conveyed by the Italians: Ibid.

33. Badoglio had given the Germans a letter: Ibid., 49–50. Note: According to Plehwe, Badoglio told the Germans about this letter on July 26.

34. Benito Mussolini, *Memoirs,* 84.

35. Goebbels, 415.

36. Units from France and the Eastern front: Plehwe, 67–68.

37. Goebbels, 408.

38. The Allies were caught off guard by the coup: Davis, *Who Defends Rome,* 163.

39. Ibid., 40 (this remark was made by Galeazzo Ciano to a friend).

40. Lacked experience as a politician: Lamb, *War in Italy,* 13.

41. Sacked in 1940: Lamb, *War in Italy,* 14.

42. A pint of champagne daily, card games and frequent naps: Lamb, *War in Italy,* 14.

43. Rarely made a move without the monarch's approval: Garland and Smyth, 267, 281.

44. Neither had developed a strategy for getting out of the war: Delzell, 233.

45. Several attempts to contact the West: Lamb, *War in Italy*, 12.

46. Inclined to reject such a harsh stance: Ibid.

47. Held out hope that they could come to an understanding with Hitler and thereby exit the war: Garland and Smyth, 282, 287.

48. Plehwe, 125.

49. Contacted Hitler and requested a summit meeting: Garland and Smyth, 286.

50. Badoglio, 55.

51. Churchill, *Onwards to Victory*, 143, 145.

52. Created uncertainty in the minds of the Allies: Delzell, 243; Denis Mack Smith, *Modern Italy*, 417; and Lamb, *War in Italy*, 13.

53. Dozens wrote letters to Badoglio: Denis Mack Smith, *Italy and Its Monarchy*, 307; and Plehwe, 73, 75.

54. Badoglio, 46.

55. Its 4 million members: Denis Mack Smith, *Italy and Its Monarchy*, 306.

56. Units were beginning to mass near the Italian frontier: Plehwe, 66.

57. Some of Badoglio's own generals believed that Italy should make a clean break: Denis Mack Smith, *Italy and Its Monarchy*, 307; and Delzell, 257. Never gave this option consideration: Davis, *Who Defends Rome,* 210.

58. Badoglio, 66.

Chapter 5

1. Skorzeny, *Secret Missions,* 57.

2. Put it on hold before canceling it altogether: Note: According to Garland and Smyth, 368, OKW cancelled Operation Student on August 5.

3. Student, 392–393.

4. About 20,000: Ibid., 394.

5. Skorzeny, *Secret Missions,* 48.

6. Sometime after 11:00 P.M.: Radl, 22–26.

7. Skorzeny, *Secret Missions,* 48.

8. Every half an hour: Radl, 22–26.

9. Forty commandos from Friedenthal: Skorzeny, *My Commando Operations,* 236.

10. Ten intelligence officers from Amt VI: Ibid.

11. Assigned to Skorzeny to aid in the search: Ibid., 233, 236.

12. Paratrooper garb and bogus IDs: Radl, 23–30.

13. A set of civilian clothes: Ibid., 23–27.

14. Dye their hair black: Ibid., 27–31.

15. Chalked up the idea to Himmler: Skorzeny, *My Commando Operations,* 233.

16. Radl ignored the hair dye order: Radl, 29–33.

17. Monk's robes: Ibid., 25–29.

18. Early on the morning of July 27: Student, 393–394.

19. Gerlach was an ace: Patricelli, 67.

20. Skorzeny, *Secret Missions,* 52.

21. Ibid., 53.

22. Ten miles from Rome: Davis, *Who Defends Rome,* 363.

23. Had worked with them for more than a year and a half: See ibid., 87.

24. Skorzeny, *Secret Missions,* 54.

25. Ibid.

26. Ibid.

27. Goebbels, 410.

28. Skorzeny, *Secret Missions,* 44.

29. Similar lecture about secrecy: Student, 393–394, 412.

30. Keep Kesselring out of the loop: See Ibid., 393–394; and Deakin, 544.

31. Kesselring, 171.

32. Liddell Hart, *Rommel Papers,* 434.

33. Over the next several days: Garland and Smyth, 286, 293.

34. Without the consent of the Italians: Student, 394; and Liddell Hart, *Second World War,* 452. Would be transferred to Sicily or southern Italy: Ibid.

35. On the evening of July 28: Radl, 48–52.

36. Detour to France on July 27: Ibid., 35–42.

37. Quartered near the airport: Skorzeny, *My Commando Operations,* 234.

38. Showed up on July 29 and informed his men: Radl, 55–56.

39. Ibid., 55.

40. One of the commandos fainted: Ibid., 56.

41. Ibid.

42. Skorzeny, *Secret Missions,* 55.

43. Worked with Langguth: Radl, 87–91; and Patricelli, 23.

44. Blue eyes: Dollmann, *Interpreter,* 241. Kappler was thirty-six: Katz, *Battle for Rome,* 46; and Davis, *Who Defends Rome,* 89. Dueling scars: Dollmann, *Interpreter,* 239; and Katz, *Battle for Rome,* 83. Training in espionage and security: Ibid., 51.

45. Spying on the Italian police: Katz, *Battle for Rome,* 51.

46. Dogs, roses, and Etruscan vases: Ibid.

47. Fondness for Rome: Ibid. Posted to Rome in 1939: Ibid.

48. Skorzeny, *Secret Missions*, 55.

49. Dollmann was in the General SS: Dollmann, *Interpreter,* 76.

50. Excellent knowledge of Italian: Katz, *Death in Rome,* 26. Blond: Ibid. Dapper: Katz, *Battle for Rome,* 291. Confidant of Eva Braun: Katz, *Death in Rome,* 26.

51. Elegant manners and knowledge of Italian culture: Katz, *Death in Rome,* 26.

52. Flair for intrigue: Ibid.

53. Dollmann, *Interpreter,* 239.

54. Ibid.

55. Ribbentrop urged the German embassy staff to arrest the "wire-pullers": Plehwe, 60; also see Hoettl, 225.

56. Three men and one female secretary: Plehwe, 60.

57. Kappler and Dollmann disliked each other: Dollmann, *Interpreter,* 237, 241; and Plehwe, 63. Kappler believed that rescuing Mussolini was a bad idea: Katz, *Battle for Rome,* 51.

58. Dollmann, *Interpreter,* 249.

59. Kappler was convinced that Fascism was finished: Plehwe, 63.

60. Ibid.

61. Kappler flew to see Himmler: Ibid., 91–92.

62. Dollmann, *Interpreter,* 240.

63. Dollmann and Mackensen drew up the list of victims: Plehwe, 84, 89; also see Radl, 72–76.

64. Resented Skorzeny as an intrusion: Dollmann, *Interpreter,* 241. A stickler for orders: Ibid; and Katz, *Battle for Rome,* 51.

65. Priebke spoke fluent Italian: Goni, *Real Odessa,* 252. Priebke was Kappler's second-in-command: Katz, *Battle for Rome,* 61.

66. He had made connections among the Italians: Radl, 71–75. Italian operatives on his payroll: Note: Radl, 87–91, indicates that Kappler used his "agents" to help find Mussolini, but it is not clear whether Radl is referring to Kappler's tiny staff or to possible Italian operatives.

67. Kappler was actively involved: Ibid., 87–91.

68. Student, 410.

69. Skorzeny, *Secret Missions,* 57.

70. Hoettl, 231.

71. Schellenberg, 386.

72. Wulff, *Zodiac,* 85 and 87.

73. Student, 408.

74. About 5,000 pounds in forged British banknotes: Skorzeny, *My Commando Operations,* 221.

75. *New York Times,* July 26, 1943.

76. A wave of popular feeling rippled through Rome: Wiskemann, 303.

77. People sang songs in the streets and wept: Ibid. They declared that the end of Fascism had arrived and cursed the name of Mussolini: Hibbert, 229.

78. Plehwe, 41.

79. Monelli, 224–225.

80. Little physical violence: Monelli, 224.

81. Shop windows already bore photographs of the king and Badoglio: Monelli, 225.

82. Badoglio, 50.

83. Outdid the Fascists regarding repressive measures: Katz, *Battle for Rome,* 27.

84. A 9:00 P.M. curfew, and meetings involving more than three people were outlawed: Plehwe, 49.

85. One of the best organizations of its kind: Davis, *Who Defends Rome,* 59.

86. Planted by Italian agents: Radl, 87–91; and Davis, *Who Defends Rome,* 286.

87. Skorzeny, *Secret Missions,* 56.

88. Student, 409.

Chapter 6

1. Benito Mussolini, *Memoirs,* 83.

2. Captain Paolo Vigneri: Davis, *Who Defends Rome,* 135, 141.

3. Benito Mussolini, *Memoirs,* 82.

4. Ibid.

5. A seat on a stretcher: Monelli, 219.

6. Hoettl, 237 (from Mussolini's *Pontine and Sardinian Musings*).

7. Benito Mussolini, *Memoirs,* 82.

8. Courtyard of the Podgora barracks in Via Quintino Sella: Hibbert, 227.

9. Thrust out his chin, hands on hips: Ibid.

10. Shown to the officers' mess, bided his time for forty-five minutes: Ibid.

11. Carabinieri cadet barracks in Via Legnano: Ibid. Arriving at 7:00 P.M.: Davis, *Who Defends Rome,* 147.

12. Benito Mussolini, *Memoirs,* 83.

13. Large white letters: Hibbert, 232. "Believe, Fight, and Obey" was a popular Fascist slogan: Denis Mack Smith, *Mussolini,* 124.

14. Green-colored envelope, "War Office," and handwritten note: Benito Mussolini, *Memoirs,* 83.

15. Ibid., 83–84.

16. Ibid., 84.

17. Ibid., 85.

18. Goebbels, 415.

19. Benito Mussolini, *Memoirs,* 84.

20. Ibid.

21. Ibid., 86.

22. About eighty miles southeast of Rome: Maugeri, 125.

23. Costanzo Ciano Wharf: Hibbert, 235. Named after the father of Galeazzo Ciano: Dombrowski, 62.

24. Maugeri, 125.

25. Ibid., 129.

26. Ibid.

27. Ibid., 130.

28. Ibid., 131.

29. Ibid.

30. Twenty-five miles northwest of Ventotene: Hibbert, 237.

31. Maugeri, 134.

32. Ibid.

33. Ibid., 135–136.

34. Ibid., 139.

35. Ibid., 139–140.

36. Ibid., 140.

37. Ibid.

38. Criticized the Italians for being too soft and artistic: See, for instance, Monelli, 181.

39. Santa Maria was a village: Hibbert, 238.

40. Gray-colored house with green shutters: Ibid.

41. Benito Mussolini, *Memoirs,* 87–88.

42. Ibid., 226 (from "In the Ras's House," an article compiled by the editors of the Rome periodical *Politica Estera*).

43. Ibid. (also from "In the Ras's House," an article compiled by the editors of the Rome periodical *Politica Estera*).

44. Ibid., 88.

Chapter 7

1. Speer, 308.

2. Approximately 30,000 German soldiers: Garland and Smyth, 371.

3. "Viva il Duce" on their helmets: Lamb, *War in Italy*, 14.

4. Badoglio was confident that he could talk the Anglo-Americans down: Badoglio, 56. The king also believed that Italy could get better terms: Denis Mack Smith, *Italy and Its Monarchy*, 308.

5. Churchill, *Closing the Ring*, 100.

6. Stalling for time: Note: According to Denis Mack Smith, *Italy and Its Monarchy*, 308, even at this stage while they were sending peace feelers to the Allies, the Italians were still hoping that Hitler would allow them to withdraw from the Axis.

7. Churchill, *Closing the Ring*, 101–102 (from a telegram dated August 7).

8. Goebbels, 412.

9. *Fuehrer Conferences*, 121 (Hitler said this to Doenitz).

10. Speer, 308.

11. Skorzeny, *Secret Missions*, 56.

12. A petty officer said he had seen the Duce boarding a vessel in Gaeta: Deakin, 544.

13. Demanded that he be kept informed of the latest leads: Ibid., 543.

14. *Fuehrer Conferences*, 110.

15. Ultimate source of the Ventotene lead was Laurich: Deakin, 544.

16. Laurich worked at a German navy signals base at Gaeta: Ibid. He received the tip from an Italian naval officer, with whom he had become friendly: Ibid., 544; and Martienssen, 189 (in a footnote).

17. *Fuehrer Conferences*, 113.

18. Ventotene lead may have been a plant by SIM: Davis, *Who Defends Rome*, 286.

19. *Fuehrer Conferences*, 110.

20. Ibid.

21. Rescue of the Duce was put on hold, as well as Hitler's plans to take over Italy by force: Deakin, 502.

22. Keitel, 188.

23. *Fuehrer Conferences*, 113.

24. Ibid.

25. Ibid.

26. Ibid., 113–114.

27. Ibid., 114.

28. Maugeri, 142.

29. Badoglio, 63.

30. Maugeri, 143.

31. Ibid.

32. Ibid., 144.

33. Ibid., 145.
34. Ibid., 147–148.
35. Benito Mussolini, *Memoirs*, 91.
36. Evacuated after a heavy bombing raid: Hibbert, 245.
37. Composed mainly of sailors and fishermen: Ibid.
38. Benito Mussolini, *Memoirs*, 92.
39. He called his journal the *Pontine and Sardinian Musings:* Hoettl, 264.
40. Ibid., 239 (from Mussolini's *Pontine and Sardinian Musings*).
41. Ibid., 242 (from Mussolini's *Pontine and Sardinian Musings*).
42. Ibid., 248 (from Mussolini's *Pontine and Sardinian Musings*).
43. Ibid., 258 (from Mussolini's *Pontine and Sardinian Musings*).
44. Benito Mussolini, *Memoirs*, 92.
45. "Live dangerously" was a Fascist motto: Denis Mack Smith, *Mussolini*, 115.
46. An enormous case: Badoglio, 64.
47. Benito Mussolini, *Memoirs*, 93.
48. The same gift that Mackensen had attempted to deliver: Plehwe, 66.
49. Badoglio, 64.
50. Polito was his senior jailer: Hibbert, 248.
51. Not certain he could prevent Mussolini from being seized by mobs: Monelli, 225.
52. Hoettl, 246 (from Mussolini's *Pontine and Sardinian Musings*).

Chapter 8

1. *Fuehrer Conferences*, 115.
2. Schmidt, 263.
3. Ibid.
4. Warlimont, 376.
5. Deakin, 506 (from *Hitler e Mussolini*).
6. Ibid. (from *Hitler e Mussolini*).
7. Ibid. (from *Hitler e Mussolini*).
8. Ribbentrop had been instructed to gauge intentions: Plehwe, 111; and Warlimont, 375.
9. Dollmann, *Interpreter,* 245.
10. The return of Italian troops: Garland and Smyth, 369–370.
11. Would refer the matter to Hitler: Ibid., 370.
12. Conference was a bust: Ibid.
13. Dollmann, *Interpreter,* 246.
14. Ibid.

15. Ibid.
16. *Fuehrer Conferences,* 114.
17. Ibid.
18. Ibid., 115.
19. Ibid.
20. Ibid.
21. Ibid.
22. Ibid.
23. "Game": Gilbert, 50–51.
24. *Fuehrer Conferences,* 115.
25. Ibid., 116.
26. Ibid.
27. Liddell Hart, *Rommel Papers,* 441.
28. *Fuehrer Conferences,* 118.
29. Kappler had traced the Duce to Ponza: Student, 410.
30. An Italian grocer who supplied the island: Radl, 88–94.
31. Sometime during the first ten days of August: Ibid., 94–98.
32. *Fuehrer Conferences,* 119.
33. Student, 411.
34. *Fuehrer Conferences,* 119.
35. Ibid., 118.
36. Doenitz was becoming one of Hitler's closest advisors during this period: Warlimont, 374.
37. *Fuehrer Conferences,* 121.
38. Ibid., 117.
39. Ibid., 118.
40. Warlimont, 374.
41. Keitel, 187.
42. A mass exodus from Berlin during August: Irving, *Hitler's War,* 612.
43. One million civilians were eventually evacuated, many of them women and children: Ibid.

Chapter 9

1. Student, 413.
2. Kamptz had run across an old navy buddy in Rome: Ibid., 411.
3. Rumor going around the island: Ibid.
4. Flew to the Wolf's Lair on August 16: *Fuehrer Conferences,* 122.
5. Ibid., 123.

6. Ibid.

7. Ibid.

8. Being held on an Italian warship in Spezia: Student, 411.

9. "Reliable source" revealed Mussolini's secret location: Ibid.

10. Ultimate source was an Italian naval officer: Skorzeny, *Secret Missions*, 57.

11. Student, 411–412.

12. Student did not know what to believe: Ibid., 412.

13. Left the Pontine islands aboard an Italian warship (destination unknown) prior to mid-August: Radl, 91–95. Note: Skorzeny, *My Commando Operations*, 248, claimed that the Germans learned this on August 10 or 11.

14. Cordon around Spezia: Davis, *Who Defends Rome*, 286.

15. Student, 412.

16. Skorzeny, *Secret Missions*, 57.

17. *Jaegerleitoffiziere* based in Spezia: Student, 412.

18. Ibid.

19. Ibid., 413.

20. Whiting, *Skorzeny*, 14.

21. Skorzeny, *My Commando Operations*, 127.

22. Skorzeny, *Secret Missions*, 13.

23. About five hundred yards west of the town: Infield, *Skorzeny*, 35.

24. Hunaeus mentioned the Villa Webber: Skorzeny, *My Commando Operations*, 249; and Radl, 102–104.

25. Multiple leads pointed to the area of Sardinia: Radl, 95–97, 103–105.

26. Flak unit commander said that Mussolini was in Santa Maria: Skorzeny, *My Commando Operations*, 248–249.

27. Skorzeny, *Secret Missions*, 58.

28. An interpreter working for Hunaeus: Skorzeny, *My Commando Operations*, 249; and Radl, 103–105.

29. Skorzeny, *Secret Missions*, 59.

30. Student, 413.

31. Skorzeny, *Secret Missions*, 60.

32. Ibid.

33. The 20,000-pound airplane: Green, *Warplanes*, 303.

34. Skorzeny, *Secret Missions*, 62.

35. Arrived in Rome on August 20: Ibid., 63. He learned of Kappler's discovery: Skorzeny, *My Commando Operations*, 250.

36. Had focused on Mussolini's family: Radl, 106–108. Vittorio had fled to Germany: Davis, *Who Defends Rome*, 287.

37. Kappler traced it to Maddalena: Radl, 107–109.

38. Had actually seen the Duce: Skorzeny, *My Commando Operations,* 250; and Radl, 108–110.

39. On August 23 he flew back to Maddalena with Radl: Skorzeny, *My Commando Operations,* 250; and Radl, 108–110.

40. Spied a bald, stocky man on the terrace: Radl, 109–111.

41. Was almost certain that it was the Duce: Ibid.

42. Returned to Rome on August 24 and conferred with Student: Ibid., 110–112.

43. Skorzeny, *Secret Missions,* 63–64.

44. Abwehr and Amt VI were separate organizations with similar agendas, and the lines of demarcation were gray: Lucas, *Kommando,* 21–22.

45. Competed for Hitler's favor: Ibid., 22–23.

46. Almost a matter of policy: Brendon, 289; Lucas, *Kommando,* 22–23; and Doenitz, *Memoirs,* xv.

47. Philosophy of "divide and rule": Brendon, 289; Lucas, *Kommando,* 22–23; and Doenitz, *Memoirs,* xv.

48. Reassured the Nazi leadership that the loyalty of the Italians was beyond reproach: Hoehne, 532.

49. On Elba or somewhere close by: Student, 414.

50. To meet with Hitler in person: Note: Contrary to what the accounts of Student and Skorzeny say, Radl, 141–146, claimed that this visit took place *after* the aborted Maddalena rescue attempt.

51. Student, 414.

52. Skorzeny, *My Commando Operations,* 251.

53. Student, 414.

54. Skorzeny, *My Commando Operations,* 252.

55. Student, 414.

56. Skorzeny, *Secret Missions,* 71.

57. Some of them were drinking wine: Radl, 142–144.

58. Skorzeny, *Secret Missions,* 71.

59. Student, 414.

60. Skorzeny, *Secret Missions,* 72.

61. Dulles, *From Hitler's Doorstep,* 111.

62. Open secret among the local population: Patricelli, 42.

63. Believed that a rescue attempt was in the making: Hibbert, 248.

64. On August 28 at around 4:00 A.M.: Benito Mussolini, *Memoirs,* 93.

65. An hour and a half: Ibid.

66. Not far from the headquarters of the Third Panzergrenadier Division: Davis, *Who Defends Rome,* 287.

67. Gueli replaced Polito after the latter was injured in a car accident: Hibbert, 248.

68. The "usual motor-ambulance," and was driven past Rieti and Cittaducale: Benito Mussolini, *Memoirs,* 93–94.

69. Fifteen miles or so: Hibbert, 249. Small inn called La Villetta: Iurato and Antonelli, "With Mussolini at the Campo Imperatore," 244.

70. Two primary guardians were Gueli and Faiola: Benito Mussolini, *Memoirs,* 94; and Iurato and Antonelli, "With Mussolini at the Campo Imperatore," 245.

Chapter 10

1. Deakin, 522.

2. Warlimont, 374.

3. Liddell Hart, *Rommel Papers,* 440 (from a diary entry dated August 11).

4. Student, 397.

5. Deakin, 519.

6. Ibid., 520.

7. Ibid., 522.

8. For several weeks to come, Ribbentrop would nurture the hope that the Nazis could reach an understanding with Badoglio: Ibid., 516.

9. Ibid., 522.

10. D'Ajeta wanted to know whether they were open to the idea of negotiating: Davis, *Who Defends Rome,* 230.

11. Suave: Strong, *Intelligence at the Top,* 146. A quick-witted Sicilian: Plehwe, 53; and Monelli, 208.

12. Left by train on August 12: Delzell, 247.

13. Castellano could have taken a plane, but was told not to hurry: Denis Mack Smith, *Italy and Its Monarchy,* 311.

14. A "motley collection of garments": Strong, *Intelligence at the Top,* 144–145.

15. Ibid., 151.

16. Not anxious to surrender: Delzell, 248; and Denis Mack Smith, *Italy and Its Monarchy,* 311.

17. Did not have the authority to surrender: Delzell, 248; and Denis Mack Smith, *Italy and Its Monarchy,* 311.

18. Trying to learn the details of the invasion plans: Denis Mack Smith, *Italy and Its Monarchy,* 312.

19. Strong, *Intelligence at the Top,* 149–150.

20. Failed to send a progress report: Denis Mack Smith, *Italy and Its Monarchy,* 311; Delzell, 249; and Clark, *Modern Italy,* 303.

21. Neglected to bring a radio: Denis Mack Smith, *Italy and Its Monarchy,* 311.

22. Italian intelligence services possessed several communications links, but no one told Castellano: Ibid.

23. Zanussi was on Roatta's staff: Delzell, 249. Arrived on August 26: Churchill, *Closing the Ring,* 107–108.

24. Created confusion: Denis Mack Smith, *Italy and Its Monarchy,* 311; and Garland and Smyth, 462.

25. Churchill, *Closing the Ring,* 107.

26. One of Eisenhower's men (Bedell Smith) considered having Zanussi shot: Davis, *Who Defends Rome,* 292.

27. *Fuehrer Conferences,* 117.

28. Would help to "clarify" intentions: *Fuehrer Conferences,* 117; and Liddell Hart, *Rommel Papers,* 441.

29. Just outside Bologna at a villa that had belonged to Federzoni: Deakin, 512.

30. Diplomats were told to stay at home: Garland and Smyth, 452.

31. Kesselring, 173.

32. Liddell Hart, *Rommel Papers,* 441.

33. Warlimont, 378. Note: Warlimont did not attend the Bologna conference.

34. On August 11: Warlimont, 377; and Plehwe, 118. Triggered the August 15 meeting: Warlimont, 377.

35. Warlimont, 378.

36. Roatta refused to answer: Garland and Smyth, 453.

37. Progress was almost nonexistent: Ibid., 452; and Badoglio, 69.

38. Fearful of a poisoning attempt: Davis, *Who Defends Rome,* 251.

39. In the center of Bologna: Ibid.

40. Jodl refused to drink his coffee: Plehwe, 119.

41. Roatta stressed the distrustful atmosphere: Garland and Smyth, 453.

42. Struck by the fact that the Nazis surrounded Federzoni's villa with SS: Ibid.

43. Badoglio cautioned everyone present: Ibid.

44. Provocations might cause the Nazis to descend on Rome: Ibid.

45. In the early afternoon of August 15: Warlimont, 378.

46. Ibid.

47. *Fuehrer Conferences,* 124.

48. Could not hold on to all of Italy without the support of the Italians: Garland and Smyth, 469.

49. *Fuehrer Conferences,* 99.

50. Eighty percent of Italian industry: Brendon, 138.

51. By mid-month, half of Army Group B had entered Italy: Garland and Smyth, 442.

52. "Showed their true colors": *Fuehrer Conferences,* 116. Kesselring's divisions would withdraw from the south and regroup in the Rome area: Davis, *Who Defends Rome,* 330.

53. At which point Rommel would assume control of all German forces in Italy: Davis, *Who Defends Rome,* 330.

54. An assignment in Norway: Westphal, 153.

55. Rommel advocating the evacuation of southern and central Italy: Kesselring, 184.

56. Ibid., 171.

57. Had quarreled with the Italians: Plehwe, 68.

58. Warlimont, 379.

59. On August 17: Warlimont, 379; and D'Este, 74. After thirty-eight days of fighting: D'Este, 75.

60. Some 40,000 German troops: Garland and Smyth, 469; and Liddell Hart, *Second World War,* 445. Note: D'Este, 74, puts the number at 55,000.

61. Brought their vehicles and equipment: Garland and Smyth, 469.

62. Kesselring and Jodl made the decision for him: Warlimont, 379.

63. Churchill, *Closing the Ring,* 102 (he wrote this in a message to Anthony Eden dated August 7 after learning that the Italians had made contact with a British diplomat in Tangier).

64. Frequently bombed Italian cities: Monelli, 228.

65. Milan, Naples, Turin, and Genoa: Ibid.

66. On August 13: Deakin, 513; and Davis, *Who Defends Rome,* 239. Declared Rome an Open City on August 14: Davis, *Who Defends Rome,* 240; and Garland and Smyth, 279–280.

67. Bombings of Italy undermined the idea that the Italians were forging a separate peace: Student, 414.

68. Eastern forces had been weakened: Davis, *Who Defends Rome,* 345. Captured Kharkov on August 23 and Taganrog one week later: Goebbels, 422 (in an editor's note).

69. Hundreds of miles away: Ibid., 423 (in an editor's note).

70. One million civilians: Irving, *Hitler's War,* 612.

71. Might not be receptive: Deakin, 517.

72. Badoglio worried about the Nazis and the Fascists: Deakin, 517.

73. Exposed or manufactured: Ibid. Note: Davis, *Who Defends Rome,* 278, maintains that Badoglio made the whole thing up.

74. Some of the plotters had been arrested after July 25 and subsequently released: Deakin, 517.

75. Preemptive strike, settle accounts, and eliminate rivals: Davis, *Who Defends Rome,* 277–278.

76. Tongue lashing from the king: Ibid., 282.

77. For having illegally enriched himself: Deakin, 518.

78. On August 27: Skorzeny, *My Commando Operations,* 235; Hoettl, 267; Edda Ciano, 26; and Moseley, 182. Three children: Edda Ciano, 27. Conducted by Kappler: Dollmann, *Interpreter,* 292; Skorzeny, *My Commando Operations,* 235; and Deakin, 518.

79. Edda Ciano, 26.

80. Believed that the Nazis would facilitate their journey to Spain: Hibbert, 268; and Ciano, *Ciano Diaries,* v, 580.

81. Edda Ciano, 28.

82. Edda Ciano, 28.

83. Hoettl helped plan the Cianos' escape: Hoettl, 265–268; and Skorzeny, *My Commando Operations,* 246 (in a footnote).

84. Hoettl, 265.

Chapter 11

1. Skorzeny, *My Commando Operations,* 254.

2. On August 27, Castellano returned: Plehwe, 135; and Delzell, 253. Note: Some sources give the date as August 28.

3. Dearly wanted to reach an understanding: Strong, *Intelligence at the Top,* 154; Lamb, *War in Italy,* 16; and Garland and Smyth, 465.

4. A majority recommended rejecting the armistice: Denis Mack Smith, *Italy and Its Monarchy,* 312.

5. To haggle over the Short Terms and learn more about the invasion: Delzell, 254.

6. Churchill, *Closing the Ring,* 109.

7. By the end of August the Nazis had more or less completed their military preparations in northern Italy: Deakin, 517; and Garland and Smyth, 474.

8. Kesselring, 171.

9. Had no desire to force an open break: Deakin, 516.

10. Clung to the hope that he could keep the Italians in the Axis camp, possibly by reinserting Mussolini: Warlimont, 374.

11. Ribbentrop believed that the Nazis might be able to do business with Badoglio, even at this late date (the end of August): Deakin, 516.

12. Warlimont, 379.

13. To probe Badoglio's state of mind and play for time: Deakin, 516.

14. On August 31, Hitler fired Mackensen and Rintelen: Westphal, 147. Note: Garland and Smyth, 473, give the date as September 1.

15. Intelligent: Dollmann, *Interpreter,* 254; and Deakin, 514. Bushy eyebrows: Dollmann, *Interpreter,* 254.

16. Designed to increase Badoglio's anxiety: Deakin, 528 (in a footnote).

17. Flew to Rome on August 30 and met with Guariglia: Ibid.

18. Ibid. (from Guariglia's book *Ricordi 1922–1946*).

19. Were aware of negotiations; would not hesitate to use force: Deakin, 528.

20. On September 3, Rahn met with Badoglio: Ibid., 529.

21. Ibid. (from Rahn's book *Ruheloses Leben*).

22. At the same moment: Deakin, 529. Olive grove: Churchill, *Closing the Ring,* 111.

23. In no hurry to hand over Mussolini (after the September 3 armistice signing): Plehwe, 146.

24. The Italians had considered handing Mussolini over to the Allies right after the coup: Denis Mack Smith, *Mussolini,* 298–299.

25. Two main guardians were Gueli and Faiola: Benito Mussolini, *Memoirs,* 94; and Iurato and Antonelli, "With Mussolini at the Campo Imperatore," 245.

26. Retrieved the knives and forks after his meals: Hibbert, 250.

27. At the beginning of September: Benito Mussolini, *Memoirs,* 95; and Hibbert, 250. Nearby cable car station: *After the Battle,* 15.

28. A ten-minute ride: Iurato and Antonelli, "With Mussolini at the Campo Imperatore," 245. Spanned 3,000 feet: Hibbert, 249; and *After the Battle,* 16 (map). First look: Iurato and Antonelli, "With Mussolini at the Campo Imperatore," 248.

29. Almost 7,000 feet: *After the Battle,* 16 (map).

30. At 9,500 feet, it was the highest peak in the Apennines: *Encyclopedia Britannica* online.

31. Benito Mussolini, *Memoirs,* 95.

32. Guests were evacuated: Iurato and Antonelli, "With Mussolini at the Campo Imperatore," 245. Note: Hibbert, 250, claimed that Mussolini was kept at La Villetta only because the Italians needed time to evacuate the Imperatore.

33. There were two hundred or so Italians guarding Mussolini: Skorzeny, *My Commando Operations,* 255. Police and carabinieri: Davis, *Who Defends Rome,* 288.

34. Comfortable second-floor suite: Iurato and Antonelli, "With Mussolini at the Campo Imperatore," 245; and *After the Battle,* 15. No. 201: Ibid.

35. Listening to the radio and playing card games such as *Scopone* with his captors: Iurato and Antonelli, "With Mussolini at the Campo Imperatore," 247. One of his new privileges: Hibbert, 250.

36. Allowed to take walks: Iurato and Antonelli, "With Mussolini at the Campo Imperatore," 246.

37. Benito Mussolini, *Memoirs*, 116.

38. Special treatment reserved for men facing the gallows: Ibid., 115.

39. Iurato and Antonelli, "With Mussolini at the Campo Imperatore," 250. Note: Other sources also indicate that Badoglio ordered that Mussolini was not to be taken alive by the Nazis: Denis Mack Smith, *Mussolini*, 300; Hibbert, 254; and Davis, *Who Defends Rome*, 473.

40. On August 31: Edda Ciano, 197. Welled up with tears: Ibid., 122.

41. Ibid., 122–123.

42. Skorzeny, *My Commando Operations*, 253. Note: Radl claimed that Student admitted that there were men on his own staff who doubted that the war could still be won. Radl, 79–81.

43. Skorzeny, *My Commando Operations*, 253.

44. Ibid.

45. Barnett, *Hitler's Generals*, 477.

46. Ibid., 474.

47. In Africa, Russia, Sicily, Italy, France, Holland, and Germany: Ibid., 473.

48. One "trustworthy" source placed Mussolini in a Roman hospital: Radl, 157–161.

49. Eugen Dollmann dispelled a rumor suggesting that Mussolini was being held in the Villa Savoia: Ibid.

50. Hints that Badoglio had hidden Mussolini somewhere near Lake Trasimene: Ibid., 160–164.

51. Skorzeny, *My Commando Operations*, 254. Note: Radl, 158–162, and Student, 414, also mention this intercept.

52. Did not attach much value to Kappler's discovery: Student, 414–415.

53. Was not convinced that he was on the mainland: Ibid.

54. On September 4 or 5: Radl, 160–164. Note: Student, 415–416, also mentions this visit.

55. In preparation for the Maddalena rescue: Student, 414–415.

56. Heard a story from the squadron captain: Ibid., 415.

57. Seemed to confirm that he was on the mainland: Ibid., 414–415.

58. If it were not for the secrecy: Ibid., 415–416.

59. "Racking his brains" for weeks: Ibid., 415.

60. Ibid., 415–416.

61. Supported by a car crash involving two Italian officers: Radl, 158–162.
62. Student, 416.
63. Brochure provided some details, including a photo: Radl, 160–162.
64. Student, 414. Note: Student seems to be referring to the period between September 3 and September 8.
65. Krutoff spoke fluent Italian: Ibid., 417. Krutoff was a charmer: Ibid.; and Radl, 168–172.
66. About seventy-five miles from Rome: Lamb, *War in Italy,* 23.
67. At least one agent had done some snooping: Radl, 159–162.
68. Skorzeny, *My Commando Operations,* 254.
69. About 230 miles per hour and its altitude was 16,400 feet: Ibid.
70. Temperature was 18 degrees Fahrenheit: Ibid.
71. Skorzeny, *Secret Missions,* 76.

Chapter 12

1. Goebbels, 429.
2. Around noon: Garland and Smyth, 522. More than 10,000 people, and almost four hundred tons: Davis, *Who Defends Rome,* 363.
3. Thousands of Frascati's residents lay dead or injured: Ibid.
4. 150 German soldiers had been killed: Katz, *Battle for Rome,* 30.
5. Kesselring was uninjured: Garland and Smyth, 522–523.
6. Kesselring, 176.
7. Minor damage: Davis, *Who Defends Rome,* 363.
8. Skorzeny, *Secret Missions,* 79.
9. At 5:45 P.M. on the American radio: Deakin, 529.
10. The U.S. media had broken the story prior to Eisenhower's announcement: Davis, *Who Defends Rome,* 372.
11. Garland and Smyth, 508.
12. At noon: Deakin, 529.
13. Ibid. (from a Rahn telegram).
14. After hearing the first broadcast: Deakin, 529–530.
15. British propaganda: Ibid.
16. Ibid. (from a Rahn telegram).
17. Ibid. (from a Rahn telegram).
18. Believed D-day was set for September 12: Badoglio, 71; and Garland and Smyth, 490. Note: Denis Mack Smith, *Italy and Its Monarchy,* 317, asserts that this so-called confusion regarding the date of the invasion was merely used as

an excuse by the king and Badoglio, who had no intention of providing military support.

19. On the evening of September 7–8: Garland and Smyth, 501; and Davis, *Who Defends Rome,* 349.

20. Victor Emmanuel convened a council: Garland and Smyth, 511.

21. Considered denying the existence of the armistice: Denis Mack Smith, *Italy and Its Monarchy,* 315.

22. At 7:45 P.M.: Garland and Smyth, 513.

23. Ibid., 509, 513.

24. Eisenhower was left guessing: Ibid., 509.

25. Could have been disastrous: Ibid., 465.

26. Italian aircraft attacked the invasion force: Denis Mack Smith, *Italy and Its Monarchy,* 315.

27. Prevented at the last minute: Ibid., 315–316.

28. Caught the Nazis by surprise: Bullock, *Hitler,* 415; Garland and Smyth, 514; Dollmann, *Interpreter,* 255; and Plehwe, 122.

29. *Times* (London), September 9, 1943.

30. Kesselring had anticipated a landing in the Salerno area: Liddell Hart, *Second World War,* 456.

31. Kesselring, 186.

32. Strong, *Intelligence at the Top,* 164–165.

33. Thanks to naval gunfire, air power, and desperate fighting: D'Este, 109.

34. Cooks and typists: Ibid., 107.

35. Strong, *Intelligence at the Top,* 164–165.

36. Clark admitted that Salerno was almost a disaster: Liddell Hart, *Second World War,* 456.

37. Garland and Smyth, 508.

38. About 140 miles: Lamb, *War in Italy,* 19; and Garland and Smyth, 449.

39. Would spook the Nazis: Garland and Smyth, 478; and Plehwe, 143–144.

40. Series of airdrops and landings: Garland and Smyth, 498–499.

41. On September 7: Denis Mack Smith, *Italy and Its Monarchy,* 314; and Delzell, 255. Downed airman: Katz, *Battle for Rome,* 29; and Garland and Smyth, 500.

42. Strong, *Intelligence at the Top,* 159.

43. Dubious assertions involving lack of fuel and ammunition and German troop positions: Denis Mack Smith, *Italy and Its Monarchy,* 317.

44. Strong, *Intelligence at the Top,* 161.

45. Five divisions in the Rome area: Garland and Smyth, 532; Shirer, 1001; and Liddell Hart, *Second World War,* 452, 459.

46. The Third Panzergrenadier Division and the Second Parachute Division: Garland and Smyth, 523.

47. Badoglio, 82.

48. Badoglio did not give the Italian Army specific orders: Garland and Smyth, 513; Delzell, 258; Clark, *Modern Italy*, 303; Denis Mack Smith, *Modern Italy*, 417.

49. On September 11, the Italian people received a call to arms (the message from Churchill and Roosevelt): Garland and Smyth, 535; and Davis, *Who Defends Rome*, 468.

50. *United States and Italy, 1936–1946:* 68.

51. Cementing their control over most of Italy at this time: Bullock, *Hitler*, 415.

52. Goebbels, 444.

53. De Courten met with Kesselring on September 7: Westphal, 147.

54. Ibid., 147–148.

55. Arrived in Malta on September 11: Churchill, *Closing the Ring*, 115.

56. Ibid.

57. Executed several Italian commanders: Garland and Smyth, 533.

58. Goebbels, 432 (from an entry dated September 10).

59. Four-fifths of Italy: Garland and Smyth, 540; and Lamb, *War in Italy*, 21.

60. Liddell Hart, *Second World War*, 455 (from the *Other Side of the Hill* by Liddell Hart).

61. Aircraft carriers were unavailable in quantity: Garland and Smyth, 261.

62. Goebbels, 429.

63. Ibid.

64. *New York Times*, September 11, 1943.

65. Ibid.

66. Ibid.

67. Ibid.

68. Seventeen thousand civilians were killed: Shirer, 826.

Chapter 13

1. *Los Angeles Times*, December 26, 1987.

2. Skorzeny, *Secret Missions*, 83.

3. Student, 417.

4. Liddell Hart, *Second World War*, 454 (from *Other Side of the Hill* by Liddell Hart).

5. Italians put up a fierce resistance: Student, 402.

6. By September 10, the task force was turning its attention to the Gran Sasso: Ibid., 417.

7. Ibid.

8. On the evening of September 10, Student decided to spring the Duce: Ibid.

9. Ibid., 416.

10. Just a mule track: Patricelli, 64.

11. Skorzeny, *Secret Missions*, 84.

12. Ibid.

13. Four inches square: Ibid.

14. Student, 416.

15. Concept originated with Hitler: McRaven, 33.

16. On a 150-foot ridge: Lucas, *Kommando*, 53. Designed to withstand artillery shelling and aerial bombardment: McRaven, 66.

17. Student and his staff developed a detailed plan: McRaven, 41, 60.

18. Eben Emael was their debut: McRaven, 62.

19. German Institute for Gliding Research: Edwards, *German Airborne Troops*, 44.

20. Early on the morning of May 10: McRaven, 45–47.

21. Dodging antiaircraft fire: Ibid., 47.

22. Shaped charges were a novelty: Ibid., 62.

23. Student's sixty-nine-man team was outnumbered by ten to one: Ibid., 55. Within twenty minutes: Ibid., 58.

24. Germans had six fatalities, the Belgians twenty-five: Ibid., 55.

25. Rehearsed for months on end: Ibid., 57, 64.

26. Had good intelligence, including blueprints: Ibid., 61.

27. Four or five acres: Ibid., 195.

28. Did not possess proper schematics: Ibid., 193.

29. Worked out many of the details himself: Student, 418, 434.

30. Mors was the primary architect: Patricelli, 60–61 and 65–66; and the *Los Angeles Times*, December 26, 1987.

31. Led troops during the invasion of the Low Countries and the assault on Crete: *Los Angeles Times*, December 26, 1987.

32. Mors received the assignment on September 11: Patricelli, 58–59.

33. *Los Angeles Times*, December 26, 1987.

34. Student, 434.

35. Berlepsch was given command of the assault team: Student, 434.

36. *Los Angeles Times*, December 26, 1987.

37. Student, 419–420.

38. Cutting telephone and telegraph lines: Skorzeny, *My Commando Operations*, 258.

39. To prevent reinforcements from aiding the Italians: Student, 418.

40. Scheduled to take place at the same time: Ibid.

41. Ibid.

42. The two hundred or so Italians: Skorzeny, *My Commando Operations*, 255.

43. Student, 419. Student was a glider pilot: McRaven, 33.

44. It was a worthy "challenge": Student, 419.

45. The FG-42 was a new type of automatic rifle built especially for the paratroopers: Edwards, *German Airborne Troops*, 29–30; and McRaven, 180, 193 (in a footnote).

46. Skorzeny, *Secret Missions*, 86.

47. Ibid., 87.

48. Student, 421.

49. Soleti was contacted on September 11: Radl, 214–218.

50. Not told the real reason: Ibid., 215–217.

51. Goebbels, 439–440 (from an entry dated September 10).

52. Had assured Eisenhower that the dictator would be in a secure location: Denis Mack Smith, *Italy and Its Monarchy*, 316.

53. Butcher, 407.

54. Made no effort: Denis Mack Smith, *Italy and Its Monarchy*, 316.

55. Had driven through the Abruzzi region not far from the Hotel Imperatore: Davis, *Who Defends Rome*, 429.

56. Gueli was Mussolini's senior jailer: Hibbert, 248; and Deakin, 547. Enhanced security measures: Benito Mussolini, *Memoirs*, 117; and Iurato and Antonelli, "With Mussolini at the Campo Imperatore," 248. A few machine guns: Dombrowski, 68.

57. Benito Mussolini, *Memoirs*, 133.

58. On the evening of September 10 while listening to Berlin radio: Ibid., 117; and Davis, *Who Defends Rome*, 473.

59. Benito Mussolini, *Memoirs*, 117. Which he missed: Davis, *Who Defends Rome*, 472.

60. *New York Times*, September 10, 1943.

61. *United States and Italy, 1936–1946*, 61.

62. Kept secret until 1945: Garland and Smyth, 550 (in a footnote).

63. Later that evening on September 10, Mussolini tried to slit his wrists with a Gillette razor blade: Davis, *Who Defends Rome*, 473.

64. It is not clear whether the Duce was really trying to commit suicide: Note: Denis Mack Smith, *Mussolini*, 300, casts doubt on whether Mussolini really intended to commit suicide.

65. Faiola removed the razors and other sharp objects: Benito Mussolini, *Memoirs*, 133.

66. More likely the Nazis would attempt to snatch Mussolini: Hibbert, 254.

67. The Nazis were not to take Mussolini alive: Denis Mack Smith, *Mussolini*, 300; Hibbert, 254; and Davis, *Who Defends Rome*, 473.

Chapter 14

1. Skorzeny, *Secret Missions*, 105.

2. Goebbels, 443 (from an entry dated September 11).

3. September 12 was a Sunday: Skorzeny, *Secret Missions*, 88.

4. Swoop down at 7:00 a.m: Ibid.

5. Operation would have to be postponed: Student, 420.

6. Mors wanted to be certain: Ibid.

7. Mors wanted a margin for error: Ibid.

8. Student pushed Zero Hour back to 2:00 P.M.: Ibid.

9. During the early hours of September 12, Mors left for Assergi in a motorized column: Ibid., 420, 418.

10. Ibid., 420.

11. Ibid.

12. Around 7:30 A.M.: Skorzeny, *My Commando Operations*, 262.

13. Appeared at 9:00 A.M. and agreed to accompany Radl: Radl, 225–229.

14. Student took Soleti aside: Ibid., 229–233.

15. Gave his consent without much fuss: Ibid.

16. Scheduled to fly from Grosseto to Pratica: Student, 422.

17. About an hour later, the gliders and tugs appeared: Skorzeny, *Secret Missions*, 92.

18. Student, 422.

19. Soleti was eating with Radl in an airport building: Radl, 231–235.

20. Student had not gone into great detail: Radl, 229–233.

21. Skorzeny, *My Commando Operations*, 262.

22. Ibid.

23. Ibid.

24. Soleti thought Radl was making a joke: Ibid., 263.

25. Soleti became ill and a doctor was summoned: Radl, 232–236.

26. Made an appeal to Student and Kappler: Skorzeny, *My Commando Operations*, 263.

27. Ibid.

28. Was kept under guard: Ibid.

29. Gave a briefing for the pilots and selected officers in an office of the airfield: Radl, 233–237.

30. Also present were Berlepsch, Langguth, Skorzeny, and Radl: Ibid.

31. Most were surprised: See Whiting, *Hunters from the Sky*, 105.

32. Student, 422.

33. The shock value of the raid would be great: Ibid.

34. Main job of the pilots was to put the paratroopers on the ground: Ibid.

35. Was regrettable that the pilots would have to make their landings in the afternoon: Ibid.

36. No guarantee that Mussolini was still on the mountain: Patricelli, 76; and Whiting, *Hunters from the Sky*, 105.

37. Italian morale was low: Student, 422.

38. The Germans were bringing Soleti: Ibid.

39. Student returned to Frascati: Ibid.

40. Langguth and Skorzeny offered additional details: Radl, 236–240; and Skorzeny, *Secret Missions*, 92.

41. Hard to discern the slope: Skorzeny, *My Commando Operations*, 254; and Radl, 193–197.

42. Ridge east of Tivoli that rose to a height of 4,265 feet: Student, 422.

43. Not certain whether the aircraft could gain enough altitude: Ibid.

44. A horizontal 360-degree turn: Ibid., 424.

45. Henschel aircraft: Skorzeny, *My Commando Operations*, 260.

46. The Hs 126 was doing a lot of glider towing: Green, *Warplanes*, 389.

47. The 131-foot-long tow cable: Green, *Warplanes*, 105. Note: This type of cable was typical, but the Germans occasionally used a rigid-tow arrangement that was much shorter. It is not clear which was used during the Gran Sasso raid of September 12.

48. Rate of one per minute: Skorzeny, *My Commando Operations*, 260.

49. Berlepsch was in command of the assault team: Student, 419, 434; and *Los Angeles Times*, December 26, 1987 (in this article, Mors identifies Berlepsch as the commander).

50. Twelve glider groups: Skorzeny, *My Commando Operations*, 260–261.

51. Langguth would fly the leading tug: Student, 423.

52. Berlepsch would ride in the glider attached to Langguth's plane: Ibid.

53. Skorzeny would fly in the DFS 230 of the second chain: Ibid.

54. FG–42 paratrooper rifles, machine guns, and light mortars: Skorzeny, *My Commando Operations*, 260–261.

55. Without the need for a bloody clash: Student, 419.

56. Skorzeny, *My Commando Operations*, 155.

57. Twin-engine Mitchells: Whiting, *Hunters from the Sky*, 107. Dropping bombs on the airport: Skorzeny, *Secret Missions*, 92. Note: Student, 423, claimed that the enemy planes did not drop bombs during this raid.

58. Dashed for cover in the bushes and trees as the sound of explosions and AA guns filled the air: Radl, 237–241.

59. Skorzeny, *Secret Missions*, 92.

60. None of the gliders had been hit: Skorzeny, *Secret Missions*, 92–93. Minor damage: Ibid.; and Radl, 237–241.

61. Radl, 240.

62. Soleti made an attempt to shoot himself: Student, 424; and Radl, 238–242.

63. Trouble controlling their bladders: Radl, 239–243.

64. Tubular steel rods surrounded by a fabric skin: Green, *Warplanes*, 104.

65. Length of thirty-seven feet and a wingspan of seventy-two feet, and it weighed less than one ton when empty: Ibid., 107.

66. Particularly vulnerable to enemy fire: Ibid., 105.

67. Came equipped with machine guns: Ibid.

68. Not planning to fire these glider guns: Student, 422.

69. A little more than 4,600 pounds: Green, *Warplanes*, 107.

70. Straddle a long bench that ran down the center: McRaven, 41.

71. Jettison its wheels (two-wheel dolly): Green, *Warplanes*, 104.

72. Barbed wire: Student, 423; and Radl, 240–244.

73. Parachute beneath rear fuselage: Green, *Warplanes*, 105.

74. At 1:00 P.M., they began lifting off: Skorzeny, *Secret Missions*, 93; and Student, 424.

75. Langguth was flying in the lead chain: Student, 423.

76. Skorzeny flew in the glider of the second chain: Ibid.

77. Skorzeny, *Secret Missions*, 93.

78. The hotel was seventy-five miles from Rome: Lamb, *War in Italy*, 23.

79. Normal towing speed was about 112 miles per hour, but could be increased to 130 miles per hour: Green, *Warplanes*, 107.

80. Former cavalry officer: Skorzeny, *My Commando Operations*, 263.

81. Skorzeny, *Secret Missions*, 93.

82. One of the commandos in Radl's glider vomited: Radl, 241–245.

83. Langguth decided to swing around in a circle: Student, 424.

84. Langguth flew a loop: Ibid.

85. None of the other chains were following suit: Ibid.

86. Ibid.

87. Bank of clouds near Tivoli: Skorzeny, *Secret Missions*, 93–94.

88. No radio contact between chains: Student, 424.

89. Failed to understand the significance of the course change: Ibid.

90. Skorzeny, *My Commando Operations*, 266.

91. Small plastic windows: Skorzeny, *My Commando Operations*, 265. Cut slits in the fuselage: Skorzeny, *Secret Missions*, 94.

92. Skorzeny, *Secret Missions*, 94.

93. Meyer relayed the information to the tug: Skorzeny, *My Commando Operations*, 266.

94. Spotted L'Aquila: Ibid.

95. Dust storm: Ibid.

96. Winding road that led to the cable car station: Ibid.

97. Timing was perfect: Ibid.

98. Altitude of 9,843 feet: Note: According to Student, 425, the gliders were flying at 9,843 feet right before the tow cables were released.

99. Skorzeny, *Secret Missions*, 95.

100. Rocks and boulders: Ibid., 96.

101. "Steep approach!": Skorzeny, *My Commando Operations*, 266. Told the pilot to land close to the hotel: Skorzeny, *Secret Missions*, 95.

102. Radl, 244.

103. Skorzeny, *Secret Missions*, 96.

104. Fifty feet from the corner of the hotel: Skorzeny, *My Commando Operations*, 266. Near the rear corner on the hotel's right shoulder: McRaven, 186 (in a diagram).

105. Benito Mussolini, *Memoirs*, 133. Note: Due to the location of Mussolini's suite, it is unlikely that the Duce saw Skorzeny's glider land; he is probably referring to one of the other DFS 230s.

106. Door was torn off: Skorzeny, *Secret Missions*, 96.

107. Skorzeny followed: Ibid.

108. "Don't shoot, don't shoot!": Radl, 244–248. Note: Iurato and Antonelli, "With Mussolini at the Campo Imperatore," 250, make a similar claim.

109. Skorzeny, *Secret Missions*, 97.

110. Saw a face at a window: Ibid.

111. Benito Mussolini, *Memoirs*, 134.

112. Ibid.

113. Skorzeny, *My Commando Operations*, 267.

114. Radl's glider landed in front: Ibid. Three hundred feet from the hotel: Radl, 244–248.

115. Could see Skorzeny and his men moving along the front: Radl, 242–246.

116. Soleti was with them: Ibid.

117. Skorzeny, *My Commando Operations*, 267.

118. Skorzeny, *Secret Missions*, 97.

119. Only three or four minutes: Ibid., 98.

120. Two Germans appeared at the window: Ibid.

121. Not a shot fired: Skorzeny, *My Commando Operations*, 267.

122. Ibid.

123. Several gliders appeared from the clouds: See Student, 425.

124. Berlepsch was among the new arrivals: Skorzeny, *My Commando Operations*, 268; and Patricelli, 85. His chain had rejoined the convoy: Patricelli, 77. Note: Contrary to Student's account, Skorzeny claimed that Berlepsch rode in the fifth glider—not the first.

125. Skorzeny, *Secret Missions*, 98.

126. Shots in the distance: Ibid.

127. Skorzeny, *My Commando Operations*, 267.

128. Ibid.

129. Ibid.

130. Treated by German and Italian medics: Skorzeny, *My Commando Operations*, 269.

131. Not life-threatening: Ibid.

132. Ibid.

133. Minor Italian casualties: Skorzeny, *My Commando Operations*, 269.

134. Deakin, 547.

135. It was signed by Senise: Ibid.

136. Shortly after Skorzeny's glider landed, Gueli gave the order not to open fire: Ibid.; and Davis, *Who Defends Rome*, 473.

137. Gave them the authority to surrender the Duce: Davis, *Who Defends Rome*, 473.

138. Student, 425.

139. Traveling overland was too risky: Skorzeny, *Secret Missions*, 100.

140. Fearful of angry civilians: McRaven, 188.

141. To be flown back to Pratica in a Stork: Student, 426.

142. Hover in mid-air: Green, *Warplanes*, 166.

143. A second Stork would transport Skorzeny: Student, 425–426.

144. Ibid., 426.

145. Gerlach was thirty: Whiting, *Hunters from the Sky*, 106. Headwind and an incline: Student, 426.

146. Had landed in the valley and damaged its undercarriage: Student, 427.

147. Skorzeny, *Secret Missions*, 102.

148. Student, 427.

149. No enthusiasm for the flight, with or without Skorzeny: Ibid., 426–427.

150. Be allowed to return to Rocca: Skorzeny, *My Commando Operations,* 270; Radl, 250–254; and Iurato and Antonelli, "With Mussolini at the Campo Imperatore," 251.

151. Mors was in charge of the entire operation: Student, 425; and *Los Angeles Times,* December 26, 1987 (in this article, Mors claimed that he was in charge of the rescue operation).

152. *Los Angeles Times,* December 26, 1987.

153. Cameraman by way of the cable car: *After the Battle,* 29.

154. Dark overcoat, which was too big for him, and black felt hat: Hibbert, 266.

155. German soldiers and some of the carabinieri raised their arms in the Fascist salute and chanted "Duce!": Iurato and Antonelli, "With Mussolini at the Campo Imperatore," 252; and Hibbert, 265.

156. At 3:00 P.M.: Benito Mussolini, *Memoirs,* 135.

157. The "runway" was a downward slope: Skorzeny, *My Commando Operations,* 270; and *After the Battle,* 25, in a photo caption. Two hundred yards long: *After the Battle,* 29; and Whiting, *Hunters from the Sky,* 111.

158. The 240-horsepower engine: Green, *Warplanes,* 168.

159. Some German soldiers were holding the plane: Skorzeny, *Secret Missions,* 104; and Hibbert, 266.

160. Rolled over half-buried stones: Skorzeny, *Secret Missions,* 104.

161. Ibid., 105.

162. Benito Mussolini, *Memoirs,* 135.

163. Radl, 261.

164. An eerie silence swept through the crowd: Radl, 259–263.

165. Ibid., 261.

166. Skorzeny, *Secret Missions,* 105.

167. Student, 427.

168. Southwesterly course: Hibbert, 266. Skimming the treetops: Skorzeny, *Secret Missions,* 105.

169. The engine was not functioning properly: Student, 428.

170. Placed a hand on Mussolini's shoulder: Skorzeny, *Secret Missions,* 105.

171. Ibid.

172. Two-point landing due to damaged left wheel: Ibid., 106.

173. Ibid.

174. Student, 428.

175. Aspern airport: Skorzeny, *My Commando Operations,* 272; and Student, 429. At about 11:00 P.M.: Skorzeny, *My Commando Operations,* 246 (in a footnote).

176. Hotel Imperial: Skorzeny, *My Commando Operations,* 272.

177. Close to midnight, a colonel appeared: Ibid., 246 (in a footnote).

178. McRaven, 187–188 (from "Mussolini Event").

179. First time it was earned and awarded on the same day: Whiting, *Skorzeny,* 43; Patricelli, 128; and *Los Angeles Times,* December 26, 1987.

180. Himmler, Goering, and Keitel spoke to Skorzeny: Skorzeny, *My Commando Operations,* 272–273.

181. Thanked Hitler briefly and went directly to bed: Hibbert, 267.

182. Goebbels, 450 (from an entry dated September 13).

183. Skorzeny walked off with Mussolini's papers: Hoettl, 232–233. Note: According to Hoettl, Skorzeny stole Mussolini's papers during the journey from Rome to Vienna.

184. Copied, translated, and presented to Hitler: Ibid., 233.

Epilogue

1. *New York Times,* September 13, 1943.

2. Boost to German morale: Wiskemann, 311; and Toland, *Hitler,* 755.

3. Bullock, *Hitler,* 417.

4. *New York Times,* September 13, 1943.

5. Ibid., September 14, 1943.

6. Ibid.

7. Ibid.

8. Ibid.

9. Churchill, *Onwards to Victory,* 200.

10. Ibid.

11. Air Force Medal in Gold from Goering: Whiting, *Skorzeny,* 44.

12. Order of the Hundred Musketeers: Ibid.

13. Radl was promoted to captain: Skorzeny, *My Commando Operations,* 276.

14. Hoettl, 230.

15. Goebbels, 451 (from an entry dated September 14).

16. Ibid., 452 (from an entry dated September 15).

17. Never thanked Student or the paratroopers: Student, 429.

18. Student, 430.

19. The one organization he could trust: See Irving, *Hitler's War,* 617. Note: Irving points out that Hitler's trust in Himmler and the SS was absolute by this point.

20. To restage the rescue: Skorzeny, *My Commando Operations,* 281.

21. *New York Times*, September 13, 1943.
22. Hitler had tears in his eyes: Hibbert, 269.
23. Goebbels, 471 (from an entry dated September 23).
24. Demanded that Ciano and the others pay with their heads: Monelli, 230.
25. Goebbels, 468 (from an entry dated September 23).
26. Ibid., 471 (from an entry dated September 23).
27. To avoid civil war: Monelli, 230.
28. Would reflect badly on Germany: Monelli, 230.
29. Goebbels, 470, 471 (from an entry dated September 23).
30. Goebbels was jealous: Hibbert, 271; and Wiskemann, 312.
31. Goebbels, 472 (from an entry dated September 23).
32. Wiskemann, 313.
33. Dollmann, *Interpreter,* 280.
34. Rachele Mussolini, 277.
35. On the western shore of Lake Garda: Deakin, 607.
36. Never saw the Eternal City again: Shirer, 1005; and Dombrowski, 73.
37. Under pressure from Hitler: Shirer, 1005; and Monelli, 235.
38. Ciano turned around to face his executioners: Monelli, 286.
39. The Villa Feltrinelli in Gargnano: Deakin, 607.
40. Monelli, 232.
41. Liked to refer to Wolff as his jailer: Ibid.
42. Dombrowski, 144.
43. Clark, *Modern Italy,* 310.
44. Churchill, *Closing the Ring,* 187.
45. The 80,000 or so Partisans: Clark, *Modern Italy,* 315. More than half of the Partisans (50,000) had joined the Communist-controlled Garibaldi brigades: Clark, *Modern Italy,* 312.
46. Assassinations, sabotage, and surprise attacks: Ibid., 311.
47. Dollmann, *Interpreter,* 322.
48. Goering, Doenitz, and Ribbentrop began to squabble: Shirer, 1056.
49. Crumbling a piece of cake and creating sculptures: Dollmann, *Interpreter,* 323.
50. Ibid.
51. Schmidt, 276–277.
52. Looked Mussolini in the eye and reaffirmed his friendship: Hibbert, 301.
53. Deakin, 713 (from *Die Gebrochene Achse* by E. F. Moellhausen).
54. Hitler drew aside Rahn: Deakin, 713.
55. Dollmann, *Interpreter,* 325.

56. Deakin, 800 (from volume 3 of Tamaro's *Due Anni di Storia, 1943–1945,* 514).

57. Outside the village of Dongo: Monelli, 257.

58. Wearing an overcoat, helmet, and sunglasses: Ibid.

59. Near the hamlet of Mezzegra: Deakin, 816. On the western shores of Como: Wiskemann, 338.

60. Piazzale Loreto: Denis Mack Smith, *Modern Italy,* 420.

61. Left the Wolf's Lair for good in November 1944: Hoffmann, *Hitler's Personal Security,* 257.

62. In January 1945, he ordered that it be destroyed: Hoffmann, *Hitler's Personal Security,* 257. Not enough explosives to finish the job: Ibid., xii.

63. Junge, 177.

64. Benito Mussolini, *Memoirs,* 139.

65. Succumbed to their illusions like madmen: Hibbert, 291; and Dombrowski, 148.

66. McRaven, 195.

67. Bradley, 467–468.

68. Summersby, 202–203.

69. *New York Times,* May 18, 1945.

70. Ibid.

71. Whiting, *Skorzeny,* 104.

72. Worked as a temporary agent of the Mossad: *Jerusalem Post,* September 20, 1989.

73. To foil an Egyptian plan to develop a missile program: Ibid.

74. *Los Angeles Times,* December 26, 1987.

75. Ibid.

76. Ibid.

77. Ibid.

78. McRaven, 192 (in a footnote).

79. Lamb, *War in Italy,* 1.

80. Westphal, 153.

81. Liberate Naples by Day Three: Liddell Hart, *Second World War,* 461.

82. Took them three weeks: Ibid. Naples fell on October 1: D'Este, 110. Fifth Army suffered 12,000 casualties: Liddell Hart, *Second World War,* 469.

83. Could be captured by the end of October 1943: D'Este, 115.

84. The 140-mile distance from Salerno to Rome: Lamb, *War in Italy,* 19; and Garland and Smyth, 449.

85. D'Este, 117.

86. About eighty miles south of Rome: Katz, *Battle for Rome,* 65.

87. Berlepsch was killed in action there: *Los Angeles Times*, December 26, 1987.

88. Katz, *Death in Rome,* 6.

89. Katz, *Battle for Rome,* 181.

90. Ultimately, 335 men were shot dead: Katz, *Battle for Rome,* 254.

91. Deakin, 725 (from a Kesselring order dated August 4, 1944).

92. Gothic Line was in the mountains north of Florence: D'Este, 181.

93. D'Este, 89.

The Story of Operation Oak

1. Deakin, 543.

BIBLIOGRAPHY

■

Published Documentary Material

Documents on German Foreign Policy, 1918–1945. Series D, vol. VI, *The Last Months of Peace*. London: Her Majesty's Stationery Office, 1956.

Documents on German Foreign Policy, 1918–1945. Series D, vol. VII, *The Last Days of Peace*. Washington, DC: U.S. Government Printing Office, 1956.

Documents on German Foreign Policy, 1918–1945. Series D, vol. VIII, *The War Years*. Washington, DC: U.S. Government Printing Office, 1954.

Fuehrer Conferences on Matters Dealing with the German Navy, 1943. Washington, DC: U.S. Navy Department, 1947.

Nazi Conspiracy and Aggression. Vol. III. Washington, DC: U.S. Government Printing Office, 1946.

Nazi Conspiracy and Aggression. Vol. VIII. Washington, DC: U.S. Government Printing Office, 1946.

United States and Italy, 1936–1946: Documentary Record. Washington, DC: U.S. Government Printing Office, 1946.

Memoirs, Diaries, and Letters

Alfieri, Dino. *Dictators Face to Face*. Translated by David Moore. Westport, CT: Greenwood, 1978.

Badoglio, Pietro. *Italy in the Second World War: Memories and Documents*. Translated by Muriel Currey. Westport, CT: Greenwood, 1976.

Bradley, Omar N. *A Soldier's Story*. New York: Henry Holt, 1951.

Butcher, Harry C. *My Three Years with Eisenhower*. New York: Simon & Schuster, 1946.

Churchill, Winston S. *Closing the Ring*. Boston: Houghton Mifflin, 1951.

Ciano, Edda Mussolini. *My Truth*. Translated by Eileen Finletter. New York: William Morrow, 1977.

Ciano, Galeazzo. *Diary, 1937–1943*. New York: Enigma, 2002.

———. *The Ciano Diaries, 1939–1943*. Edited by Hugh Gibson. Safety Harbor, FL: Simon, 2001.

Doenitz, Karl. *Memoirs: Ten Years and Twenty Days*. Translated by R. H. Stevens and David Woodward. Cambridge, MA: Da Capo, 1997.

Dollmann, Eugen. *The Interpreter*. Translated by J. Maxwell Brownjohn. London: Hutchinson, 1967.

Eisenhower, Dwight D. *Crusade in Europe*. Garden City, NY: Doubleday, 1948.

Goebbels, Joseph. *The Goebbels Diaries, 1942–1943*. Edited and translated by Louis P. Lochner. Garden City, NY: Doubleday, 1948.

Hitler, Adolf. *Mein Kampf*. Translated by Ralph Manheim. New York: Houghton Mifflin, Mariner, 1999.

Hoettl, Wilhelm. *The Secret Front: The Story of Nazi Political Espionage*. Translated by R. H. Stevens. New York: Frederick A. Praeger, 1954.

Irving, David. *The Secret Diaries of Hitler's Doctor*. New York: Macmillan, 1983.

Junge, Traudl. *Until the Final Hour: Hitler's Last Secretary*. Edited by Melissa Müller and translated by Anthea Bell. New York: Arcade, 2004.

Keitel, Wilhelm. *The Memoirs of Field-Marshal Keitel*. Edited by Walter Gorlitz and translated by David Irving. London: William Kimber, 1965.

Kesselring, Albert. *The Memoirs of Field-Marshal Kesselring*. Translated by Lynton Hudson. London: William Kimber, 1953.

Liddell Hart, B. H. *The Rommel Papers*. Translated by Paul Findlay. New York: Da Capo, 1953.

Maugeri, Franco. *From the Ashes of Disgrace*. Edited by Victor Rosen. New York: Reynal and Hitchcock, 1948.

Mussolini, Benito. *The Mussolini Memoirs, 1942–1943*. Edited by Raymond Klibansky and translated by Frances Lobb. London: Orion, Phoenix, 2000.

———. *My Rise and Fall*. New York: Da Capo, 1998.

Radl, Karl. *Die Blitzbefreiung Mussolinis: Mit Skorzeny am Gran Sasso*. Selent: Pour le Mérite, 1996.

Ribbentrop, Joachim von. *The Ribbentrop Memoirs*. Translated by Oliver Watson. London: Weidenfeld and Nicolson, 1954.

Schellenberg, Walter. *The Schellenberg Memoirs*. Edited and translated by Louis Hagen. London: Andre Deutsch, 1956.

Schmidt, Paul. *Hitler's Interpreter*. Edited by R.H.C. Steed. London: William Heinemann, 1951.

Semmler, Rudolf. *Goebbels: The Man Next to Hitler*. London: Westhouse, 1947.

Skorzeny, Otto. *My Commando Operations: The Memoirs of Hitler's Most Daring Commando.* Translated by David Johnston. Atglen, PA: Schiffer, 1995.

_____. *Skorzeny's Secret Missions: War Memoirs of the Most Dangerous Man in Europe.* Translated by Jacques Le Clercq. New York: E. P. Dutton, 1950.

Speer, Albert. *Inside the Third Reich.* Translated by Richard and Clara Winston. New York: Simon & Schuster, Touchstone, 1997.

Starhemberg, Ernst Rudiger. *Between Hitler and Mussolini: Memoirs of Ernst Rudiger Prince Starhemberg.* New York: Harper, 1942.

Strong, Kenneth. *Intelligence at the Top.* Garden City, NY: Doubleday, 1969.

Student, Kurt, and Hermann Götzel. *Generaloberst Kurt Student und seine Fallschirmjäger: die Erinnerungen des Generaloberst Kurt Student.* Friedberg: Podzun-Pallas, 1980.

Summersby, Kay. *Eisenhower Was My Boss.* Edited by Michael Kearns. New York: Prentice-Hall, 1948.

Trevor-Roper, H. R. *The Bormann Letters: The Private Correspondence Between Martin Bormann and His Wife from January 1943 to April 1945.* Translated by R. H. Stevens. London: Weidenfeld and Nicolson, 1954.

Warlimont, Walter. *Inside Hitler's Headquarters, 1939–45.* Translated by R. H. Barry. Novato, CA: Presidio, 1964.

Westphal, Siegfried. *The German Army in the West.* London: Cassell, 1951.

Books About Hitler, Mussolini, and the Axis

Bosworth, R.J.B. *Mussolini.* London: Arnold, 2002.

Bullock, Alan. *Hitler: A Study in Tyranny.* New York: HarperCollins, Harper-Perennial, 1991.

Corvaja, Santi. *Hitler and Mussolini: The Secret Meetings.* Translated by R. L. Miller. New York: Enigma, 2001.

Davis, Melton S. *Who Defends Rome? The Forty-Five Days, July 25-September 8, 1943.* New York: Dial, 1972.

Deakin, F. W. *The Brutal Friendship: Mussolini, Hitler and the Fall of Italian Fascism.* London: Orion, Phoenix, 2000.

Dombrowski, Roman. *Mussolini: Twilight and Fall.* Translated by H. C. Stevens. London: William Heinemann, 1956.

Hibbert, Christopher. *Benito Mussolini: The Rise and Fall of Il Duce.* Harmondsworth, England: Penguin, 1975.

Monelli, Paolo. *Mussolini: The Intimate Life of a Demagogue.* Translated by Brigid Maxwell. New York: Vanguard, 1954.

Mussolini, Rachele. *Mussolini: An Intimate Biography by His Widow.* New York: Simon & Schuster, Pocket Books, 1977.

Plehwe, Friedrich-Karl von. *The End of an Alliance: Rome's Defection from the Axis in 1943.* Translated by Eric Mosbacher. London: Oxford University, 1971.

Ridley, Jasper. *Mussolini: A Biography.* New York: Rowman & Littlefield, Cooper Square, 2000.

Smith, Denis Mack. *Mussolini.* New York: Random House, Vintage, 1983.

Taylor, A.J.P. *The War Lords.* London: Hamish Hamilton, 1977.

Toland, John. *Adolf Hitler.* New York: Random House, Anchor, 1992.

Trevor-Roper, Hugh. *The Last Days of Hitler.* 6th ed. Chicago: University of Chicago, 1992.

Wiskemann, Elizabeth. *The Rome-Berlin Axis: A History of the Relations Between Hitler and Mussolini.* London: Oxford University, 1949.

Books About the German Paratroopers and the Luftwaffe

Ailsby, Christopher. *Hitler's Sky Warriors: German Paratroopers in Action, 1939–1945.* Dulles, VA: Brassey's, 2000.

Edwards, Roger. *German Airborne Troops, 1936–45.* Garden City, NY: Doubleday, 1974.

Farrar-Hockley, A. H. *Student.* New York: Ballantine, 1973.

Green, William. *The Warplanes of the Third Reich.* New York: Galahad, 1990.

Kurtz, Robert. *German Paratroopers: Uniforms, Insignia, and Equipment of the Fallschirmjäger in World War II.* Atglen, PA: Schiffer, 2000.

Lucas, James. *Storming Eagles: German Airborne Forces in World War II.* London: Cassell, 2001.

Nasse, Jean-Yves. *Green Devils: German Paratroops, 1939–45.* Translated by W. Mühlberger, G. Schubert, and Jean-Pierre Villaume. Paris: Histoire & Collections, 1997.

Whiting, Charles. *Hunters from the Sky: The German Parachute Corps, 1940–1945.* New York: Random House, Ballantine, 1975.

Wood, Tony and Bill Gunston. *Hitler's Luftwaffe: A Pictorial History and Technical Encyclopedia of Hitler's Air Power in World War II.* London: Salamander, Leisure, 1977.

Books About Skorzeny

Foley, Charles. *Commando Extraordinary: A Biography of Otto Skorzeny.* Costa Mesa, CA: Noontide, 1992.

Infield, Glenn B. *Skorzeny: Hitler's Commando*. New York: St. Martin's, 1981.

Whiting, Charles. *Skorzeny: The Most Dangerous Man in Europe*. Revised and expanded ed. Conshohocken, PA: Combined, 1998.

Other Works

Barnett, Correlli. *Hitler's Generals*. New York: Grove, 1989.

Beevor, Antony. *The Fall of Berlin, 1945*. New York: Penguin, 2003.

_____. *The Spanish Civil War*. New York: Penguin, 2001.

_____. *Stalingrad*. New York: Penguin, 1999.

Bessel, Richard. *Life in the Third Reich*. Oxford: Oxford University, 1987.

Brendon, Piers. *The Dark Valley: A Panorama of the 1930s*. New York: Knopf, 2000.

Buderi, Robert. *The Invention That Changed the World: How a Small Group of Radar Pioneers Won the Second World War and Launched a Technological Revolution*. New York: Simon & Schuster, 1996.

Churchill, Winston S. *Onwards to Victory*. Compiled by Charles Eade. London: Cassell, 1944.

Clark, Martin. *Modern Italy, 1871–1995*. 2d ed. London: Longman, 1996.

Craven, Wesley Frank, and James Lea Cate. *The Army Air Forces in World War II*. Vol. 2, *Europe: Torch to Pointblank, August 1942 to December 1943*. Chicago: University of Chicago, 1949.

Cross, Robin. *The Battle of Kursk: Operation Citadel 1943*. London: Penguin, 2002.

De Felice, Renzo. *The Jews in Fascist Italy: A History*. New York: Enigma, 2001.

Delzell, Charles F. *Mussolini's Enemies: The Italian Anti-Fascist Resistance*. New York: Howard Fertig, 1974.

D'Este, Carlo. *World War II in the Mediterranean*. New York: Workman, Algonquin, 1990.

Dulles, Allen. *From Hitler's Doorstep: The Wartime Intelligence Reports of Allen Dulles, 1942–1945*. University Park, PA: Pennsylvania State University, 1996.

Fellgiebel, Walther-Peer. *Elite of the Third Reich: The Recipients of the Knight's Cross of the Iron Cross, 1939–45*. Translated by C. F. Colton and Duncan Rogers. Solihull, England: Helion, 2003.

Garland, Albert N., and Howard McGaw Smyth. *Sicily and the Surrender of Italy*. Washington, DC: Center of Military History (United States Army), 1986.

Gilbert, Felix. *Hitler Directs His War: The Secret Records of His Daily Military Conferences*. New York: Oxford University, 1950.

Goñi, Uki. *The Real Odessa: Smuggling the Nazis to Perón's Argentina*. London: Granta, 2002.

Hoffmann, Peter. *Hitler's Personal Security: Protecting the Führer, 1921–1945*. New York: Da Capo, 2000.

Hoehne, Heinz. *Canaris*. Translated by J. Maxwell Brownjohn. Garden City, NY: Doubleday, 1979.

Irving, David. *Hitler's War*. London: Focal Point, 2002.

Kahn, David. *Hitler's Spies: German Military Intelligence in World War II*. Cambridge, MA: Da Capo, 2000.

Katz, Robert. *The Battle for Rome*. New York: Simon & Schuster, 2003.

_____. *Death in Rome*. New York: Macmillan, 1967.

Keegan, John. *The First World War*. New York: Knopf, 1999.

_____. *Waffen S.S.: The Asphalt Soldiers*. New York: Random House, Ballantine, 1970.

Kessler, Leo. *Kommando: Hitler's Special Forces in the Second World War*. London: Leo Cooper, 1995.

Knox, MacGregor. *Hitler's Italian Allies: Royal Armed Forces, Fascist Regime, and the War of 1940–1943*. Cambridge: Cambridge University, 2000.

Kursietis, Andris J. *The Wehrmacht at War, 1939–1945: The Units and Commanders of the German Ground Forces During World War II*. Soesterberg, Netherlands: Aspekt, 1999.

Lamb, Richard. *War in Italy, 1943–1945: A Brutal Story*. New York: Da Capo, 1993.

Levenda, Peter. *Unholy Alliance: A History of Nazi Involvement with the Occult*. 2d ed. New York: Continuum, 2002.

Liddell Hart, B. H. *History of the Second World War*. New York: Da Capo, 1999.

Lucas, James. *Kommando: German Special Forces of World War Two*. London: Cassell, 1998.

Lukacs, John. *Five Days in London: May 1940*. New Haven, CT: Yale University, Yale Nota Bene, 2001.

Martienssen, Anthony K. *Hitler and His Admirals*. London: Secker and Warburg, 1948.

McRaven, William H. *Spec Ops: Case Studies in Special Operations Warfare: Theory and Practice*. Novato, CA: Presidio, 1996.

Moseley, Ray. *Mussolini's Shadow: The Double Life of Count Galeazzo Ciano*. New Haven, CT: Yale University, 1999.

Muggeridge, Malcolm. *Ciano's Diplomatic Papers*. Translated by Stuart Hood. London: Odhams, 1948.

Neufeld, Michael J. *The Rocket and the Reich: Peenemünde and the Coming of the Ballistic Missile Era*. Cambridge, MA: Harvard University, 1996.

Patricelli, Marco. *Liberate Il Duce*. Milano: Mondadori, 2001.

Rhodes, Richard. *Dark Sun: The Making of the Hydrogen Bomb*. New York: Simon & Schuster, Touchstone, 1996.

_____. *The Making of the Atomic Bomb*. New York: Simon & Schuster, Touchstone, 1988.

Shirer, William L. *The Rise and Fall of the Third Reich: A History of Nazi Germany*. New York: Simon & Schuster, Touchstone, 1981.

Showell, Jak P. Mallmann. *The German Navy in World War Two: A Reference Guide to the Kriegsmarine, 1935–1945*. Annapolis, MD: Naval Institute, 1979.

Smith, Denis Mack. *Italy and Its Monarchy*. New Haven, CT: Yale University, 1989.

_____. *Mussolini's Roman Empire*. New York: Viking, 1976.

_____. *Modern Italy: A Political History*. Revised ed. Ann Arbor, MI: University of Michigan, 1969.

Smith, R. Harris. *OSS: The Secret History of America's First Central Intelligence Agency*. Berkeley, CA: University of California, 1972.

Stokesbury, James L. *A Short History of World War I*. New York: William Morrow, 1981.

_____. *A Short History of World War II*. New York: William Morrow, 1980.

Toland, John. *The Last 100 Days: The Tumultuous and Controversial Story of the Final Days of World War II in Europe*. New York: Random House, Modern Library, 2003.

Treadgold, Donald W., and Herbert J. Ellison. *Twentieth Century Russia*. 9th ed. Boulder, CO: Westview, 2000.

Trevor-Roper, H. R. *Hitler's Table Talk, 1941–1944: His Private Conversations*. Translated by Norman Cameron and R. H. Stevens. New York: Enigma, 2000.

_____. *The Testament of Adolf Hitler: The Hitler-Bormann Documents, February–April, 1945*. Edited by François Genoud and translated by R. H. Stevens. London: Icon, 1962.

Weinberg, Gerhard L., Helmut Heiber, and David M. Glantz. *Hitler and His Generals: Military Conferences, 1942–1945*. New York: Enigma, 2003.

Wulff, Wilhelm. *Zodiac and Swastika: How Astrology Guided Hitler's Germany*. New York: Coward, McCann & Geoghegan, 1973.

Book Chapters and Periodicals

"Berlin Fails to Mention Place." *New York Times*, 13 September 1943.

"Berlin on 'This Open Treason.'" *Times* (London), 9 September 1943.

Brigham, Daniel T. "Arrests Reported." *New York Times,* 26 July 1943.

De Felice, Renzo. Preface to *Diary, 1937–1943,* by Galeazzo Ciano. New York: Enigma, 2002.

"Ex-SS Man Worked for Mossad Against Egyptian Rocket Project." *Jerusalem Post,* 20 September 1989.

"He is in a 'Big City,' Berlin Says." *New York Times,* 14 September 1943.

"In the Ras's House." In *The Mussolini Memoirs, 1942–1943,* by Benito Mussolini. Edited by Raymond Klibansky and translated by Frances Lobb. London: Orion, Phoenix, 2000.

Iurato, Flavia, and Domenico Antonelli. "With Mussolini at the Campo Imperatore." In *The Mussolini Memoirs, 1942–1943,* by Benito Mussolini. Edited by Raymond Klibansky and translated by Frances Lobb. London: Orion, Phoenix, 2000.

Lamb, Richard. Introduction to *My Rise and Fall,* by Benito Mussolini. New York: Da Capo, 1998.

"Mussolini Is Taken by Nazis from Italians, Berlin Reports." *New York Times,* 13 September 1943.

"Mussolini Was in Ventotene." *New York Times,* 13 September 1943.

"Nazis' Arch-Killer Captured by Yanks." *New York Times,* 18 May 1945.

Pertinax. "Trial of Mussolini Reported Planned." *New York Times,* 10 September 1943.

"Text of Hitler's Broadcast on the Defection of Italy." *New York Times,* 11 September 1943.

"The Rescue of Mussolini." *After the Battle,* no. 22 (1978): 13–31.

Tuohy, William. "SS Officer Skorzeny Wrongly Credited with Deed, Historian Says; Mussolini Rescue: A New Version." *Los Angeles Times,* 26 December 1987.

Videos

German Fallschirmjägers in Action, 1939–1944. Black and white, 30 min. RZM Imports/Home Video, 1993.

Through Enemy Eyes: A Newsreel History of the Third Reich at War. Vol. 60, #760. Black and white, 49 min. International Historic Films, 1994.

Index

■

Abwehr, 92, 147
Abyssinia. *See* Ethiopia
Addis Ababa, Ethiopia, 41
Aircraft, 11, 33, 43, 144–145, 151,
    152, 179, 181–182, 186, 195,
    219, 220, 230–232
    aerial photography, 144–145,
      181–182, 182(n), 261
    See also Bombing raids
    (Allied); Gliders
Air raid sirens, 179(n), 220
Albania, 47
Albergo-Rifugio, 174
Alfieri, Dino, 33, 42, 68
Alto Adige, 16
Ambrosio, Vittorio (General),
    123, 125
Anschluss, 14, 38–39, 40, 43–44
Antiaircraft guns, 13, 190, 203, 220
Anti-Semitism, 45
Anzio, Italy, 257–258
Apennine Mountains, 84, 152, 153,
    174, 195
Armistice terms, 169, 170, 173,
    173(n), 185, 210–211. *See also*
    Unconditional surrender
Artillery, 43
Assergi, Italy, 174, 206, 215, 217

Astrologers, 81, 92–93, 93–94, 114
Atrocities, 259
Austria, 16. *See also Anschluss*
Automatic rifles, 207
Axis conference in Tarvisio,
    123–126, 130
Axis metaphor, 42, 42(n)
Axis summit proposal, 126
Axis war council at Bologna, 160–162

Badoglio, Pietro (Marshal), 6–7, 18,
    30, 31, 40, 59, 63, 66, 69, 72,
    74, 75, 76, 86, 95, 110, 111,
    126, 146, 148, 155, 190
    announcing Italy's capitulation, 186
    and Army Group B in northern
      Italy, 77
    background of, 73
    and Cavallero plot, 166–167
    exit from Rome, 191
    and first approach to Allies,
      77–78
    kidnapping of, 111, 126. *See also*
      Operation Student
    letter from Mussolini to, 70–71,
      101–102
    and Rahn, 172
    repressive measures of, 96–97, 166

Balkans, 60, 77, 125, 134, 161, 187, 193, 197
Battle of the Atlantic, 23
Battle of the Bulge, 250–251
Bedell Smith, Walter (General), 158, 159(n), 170
Belgium, 177, 252. *See also* Eben Emael
Berio, Alberto, 110(n)
Berlepsch, Baron Otto von (Lieutenant), 206, 217, 219, 219(n), 227, 254, 262
    death of, 257
Berlin, 134–135, 166, 249
Big business, 48
Bombing raids (Allied), 23–24, 24(n)
    Berlin, 134–135, 166, 214
    Frascati, 183, 202
    Hamburg, 26, 27, 28(n), 134–135, 214
    Italian cities, 165
    Rome, 32(n)
Bonaparte, Napoleon, 105, 105(n)
Bormann, Martin, 33–34, 61, 67
Bouquet of Violets (Dürer painting), 14
Bradley, Omar (General), 151
Braun, Eva, 50, 90, 250
Braun, Wernher von, 25
Brenner Pass, 39, 44, 110, 125
Bribery, 94–95
Brindisi, Italy, 191
Bullock, Alan, 57, 238
Butcher, Harry (Captain), 209

Campo Imperatore (ski resort/hotel), 174, 178, 180–182, 200, 201–202, 209–210, 214, 218, 224, 225–230
    raid on compared with Eben Emael raid, 204
    surrender of, 228

Canaris, Wilhelm (Admiral), 92, 147–148
    execution of, 247(n)
Carabinieri, 6, 7. *See also* Soleti, Fernando
Carboni, Giacomo (General), 190
Casablanca Conference, 24
Cassino, Italy, 257–258
Castellano, Giuseppe (General), 158–159, 159(n), 160, 166, 169, 170, 173, 185
Casualties, 23, 26, 198, 228, 256, 258
Cavallero, Ugo, 166
Christian, Eckard (Colonel), 27
Churchill, Winston, 24, 37(n), 75, 110–111, 129, 130(n), 159, 165, 170, 192, 246
    and rescue of Mussolini, 239
CIA, 253, 253(n)
Ciano, Edda, 42, 146, 167–168, 175, 245, 245(n)
Ciano, Galeazzo (Count), 2, 41–42, 46, 47, 52, 55, 56, 57, 73, 175
    execution of, 245
    flown to Germany by Nazis, 167–168
    memoirs of, 242
Clairvoyants, 81, 93
Clark, Bruce (General), 251
Clark, Mark (General), 187, 188, 189, 256, 258
Clark, Martin, 246
Communism, 48, 53, 247
Concentration camps, 93
Corsica, 138, 146
Crete, 177
Croatia, 67
Crowd, The (Le Bon), 49
Czechoslovakia. 44, 46, 47, 252

D'Ajeta, Lanza, 110, 157–158
Deakin, F. W., 168(n), 261
De Courten, Raffaele (Admiral), 117,
    193–194
Denmark, 177
Dessauer (Aviation Engineer), 113, 114
D'Este, Carlo, 257, 260
Disguises, 84, 251, 252, 253
Doenitz, Karl (Admiral), 23, 65, 66,
    113, 114, 115, 116–117,
    127–128, 130, 132, 133, 134,
    138, 149, 163, 247, 250
Dollmann, Eugen, 22, 43, 56, 57(n),
    89–90, 91–92, 125, 126–127,
    178, 244, 247, 248
Dulles, Allen, 151–152

Eastern front, 72, 133, 166, 214.
    See also Russia, Nazi invasion of
Eben Emael (Belgian fort), 177–178,
    202–204
Eisenhower, Dwight D. (General),
    169, 184, 185, 186, 209
security measures for, 251
Elba (island), 105(n), 147, 148
England, 40, 41, 43, 72, 93
British commandos, 141
Ethiopia, 40–41, 46, 73, 107
Executions, 194, 208, 245, 249, 259

Faiola, Alberto (Lieutenant), 153,
    173–174, 211, 225, 229
Fascism, 8, 37, 54, 62, 65, 91, 96, 118,
    238. *See also* Italy, Fascist Party in
Federzoni, Luigi, 160
Feltre, Italy. *See* Hitler/Mussolini
    relationship, conference at Feltre
Ferone, Ernesto (General), 101
FG–42 automatic rifles, 207, 220
Firestorms, 26

France, 40, 41, 43, 72, 77, 117, 161,
    162, 177, 193, 202
Franco, Francisco (General), 11
Frascati, Italy, 85, 88, 90, 176
air attack on, 183, 202
Frick, Wilhelm, 166
F.R. 22 (destroyer), 117–118

Gaeta, Italy, 103, 113, 116
Galbiati, Enzo (General), 4
Gardner (Colonel), 190
Gargnano, Italy, 245
Garibaldi brigades, 247
Geraud, Andre, 210
Gerlach, Heinrich (Captain), 84, 84(n),
    231–232, 233–234, 240(n)
German Institute for Gliding Research
    (DFS), 203
German military
    Army Group B, 72, 72(n), 76, 77,
        139, 163, 164
    disarming/capturing Italian
        soldiers, 193, 193(n)
    Friedenthal Battalion, 82, 83, 88,
        141–142, 206, 219
    German High Command, 29
    Military Intelligence, 82
    navy, 116, 123, 131, 133, 137, 149.
        See also Submarines
    Tenth Army at Salerno, 188
    Third Panzergrenadier Division,
        82, 152, 191, 199
    See also Italy, German military forces
        in/moved to; Luftwaffe; Sicily,
        German troops in; Waffen SS
Gliders, 201–204, 207, 214–215,
    216–217, 218, 221–228,
    228(n), 229–230, 262–263
command of glider assault team,
    219(n), 262

Gliders (continued)
    design of DFS 230 gliders, 221–222
Goebbels, Joseph, 33(n), 59, 61, 62,
    63, 63(n), 67, 69, 72, 86, 102,
    111, 136, 183, 193, 195, 196,
    208, 214, 235, 240, 242, 243
    death of, 250
    and Mussolini letter to Badoglio,
    70–71
Goering, Hermann, 31–32, 51, 63,
    64, 128, 149, 155, 235, 239,
    247, 254
Goose step, 44
Gothic Line, 260
Grand Council of Fascism, 1, 2–3, 5,
    22, 29, 68(n), 70, 90, 124–125,
    130, 167, 242, 245
Grandi, Dino, 1–2, 129, 130, 160,
    160(n), 245
Gran Sasso (mountain), 174, See also
    Campo Imperatore
Greece, 73, 125
Guariglia, Raffaele, 78, 110, 123, 124,
    127, 157, 167, 172, 185
Gueli, Giuseppe, 152, 153, 173–174,
    210, 229
Guensche, Otto (Lieutenant),
    13–14, 18
Gulf of Genoa region, 60, 72
Gustav Line, 257

Hackett, Sir John (General), 177
Hamburg, Germany. See Bombing
    raids (Allied), Hamburg
Heinkel 111 bomber, 144–145,
    181–182, 235
Henschel 126 aircraft, 219, 222
Hess, Rudolf, 93
Hewel, Walter, 28–29
Hibbert, Christopher, 44

Hidaka, Shinrokuro, 3, 4, 25, 26
Himmler, Heinrich, 18–19, 63, 67, 81,
    84, 89, 91, 114, 115, 116, 128,
    130, 148, 199, 214, 235
    as Minister of Interior, 166
Hitler, Adolf, 8, 12, 241
    addressing German people about
    Italian question, 111–112,
    196–198
    assassination attempt on, 67(n),
    247, 247(n), 248, 256(n)
    characterized, 50–51, 51–52
    and Edda Ciano, 175
    and Eva Braun, 50, 250
    and Galeazzo Ciano, 42, 57
    health of, 24–25, 25(n), 44(n), 50
    and Italian coup, 18, 21, 25, 29,
    30, 31, 32, 59, 60–61, 62, 63,
    66–67, 72, 79
    and Italian royal house, 21,
    21(n), 126
    medals of, 14
    military headquarters of.
    See Wolf's Lair
    pitting subordinates against each
    other, 147
    and proposed summit meeting
    after coup, 75
    and retaliation for Allied bombing
    raids, 27–28
    and Rommel/Kesselring rivalry,
    164, 188
    and secrecy, 87(n)
    and Skorzeny, 15–17, 150
    and Student, 81–82
    suicide of, 250
    suspicions of Badoglio regime, 60,
    114–115, 129–130, 155–156,
    160, 160(n), 163, 171, 183,
    195–196

underground bunker in Berlin,
249–250
and violence, 39, 49
See also Hitler/Mussolini
relationship
Hitler/Mussolini relationship, 8, 21(n)
and *Anschluss*, 44
common ground of
Hitler/Mussolini, 48–51
conference at Feltre, 3, 32, 34–35,
74, 106
and Czechoslovakia, 47
Hitler's affection/concern for
Mussolini, 53, 54–55, 112, 129,
168, 175, 197, 238, 242, 248
Hitler's birthday gift to Mussolini,
120–121
Hitler's motives for rescuing
Mussolini, 67–68
meeting in Berlin in 1937, 43
meeting in Venice in 1934, 39
and *Mein Kampf*, 37–38
Mussolini as Hitler's equal, 54, 55
Mussolini as junior partner, 46,
57, 58
Mussolini's attitude/feelings
concerning Hitler, 39–40,
55–56, 57–58
in 1920s, 37–38
and requested aid for Italy, 34, 125
reunion after Mussolini's liberation,
241–242, 243–244
and summit of 1941, 37
Hoettl, Wilhelm, 93, 168, 240
Holland, 202
Hotel Imperatore. *See* Campo
Imperatore
Hunaeus, Helmut (naval Commander),
137, 143
Hungary, 67, 171, 196

Individualism, 119
Intelligence issues, 22, 83, 89, 89(n),
141, 142, 158, 159, 178
and Campo Imperatore raid, 204,
217, 226
German intelligence organizations,
92, 147, 247(n)
Italian Military Intelligence Service,
97–98, 114, 139–140
undercover operations on
La Maddalena, 143–144
See also Reich Security Main Office
Israel, 253
Italia (ship), 194
Italy, 15–16, 37, 76
Abruzzi region, 152, 173, 180, 223
agriculture in, 163
alliance with England/France
(1935), 40
Allied bombing of cities, 165
Allied invasion of, 21, 59–60, 61,
158, 160, 163, 169, 170, 185,
186, 187–189, 188(n), 213,
255, 256–258
and Allied invasion of Balkans, 60
Allied POWs in, 247(n)
army, 29, 42–43, 68, 125–126
civil war in, 246
communications networks in, 193
Fascist Party in, 45, 49, 65, 68,
70, 76, 95, 102, 156. *See also*
Fascism; Grand Council
of Fascism
formal military alliance with
Germany, 47–48, 78
German invasion/occupation of,
44, 63, 64, 66, 140, 150(n),
155, 171, 187, 247, 260.
See also Rome, German
occupation of

German military forces in/moved
to, 60, 65, 71–72, 74, 76, 77,
78, 82, 85, 110, 115, 125, 127,
133, 139, 157, 163, 164, 170,
187, 237–238, 255, 260
industry in, 163
Italian Empire, 41
Italian High Command, 6, 200
as Italian Social Republic, 244–245
navy, 64, 186, 193–194
popular feeling after coup,
95–96, 121
Po Valley, 260
provisional government in, 30
racial laws in, 45
as Salò Republic, 244–245, 258(n)
sanctions against, 41
and separate peace with Allies, 8,
19, 31, 34, 35, 59, 74, 110, 111,
125, 130, 165, 171, 172,
183–186. *See also* Armistice
terms; Unconditional surrender
Servizio Informazione Militare (SIM),
97–98, 114, 139–140
surrender of German forces in, 260
troops in foreign lands, 125–126,
161, 162, 193
See also Rome

Japan, 3, 238
Jews, 45, 258, 258(n)
Jodl, Alfred (General), 30, 31, 51,
65–66, 115, 130, 134, 148, 160,
161–162, 162–163
Junge, Traudl, 32, 249
Junkers 52 cargo plane, 11

Kaltenbrunner, Ernst, 141–142
Kamptz, Gerhard von (Captain), 130,
132, 137–138, 149

Kappler, Herbert, 89, 90, 91, 92, 112,
131, 146, 167, 178, 213, 240,
240(n), 259, 259(n)
Keitel, Wilhelm (Marshal), 29, 31,
65–66, 87(n), 115, 123, 125,
126, 134–135, 148, 235
Kesselring, Albert (Marshal), 17,
50–51, 66, 69, 72(n), 85–86,
86–87, 88, 90, 139, 156, 161,
171, 187, 193, 194–195,
257, 259
and Rommel, 163–165, 256
and Salerno invasion, 188, 191
war crimes of, 260(n)
Krutoff, Leo, 181, 200

Lake Garda (Italy), 164, 244, 245
La Maddalena (island), 117, 119–121,
127, 137–138, 142–145,
148–152, 175
aerial photos of, 144–145
Lamb, Richard, 255
Langguth, Gerhard (Captain), 89,
181–182, 217, 218, 219,
222–223, 261
L'Aquila, Italy, 180, 223
La Spezia, Italy, 139–140
Laurich, (Petty Officer), 113–114,
127–128
League of Nations, 41
Lebensraum, 22, 47
Le Bon, Gustave, 49
Lisbon, 110, 129, 157, 158, 169, 171
Los Angeles Times, 254
Luftwaffe, 17, 27, 31, 140, 192, 194,
203, 240, 254, 262
attack on Belgrade, 198
Second Parachute Division, 82, 87,
192, 199
See also Paratroopers

Mackensen, Hans Georg von, 22, 29,
  68, 86, 90, 92, 121, 156
  firing of, 172
  meeting with King Victor
    Emmanuel, 69–70
  recalled to Germany, 127
McRaven, William H., 204(n),
  250, 254
Maddalena Island. *See* La Maddalena
Malta, 194
Marini (Sergeant-Major), 107
Masuria (East Prussia), 11–12
Maugeri, Franco (Admiral), 103–104,
  103(n), 105–106, 113,
  117, 118
Media, 45, 95, 184, 186, 187, 196,
  214, 238, 239
Mein Kampf (Hitler), 37–38
Meyer, Elimar, 223, 240(n)
Mezzasoma, Fernando, 52, 246
Milan, Italy, 249
Mines, 27
Monelli, Paolo, 49, 58, 245
Montgomery, Sir Bernard (General),
  187–188, 189
Morell, Professor (Theodor), 24–25
Mors, Harold (Major), 199, 205,
  205(n), 206–207, 215, 217,
  219(n), 223, 232, 240, 240(n),
  241, 254
Mossad, 253
Munich, Germany, 235, 241(n)
  Munich peace conference of
    1938, 46
Mussolini, Benito, 1–8, 17, 25, 26, 250
  affairs/mistresses of, 41, 45, 50
  and *Anschluss*, 38–39, 43–44
  arrest of, 7, 22, 30, 32, 35, 74.
    See also Mussolini, Benito,
    after coup

at Campo Imperatore, 225, 226,
  227, 230–233
  characterized, 52, 58
  after coup, 99–108, 117,
    118, 137–138, 149(n),
    152–153, 173–174. *See also*
    Campo Imperatore
  crimes of, 49
  daughter of, 42, 146
  death of, 249
  diary and papers of, 235
  German plan to rescue and
    reinstate, 63. *See also*
    Operation Oak
  health of, 2, 3, 10, 22, 50, 246
  and Italian people, 4, 6, 7, 107,
    118–119
  and Jews, 45, 258(n)
  on Nazism, 39–40
  rumors about after coup, 97–98,
    117, 143, 156, 178
  sixtieth birthday of, 108, 121
  suicide attempt of, 211
  trial of, 209, 210–211
  and Victor Emmanuel, 5–7, 7(n)
  at Villa Feltrinelli, 245–246
  See also Hitler/Mussolini
    relationship
Mussolini, Rachele (wife), 5, 39,
  54–55, 56, 232, 235, 244
Mussolini, Vittorio (son), 146

Naples, Italy, 195, 256
Nationalism, 48
Nebe, Arthur (General), 94
New York Times, 210, 237, 238, 241
Nietzsche, Friedrich, 119–120
Night of the Long Knives, 39
North Africa, 21, 23, 197, 200
Norway, 164, 177, 256

Oberbefehlshaber Sued (OB SUED), 85
Oberkommando der Wehrmacht
    (OKW), 29
Odessa network, 253
Office of Strategic Services
    (OSS), 151
OKW. *See Oberkommando der*
    Wehrmacht
Olympic Games of 1936, 14
Operation Avalanche, 185, 210
Operation Axis (Achse), 64, 115,
    171, 187. *See also* Italy, German
    invasion/occupation of
Operation Barbarossa, 12, 54. *See also*
    Russia, Nazi invasion of
Operation Black (Schwarz), 64, 115
Operation Citadel, 26
Operation Dragoon, 260
Operation Gomorrah, 26
Operation Greif, 251, 252
Operation Oak (Eiche), 63, 71(n),
    81, 83, 85, 86, 88, 89, 94,
    114, 115, 123, 130, 138, 142,
    148, 176, 178, 214, 255,
    261–263
    glider sequence in Campo
        Imperatore raid, 219, 262–263
    as jailbreak, 237, 238
    mission planning and command
        structure, 262
    and placing blame on Italian
        Fascists, 129
Operation Student, 63, 66, 81, 87,
    87(n), 88, 90–92, 91(n)
Osborne, Sir D'Arcy, 78
OSS. *See* Office of Strategic Services
Owens, Jesse, 14

Pact of Steel, 47–48, 48(n)
Panthère (destroyer), 117, 117(n)

Paratroopers, 17, 82, 128, 129,
    131–132, 176, 181, 190, 191,
    200, 201, 202–207, 219, 227,
    253, 254, 262
    battles fought in, 177–178, 257(n)
Partisans, 246–247, 249, 259
Passo Romano, 44
Patricelli, Marco, 205(n), 229(n)
Patton, George (General), 3
Pelaghi (Colonel), 104, 105, 107
Peron, Juan and Evita, 253
Persefone (corvette), 103–104, 105, 113
Personality cult, 51
Pertinax (French journalist), 210
Petacci, Claretta, 41, 50, 246, 248–249
Pirelli, Alberto, 110(n)
Plehwe, Friedrich von, 74, 91, 95–96
Poison, 124, 161, 162
Poison gas, 40
Poland, 47
Polito, Saverio (General), 104, 105,
    107, 121, 152, 180(n)
Pontine and Sardinian Musings
    (Mussolini), 120
Ponza (island), 105, 107–108, 114,
    117, 118, 131, 151, 167
Portugal, 19. *See also* Lisbon
Pratica di Mare airfield, 263
Priebke, Erich, 92, 240(n), 259, 259(n)
Propaganda, 49, 50, 89, 106, 110,
    185, 232–233, 238, 239, 240

Quebec conference (Allies), 130(n)

Race issues, 39, 45–46, 56
Radar, 28(n), 132
Radl, Karl (Lieutenant), 11, 82, 83–84,
    88, 89, 131, 139, 146–147, 150,
    180, 181–182, 205(n), 208, 219,
    221, 224, 226, 233–234, 239

and Skorzeny, 261
and Soleti, 216–217
Rahn, Rudolf, 172, 184–185, 248
Raised arm salute, 44–45
Raw materials, 67
Reich Security Main Office (RSHA),
    83, 92, 141–142, 147, 148
Rhineland, 41
Ribbentrop, Joachim von, 22, 46, 47,
    51, 63(n), 64, 91, 123, 124,
    125, 126, 127, 128, 130, 148,
    167, 171, 247
    memo regarding Italian situation,
    156–157
Ridgway, Matthew (General), 190
Rintelen, Enno von (General), 34,
    86–87, 87(n), 156
    firing of, 172
Roatta, Mario (General), 160, 162, 185
Roma (ship), 194
Rome, 1–8, 17, 22, 28–29, 81, 89–90,
    94, 109, 117, 199
    airfields near, 170
    Allied airborne insertion into,
    189–191
    Allied bombing of, 32(n), 165
    Allied capture of, 255, 256, 258
    carabinieri barracks in Via
    Quintino Sella and Via Legnano,
    100–101, 112–113
    German occupation of, 30, 63, 66,
    71, 103(n), 152, 258–259
    Jews in, 258
    march on Rome in 1922, 53
    martial law in, 96–97
    popular feeling in after coup,
    95–96, 121, 244
    Roman Empire, 54
    Roman resistance, 259.
    See also Partisans

surrender of, 192, 210
University of Rome, 51
Rommel, Erwin (Marshal), 23, 25, 61,
    63, 65–66, 72, 72(n), 87, 130,
    134, 156, 160, 161, 187,
    194–195
    and assassination attempt on
    Hitler, 256(n)
    and Kesselring, 163–165, 256
    and La Spezia, 139
Rommel, Manfred (son), 161
Roon, Arnold von (Major), 254
Roosevelt, Franklin, 24, 129,
    130(n), 192
RSHA. *See* Reich Security Main Office
Rumania, 67, 171, 196
Rumors, 132, 164, 253. *See also*
    Mussolini, Benito, rumors
    about after coup
Russia, 8, 24, 177
    Kharkov, 166
    Kursk region, 26
    Nazi invasion of, 22–23, 26, 33,
    213–214. *See also* Eastern front;
    Operation Barbarossa
    Taganrog, 166

Sabotage, 247, 251
Salerno, Italy, 187–189, 191,
    195, 255
Santo Stefano (island), 128–129,
    130–131, 131–132, 137, 213
Sardinia, 117
Schellenberg, Walter, 93, 114, 142,
    148, 247(n)
Schmidt, Paul, 13(n), 58, 124
Schulz, Max, 149
Schutzstaffel (SS), 141(n). *See also*
    Waffen SS
Schwerdt (Lieutenant), 227

Secrecy, 17, 86, 87(n), 127,
179–180, 185
Semmler, Rudolf, 33(n), 63
Senise, Carmine, 229
Shaped charges, 203
Shortages, 26, 27, 28
Sicily, 170, 177, 188
Allied invasion of, 3, 23, 30–31,
32–33, 133
and conflict between Italy and
Germany, 33–34, 61
fall of to Western Powers, 165
German evacuation of, 134,
165, 187
German troops in, 30–31, 31(n),
32(n), 34, 60, 82, 165
SIM. *See* Italy, *Servizio Informazione
Militare*
Skorzeny, Otto (Captain), 9–17, 18,
79, 81, 82–85, 87, 89, 92, 94,
112, 131(n), 137, 139,
140–147, 148, 150, 199, 202
and Campo Imperatore raid, 206,
213, 217, 218, 219, 219(n),
220, 222, 223, 224–225,
226–227, 228, 237, 239–240,
252, 253, 254–255
death of, 253
in detention camp and escape,
252–253
exploits during World War II,
250–251
and flight to Rome after Campo
Imperatore raid, 231–232
medals awarded to, 235, 239
meetings with Hitler, 15–17, 150
and Mussolini, 228, 231, 235
and paratroopers, 176, 253,
262–263
and Radl, 261

Smith, Denis Mack, 43, 52,
56–57, 209(n)
Soleti, Fernando, (General), 208,
215–217, 219, 221, 222, 225,
225(n), 229, 254, 263
South Tyrol, 16
Spanish Civil War, 11
Speer, Albert, 27(n), 63, 109, 112
SS. *See Schutzstaffel*
Stalingrad, Battle of, 23
Steinbeck, John, 241
Storch (Stork) aircraft, 230–232,
233–234
Stresa front, 40
Strong, Kenneth W. D. (Brigadier),
158, 159, 189, 191
Student, Kurt (General), 17, 18, 79,
81–82, 87, 89, 92, 113, 123(n),
128, 130, 131, 137, 138,
139–140, 144, 147, 149,
156, 182(n)
and Campo Imperatore, 178–179,
180, 200, 205, 205(n), 206,
207–208, 215, 217, 219(n),
223, 229–230, 234, 240,
241, 254
career of, 176–177
death of, 253
and paratroopers, 261
Submarines, 23, 27, 116, 129, 149(n)
Summersby, Kay, 251
Switzerland, 110(n), 157

Tangier, 110(n), 157
Tanks, 43
Taranto, Italy, 188(n)
Tarvisio, Italy, 123–126, 127, 130
Taylor, A.J.P., 54
Taylor, Maxwell (General), 190
Tazzari (Lieutenant-Commander), 104

Torpedo boats, 149
Torture, 200(n)
Trettner, Heinz (General), 177

Unconditional surrender, 24, 74, 110,
    157, 158, 169, 170, 184,
    192(n). *See also* Armistice terms
United Nations, 184, 209, 211

Vatican, 63(n), 78, 110, 157
Ventotene Island, 103, 104, 114,
    115–116, 127, 128, 241
  blockade of, 116
  radar station at, 132
Versailles Treaty, 12, 40
Victor Emmanuel III (King), 2, 5–7, 8,
    29, 30, 35, 47, 62, 63, 73–74,
    75, 76, 95, 96–97, 110, 126,
    155, 167, 173, 184–185, 209
  and armistice terms, 170, 185–186
  arrest of, 87. *See also* Operation
    Student
  as banned from Italy, 260(n)
  exit from Rome, 191
  and first approach to Allies, 77–78
  kidnapping of, 111, 126. *See also*
    Operation Student
  and left-wing radicals, 96(n)
  meeting with Mackensen, 69–70
Vienna, Austria, 14, 235
Vigna di Valle (Italian seaplane base),
    152, 179
Vigneri, Paolo (Captain), 100
Villa Savoia, 5–7, 178
Villa Torlonia, 5

Waffen SS, 10, 84, 141(n), 146,
    161, 162, 176, 237, 241,
    247(n), 259
Wansee group, 93, 114
War crimes, 259(n), 260(n)
Warger, Robert, 143–144, 146–147,
    149, 150
Warlimont, Walter (General), 26, 124,
    134, 155, 161, 162, 165, 171
Webber, James, 119, 119(n)
Wehrmacht, 77. *See also* German
    military
Westphal, Siegfried (General), 23,
    194, 255
Whiting, Charles, 253
Wiskemann, Elizabeth, 52, 244
Wolff, Karl, 245
Wolf's Lair (*Wolfsschanze*), 9–10, 21,
    59, 61, 81, 83, 87(n), 111, 113,
    115, 138–139, 148, 175
  afternoon Fuehrer Conference at,
    25, 129
  last Axis summit at, 247–248
  meetings after Italian coup,
    63–64, 66
  Mussolini at, 241–242, 243–244
  Sperrkreis I, 12, 13
World War I, 11–12, 14, 16, 48
Wulff, Wilhelm, 93–94, 114

Yeo-Thomas, Forrest (Wing
    Commander), 252, 253
Yugoslavia, 197–198

Zanussi, Giacomo (General), 159–160